Small Town and Village in Bavaria

SMALL TOWN AND VILLAGE IN BAVARIA
The Passing of a Way of Life

Peter H. Merkl

Berghahn Books
New York • Oxford

Published in 2012 by
Berghahn Books
www.berghahnbooks.com

©2012 Peter H. Merkl

Library of Congress Cataloging-in-Publication Data

Merkl, Peter H.
  Small town and village in Bavaria : the passing of a way of life / Peter H. Merkl.
    p. cm.
  ISBN 978-0-85745-347-1 (hardback : alk. paper) — ISBN 978-0-85745-348-8
(ebook)
  1. Villages—Germany—Bavaria—Case studies. 2. Sociology, Rural—Germany—
Bavaria—Case studies. 3. Social change—Germany—Bavaria—History—20th
century. I. Title.
  HT431.M527 2012
  307.76'209433—dc23

                                                                  2011039292

British Library Cataloguing in Publication Data

A catalogue record for this book is available from the British Library

Printed in the United States on acid-free paper.

ISBN 978-0-85745-347-1 (hardback)
ISBN 978-0-85745-348-8 (ebook)

To my wife, Elisa, my son, John, and his wife, Lisa Goodman,
for their extraordinary efforts.

CONTENTS

FIGURES

ILLUSTRATIONS

MAPS

IN-TEXT TABLES

ACKNOWLEDGMENTS

I hardly know where to begin acknowledging all the influences on my awareness of German small town and village life, and what not to leave out. Of course, I became intrigued by the topic long before the great local territorial reforms of the 1970s, as this was the cultural and social environment of my generation and scores of earlier generations. Small towns or the countryside was where most people came from and where one spent vacations. I grew up deeply immersed in rural and small town tales of Old Europe, the traditional Bavarian and German *Heimatliteratur* (homeland literature)[1] of writers like Ludwig Ganghofer or Ludwig Thoma, which were either romantic-sentimental or bitingly satirical. Even though I was born in Munich, my family had origins in small-town Franconia and they felt more at home on the edges of the big city. My paternal grandfather, in fact, was a newspaper theater critic who often crossed swords with the day's most popular Bavarian playwright, Ludwig Thoma. Thoma also wrote the legendary *Bad Boys' Stories* (*Lausbubengeschichten*), which, of course, I devoured. German folklore and folksongs were similarly replete with small-town stories of wandering handicraft *Gesellen* (associates), leaving one place and its trade master—and their sweethearts—for another during their *Wanderjahre*.

The culture was deeply tinged with nostalgia for the simpler life of the past. Most novels dwelt upon an idealized version of country life, often emphasizing an alleged small-town or village harmony where later versions might reveal the tensions and conflicts between social strata, generations, or those who had left the countryside behind and those who remained there. Some dwelt upon the conflicts between farmers and their sons or between a rich farmer and his young attractive *Magd* (female farm hand) who hoped that her (or his) seduction might lead to her rise to the status of a farm wife. As a teenager, I read Gottfried Keller's stories of a mythical small Swiss town named Seldwyla and its people, a philosophical microcosm of moral choices and the human condition. Growing up in the old country one could hardly be unaware of the hundreds of such stories all around, including the humorous tales of mythical, walled, and turreted German Schilda and its foolish *Schildbürger*, who, among other stories, pulled a cow with a rope around its neck up the city wall so that it might graze on the grasses growing out of the old masonry. The poor animal, of course, did not survive. As a young adult I was deeply impressed by Laurence Wylie's *Village in the Vaucluse* about the life of the people of a small Provençal town (Rousssillon) and by the morality tales of Marcel Pagnol, also in motion picture form, about the greedy schemes of French rural and small-town folk. And there was *Akenfield*, Ronald Blythe's story of a village nurse before the British welfare state and Blythe's later account of how British seniors often go to live out their lives in such gentle rural and small-town places as they may have grown up in. Much of German high literature, from Theodor Storm to Thomas Mann's *Buddenbrooks*, is set in small town contexts. The list goes on and on.

Many an American or British tourist and traveler, looking down from a plane on a clear day or traveling along the Romantic Road in Bavaria—from Rothenburg ob der Tauber to Dinkelsbühl and Augsburg—has been charmed at seeing small-town and village idylls that time forgot. The neat patchwork of fields and forests with toy-like small settlements around churches and city squares surrounding the better-known tourist attractions increases the impression of fairy tale quilts and orderly town planning. This book, however, describes a major crisis in this Bavarian paradise, an earthquake brought about by what we may call the ghosts of state absolutisms past. Following the modernizing trends elsewhere, the Bavarian state in the 1970s and 1980s decided to reorder its over seven thousand small communities of less than two thousand inhabitants by taking away their autonomy and consolidating most of them with larger local administrative units with the capacity for modern administration. This was the object of our investigation, which began in the 1980s and was concluded only in the late 1990s and early 2000s. Writing up the results and thinking about their deeper significance, of course, took longer.

At the end of an undertaking of such duration and complexity, the author clearly owes gratitude and acknowledgments to many people and institutions, beginning with the Volkswagen Foundation of Wolfsburg, which provided the initial grant. The Academic Senate Committee on Research of the University of California, Santa Barbara, and the Peter Atteslander Chair of Sociology at the University of Augsburg supplied further travel and material support. I was a visiting professor at the University of Augsburg in 1983 and owe particular gratitude to Professor Atteslander, who at that time had already been involved in other local government research in Germany. He helped me formulate my own project, select small communities, and made one of his assistants, Elfriede

Offergelt, Dipl. Oec., available as an interviewer. The project was named "Social Change in Small Towns in West Middle Franconia." Ms. Offergelt visited all the fifteen small communes in West Middle Franconia, interviewing mayors, teachers, and clergymen. I later concentrated on state and county officials, including some in other areas, and corresponded with some of the mayors of "losing communities," i.e., those which lost their autonomy to an administrative union (*Verwaltungsgemeinschaft*, or VG) or (by annexation) to a neighboring integrated community (*Einheitsgemeinde*, or EG). I am greatly indebted to the many local and state officials I interviewed and corresponded with, in particular, Mayors Anton Seitz and Michael Dörr of Wolframs-Eschenbach. I spent many summers collecting relevant statewide data at the State Statistical Office in Munich and benefited a lot from the advice of colleagues at the Institute of Political Science at the University of Munich, in particular Professor Emil Hübner. I also obtained comparative material about similar reforms in other states of the old Federal Republic, particularly in Baden-Württemberg and in the north of West Germany.

A very important role fell to my collaborator and erstwhile coauthor, Patricia R. Gibson Heck (Pat Heck), emerita professor of anthropology of the University of the South in Sewanee, TN. Pat was a graduate student in anthropology at UCSB and obtained a PhD in that discipline with emphasis on political anthropology. She went with her children to live in small town Bavaria for several years and do research as a participant observer of everyday life and politics in the city and county of Rosenheim and in declining (and rivaling) nearby Wasserburg on the river Inn in Catholic Bavaria. Our original plans called for her to take booming Rosenheim, which is about the size of Ansbach, the county seat for many of our fifteen small places in West Middle Franconia, and examine the course of the local territorial reform and its impact on the surrounding smaller and subordinate communities. Rosenheim and Wasserburg are a reversed match for stagnant Ansbach and small but booming Rothenburg ob der Tauber where she also spent time in research. Pat also became interested in local democracy in Rosenheim and Wasserburg and, eventually, in East German local government after the fall of communism. Her work in Bavaria would have taken up about half of a co-authored book except that it made for a huge and somewhat unfocussed manuscript that could not find a publisher. After years of frustrating delays, we finally decided to divide the manuscript into her parts and mine, for each to pursue separate publication in a smaller format. In any case I greatly owe Pat for helping prepare my part of the manuscript and for many an anthropological insight that has enriched my approach. I also hope that she will proceed with revisions of her part and that it will eventually appear and supply comparative and complementary visions. Preliminary reports on parts of this project by both Pat and myself appeared in my *New Local Centers In Centralized States* (Lanham, MD, 1985), 3–121. Some of the results were also presented at different scholarly meetings of the American Political Science Association and at various anthropological and international gatherings.

I am also very grateful for the help and guidance of Berghahn Books, in particular Associate Editor Ann Przyzycki De Vita and Production Editor Melissa Spinelli. Sincere thanks should also go to my son, John Merkl, and to his wife, Lisa Goodman, for their tremendous efforts with photographs and tables, and to my daughter, Jackie Burrell and to the mapmaker, Jeff Durham. Likewise to my good friend and colleague, Michael O'Connell, for his advice and the production of pictures. A special debt of gratitude also goes to the town of Wolframs-Eschenbach and its mayor, Michael Dörr, for letting me use pictorial material in its possession. Last but by no means least, I am deeply in debt to my wife, Elisa, who not only endured the years of my preoccupation with this work but labored tirelessly and contributed, among many other things, considerable tech support to its final fruition.

Notes

1. Typical of the *Heimatliteratur* was the early media star Ludwig A. Ganghofer (1855–1920) whose numerous homeland stories about life in Bavaria, the Alps, and Tyrol led to the production of more than thirty movies, with titles such as *Der Jäger* (The Hunter), *Das Schweigen im Walde* (Silence in the Forest), and *Der Ochsenkrieg* (The Oxen War). But there were many others, for example Michael Georg Conrad, Heinrich Schaumberger, Joseph Baierlein, and Oskar Maria Graf, and some more contemporary, such as Otmar Franz Lang, Anna Winschneider, and Herbert Rosenberger.

Introduction

At the center of this investigation is the great modernization effort of a West German state, Bavaria, in the 1970s and 1980s by means of a reform of the smaller units of local government. It began with an ambitious scheme to reorder local and county (*Kreis*) territorial boundaries and, most controversially, the pecking order among small and larger communities. In particular, the reformers wanted to eliminate the autonomy of all units smaller than a population of two thousand inhabitants and subordinate them to larger centers that could support modern local administration—in a state where the vast majority of local communes (more than seven thousand) were of that description. Both the details and the entire plan smacked to me of the spirit of state absolutisms past. When I learned, for example, of the intention to merge four walled medieval towns near Rothenburg ob der Tauber—Wolframs-Eschenbach, Mitteleschenbach, Merkendorf, and Ornbau—with two old market towns into one, an administrative union, VG (*Verwaltungsgemeinschaft*) Triesdorf, I thought I had never heard anything so preposterous in my life. After more than five hundred years of autonomy and a modicum of self-government, it seemed that bureaucratic centralization had finally overcome what dozens of hostile armies and domestic enemies had not achieved over the centuries: To break the pride and spirit of the citizens of these towns, symbolically to raze their walls forever, and cast their traditions and perhaps even their ancient names into oblivion.

Well, upon closer examination, this funereal undertaking turned out not to be quite as devoid of common sense as it at first appeared to our sentimental regard for the old European hometown. Also, the reform was repeatedly bogged down in political controversies and was crucially frus-

trated by the dwindling of West German financial resources that had resulted from the energy crises and economic downturns of the 1970s and
1980s. Important parts of the original reform agenda (such as the functional reform) were addressed only timidly or belatedly if at all—in striking contrast to the rather high-handed first steps of the reform: Among
other things, the reformers muzzled all political protest and resistance to
its implementation, including lawsuits. Germans, like Americans, often
rebel against local territorial changes such as annexations and incorporations, and this of course involved thousands of such changes, not to mention the indignities of the subordination of one's own small communities.
Yet, once the changes in status and territory had been completed and
new sets of officials elected, a curious, amnesic peace settled in among the
antagonists. With the exception of the older generation that still remembered the past and office-holders whose positions had disappeared, the
succeeding generations seemed to accept the new status quo. They went
with the changes or, more commonly, appeared to have forgotten just
how different things were not too long ago.

Even local government experts and knowledgeable journalists are still
divided today in their judgments about how "successful" these imposed
reforms were. The authors of the changes, especially the minister of the
interior then in charge, Dr. Bruno Merk, are still convinced that it was a
long-overdue reform. As the former minister wrote to me, the old structures and functions of Bavarian small towns and villages "had long been
hollowed out" by social change. Worse, the status quo ante had become
an increasingly serious impediment to equal opportunity and to equal living conditions among the citizens of his state. Many state officials agreed.
Midway through the reforms, in 1976, the conservative state government
also expressed its hopes that the reforms would overcome major deficien-
cies in the administrative services to the needs of business and to the
protection of the environment.

So what were the reform measures contemplated at the lowest level
of local government? There had been extensive explorations in regional
planning by the federal government of West Germany in the 1960s upon
which most other states had undertaken major local government reforms.
Some other European countries had also modernized their local structures. France, which resembles Bavaria in its very high number of small
and micro-communes and in its preference for the père de famille type of
small-town and village mayor, had begun major reforms ever since Charles
DeGaulle came to power, in 1958, though more in the direction of decentralization and overcoming the blockages of the "société bloquée."[1]

Bavaria followed with a Regional Planning Law in 1970 that established a Development Program for Bavaria. Two years later came a

County (*Kreis*) Reform, which halved the number of Bavarian counties: Now there were only seventy-one, averaging about one hundred thousand inhabitants each. An Independent City Reform the same year demoted some county capitals and redrew urban boundaries. It also annexed some adjacent communities to the larger cities and allowed others, after some augmentation, an independent status. Finally, there was the Communal Reform on which we are focusing here: It had a voluntary phase (1971–1973) during which mergers of territory and population were encouraged and subsidized. This reduced the number from over 7,000 to 4,374 communes. This was followed by mandatory consolidation in 1978 which only 2,052 of them survived.

The planners had originally envisioned an ideal size of 5,000 in population for the optimal delivery of services, but in the end there were still over 1,600 communities below this level, including almost 1,000 under a population of 2,000. The solution for thinly settled areas with several small communities was the administrative union or VG, a kind of federation of small units with a designated center. In spite of the efforts to muzzle resistance, there were still many politically potent complaints facing a newly elected minister president, Franz Josef Strauss. In 1978–1979 his new administration worked out acceptable compromises in a number of cases, though perhaps in too political a manner in the eyes of his critics. Bavaria has long been dominated by his conservative Christian Social Union (CSU), which is affiliated with the national Christian Democrats (CDU). Strauss's "reform of the reform" allowed even more of the smaller communes to survive the cull.

The Plan for this Book

Our investigation began by selecting fifteen small communities with interviews and on-site inspections from a rather thinly settled area of West Middle Franconia, mostly near Ansbach, which was underdeveloped and poorly connected to the more prosperous parts of Bavaria, Throughout this book, we are contrasting this rural slice of reality with relevant statistical trends for Bavaria, a state that was long considered one of the most rural and least developed of the eleven *Länder* (states) of the western Federal Republic. In fact, it had received substantial federal tax subsidies through the horizontal redistribution program (*horizontaler Finanzausgleich*) during the first decades of West Germany. These charming small places are also adjacent to the medieval town of Rothenburg on the Tauber river, which many American travelers know, the tourism-rich cousin of impoverished Wolframs-Eschenbach of our selection.

Chapter 1 examines the impact of social change in the three decades or more prior to the reform, both on the fifteen selected small towns and villages and the state at large, with emphasis on population trends and employment patterns. Changing agriculture, the predominant activity at the outset, is analyzed in some detail, and so is the state of education of the farmer in the countryside that played such a major role in freeing small towns and villages from their geographic isolation.

Chapter 2 turns to the decline of the iconic small-town and village community that is implied by the slogan of the "hollowing out" of its functions and sense of identity. The traditional small Bavarian community, described so sentimentally in Bavarian *Heimatliteratur* (native homeland fiction), was held together by the trinity of church, elementary school, and social life. The dominant role of the priest or pastor was gradually eroded by secularization. The church-approved and usually male teachers were finally freed from their village or small-town bonds by the great school reform of 1967 that replaced the multi-grade, one- or two-room schools with distant school centers. Both church and school—not to mention the village taverns—lost their central roles in the social life of the community, as new groups and associations, step by step, created cross-community patterns of entertainment and festivals. As our survey of the fifteen communities and the state reveals, markets, services, and commuting habits have generally followed this slow erosion of the old, self-contained community. Last but not least, the glorious isolation of the past from the outside world broke down under the impact of motorization, television, and the increasing mobility of the denizens of these villages and small towns.

Chapter 3 addresses the preliminary thinking and planning of the great reform, both at the federal and the state level. The 1970s marked a new era in West Germany: The opposition Social Democrats (SPD) under chancellors Willy Brandt and Helmut Schmidt launched an era of reforms in many parts of society. Toward the end of the previous administration, federal planners had already begun to look into dimensions of regional planning and spatial order (*Raumordnung*) with regard to the entire Federal Republic and against a background of massive rural-urban migration. The goal was optimal economic development and the deepening of the welfare state to the benefit of all citizens throughout the land, regardless of where they lived. After the federal Reports on Spatial Order (*Raumordnungsberichte*) there soon came state-level reports and action, and Bavaria after a while followed suit, even though there were critics who questioned that its reform needs were comparable to those of the more industrialized states, such as North Rhine Westphalia. By the mid seventies, a slew of reports had issued forth from its Bavarian Ministry of Land Development and Environmental Concerns and the State Statistical Office, including a post-reform Land Development Program, a Report on West Middle Franconia, all with plenty of maps and charts, a Report on Agriculture, and copious statistics before and after the reform on all the local communities and their new *Bürgermeisters* and community councils.

The state now proceeded to map out its regions and places of centrality, applying all this planning theory and information to cities and towns in the different regions and localities of Bavaria, which ranges from the Alps and their foothills to the flatlands and river valleys of the north and in between. As the County Reform halved the number of counties in the states, only three were left of the original nine counties in West Middle Franconia: Ansbach, Neustadt on the Aisch/Bad Windsheim, and Weissenburg/Gunzenhausen. Most of our fifteen communities are in County Ansbach and associated with six VGs there. Rothenburg o.T. is in the same county and, in fact, is the external VG seat of three of them without being part of their VG. It is an independent city. Four are in the other two counties named above. The fifteen small communities were chosen according to their low population density in 1972, their low average size of agricultural holdings, their high average percentage of daily out-commuters (40 percent of the gainfully employed), and their average per capita tax revenues. Among them, only Wolframs-Eschenbach was restored as an undersized "unified commune" or EG (*Einheitsgemeinde*) by minister president Franz Josef Strauss's "reform of the reform" in 1978–1980, rather than remaining dependent on a VG. The interviews were conducted with mayors, teachers, and priests or ministers in these communes and included changes in their public roles since 1945, as well as agricultural, economic, political, and social changes in general. The length of this time span, which had the effect of favoring older respondents of long years of service, highlighted the changes they went through.

Chapter 4 inspects the actual implementation of the reforms in our communities, the region, and the state. Their effect on the status quo ante, the changes after the reform, and longer-range perspectives were one focus. The other was a survey of mayors throughout the state regarding their opinions about the reforms, with particular emphasis on the "losers" of the reform, i.e., mayors whose communities had lost their independence and been placed into a VG. Aside from a welter of bottled-up complaints, and frustration about their protests having been muzzled, two major themes emerged from this post facto opinion survey: One was that the old-time communes and their functions and identity had indeed been "hollowed out" long before the reforms. The mayors expressed their full agreement with the public preference that every local government office ought to deliver desired services equally and efficiently to all of its rural constituents, which it evidently had not done before the reform. The other was that this was the final straw for the old authoritarian (*obrigkeitlich*) concept of local government and that from now on, the service state (*Dienstleistungsstaat*) would entirely take its place. Even under the Weimar Republic, prior to 1933, some rural communal laws had still referred to the mayor (then always a male) as the "authority" (*Obrigkeit*) of the community and he was granted police powers, shared with the state. The Communal Statute of 1935 of the Third Reich made the mayor a kind of "viceroy" exercising authority on behalf of the state until, in 1945, local elections were reintroduced. In Bavaria, a new Communal Statute of 25 January 1952 instituted the new system. And after the completion of the reform, the final version of the Communal Statute (7 August 1992) sealed the incorporation of the service state down to the local level.[2]

Chapter 5 attempts to set these lowest-level communities and their officials and citizens into the wider setting of government in Germany. Above the member communes of a VG and the smallest unified town communities in Bavaria, there is the County (*Kreis*), represented by an elected county executive officer or prefect (*Landrat*) who is also appointed by the state government and, both, represents the Kreis toward the state and the state toward the Kreis. It was this key official, for example, who was entrusted with talking the small communes into joining a VG and negotiating the mergers and annexations necessary for optimal reform. Above the Kreis, Bavaria also has seven provinces or districts (*Regierungsbezirke*). There are elected assemblies at all levels. Above the provincial level, then, there is the state (*Land*) with its parliamentary system: A parliament (*Landtag*, and formerly also a Senate) forms the executive cabinet with ministers and a minister president.

Above the states, there is the federal government, another parliamentary system whose bicameral legislature represents both the individual citizens via political parties in an elected federal parliament (*Bundestag*) and each state in the non-elective Federal Council (*Bundesrat*). The state delegations in the *Bundesrat* consist of varying numbers of state officials specifically instructed by their respective state governments and they have to vote en bloc. This system has not changed a lot, only expanded in 1990 with German unification. And even this government, the Federal Republic of Germany, is only partly sovereign because it belongs to the European Union, yet another level. Its citizens are represented in a weak European Parliament, which imposes laws and advisories on them and via a strong member government with a voice in the executive councils of the union. At the bottom of this hierarchy, is it any wonder if the people and officials in the smallest Bavarian communes feel a bit helpless, powerless to shape their own lives and ward off bad developments?

Within the German federal system, of course, there have been dramatic changes since the beginnings of the western Federal Republic in 1949. The forceful economic development of the first decades also led to a series of de facto and constitutional changes that tended to centralize the federal system. The finance reforms of 1969 and the subsequent reordering of intergovernmental relations, in particular, made for a greatly modified federalism as compared to the rather old-fashioned design of 1949. The widening and deepening of the European Union over sixty years also left its impact on German society from top to bottom. German unification in 1990, furthermore, added not only greater size but also more uneven weight to the structure because the new states were generally smaller and far poorer than the old ones. The addition of East German local governments that had evolved quite differently from those in the West was another significant feature in the resulting system that in some ways has become almost unrecognizable from its postwar origins. One recurrent trait, on the other hand, has not changed and it is a trait that had surfaced already in the Weimar Republic, ever since the great finance reform of 1919: German local governments large and small continue to cry out for a better share of taxes and fees, a secure part of the total revenues of the country. It is difficult for them to function optimally, not to mention filling out the frame of the great local territorial reforms of the 1970s and 1980s, without adequate resources.

Finally, chapter 6 explores the seemingly perennial appeal of small-town and village life in Germany and the United States, in spite of the modern desire for comprehensive and well-integrated services for everyone. This underlying paradox also plays a role in our final judgment of the great local government reform in Bavaria. Some time having passed since the actual implementation of these measures, we attempted a summing up by interviewing the *Bürgermeisters* once more. We also revisited the one example of undeniable success—if by an act of grace, by the Strauss "reform of the reform"—Wolframs-Eschenbach. This small, if now enhanced, town indeed makes the impression of relative prosperity and survival amid an uncertain world of small places in a modernized world.

Notes

1. See Gary Meyers, "Reforming la Société Bloquée: Decentralization Through Neighborhood Democracy," in *New Local Centers in Centralized States*, Peter H. Merkl, ed. (Lanham, MD, 1985), 143–191.

2. For the original postwar version of the current Bavarian Communal Statute (*Bayerische Gemeindeordnung*) of 25 January 1952 and its updated versions of 1992 and 1993, see GV Bl. (*Gemeindeverwaltungsblatt*) 1952, 19 ff.; and GV Bl. 1993, 65 ff. Articles 29–35 of the Statute describe the structure of Bavarian local government.

Chapter 1

CHANGING VILLAGES AND SMALL PLACES IN BAVARIA

Bavaria is a land of villages and small towns, quite different from the contemporary United States and therefore not so easily understood by Americans unaccustomed to European anthropology. What is a village (*Dorf*) in the Bavarian context? What is a town (*Stadt*)? Not so many years ago, a traveler might encounter quite a variety of small and seemingly self-sufficient entities in rural Bavaria. Some of the smallest were called *Einöde* or *Weiler*. The word *Einöde* had connotations of desolation and loneliness and usually denoted a farm surrounded by its own fields, miles from the next village to which it might formally belong. Sometimes, also, a charcoal burner or an operator of an abattoir, for obvious reasons, dwelt far from the village community. A *Weiler* or *Flecken* (hamlet) might be a small group of families and their rural buildings, perhaps a group of farms forming a small village. Until just over thirty years ago, the more than 7,000 local communities of Bavaria included more than 1,000 communes of less than 200 inhabitants, 2,500 between 200 and 500, 1,700 between 500 and 1,000, and another 1,000 between 1,000 and 2,000 residents. One hundred years earlier, the small places with less than five hundred residents alone numbered 5,435, and the image of the closed village community—but also of rural isolation and poverty, of dirt roads nearly impassable in bad weather, and of the near-invisibility of government—probably fit most of these agrarian communes (*Landgemeinden*). The people in these small places overwhelmingly supported themselves by agriculture that, even in good harvest years, and depending, of course, on their property and status in rural society, promised for most of them little more than survival.

Many of the names for these villages and small towns still tell of their earliest history, of migrations and peasant settlements in the river valleys and forests of what had long been part of the declining Celtic civilization and the extension of the Roman empire north of the Alps.[1] Many Old Bavarian place names of villages end in *-ing,* as in Manching, or in Suebian Bavaria west of the river Lech, in *-ingen,* as in Dillingen or Donaueschingen—often preceded by the proper name of a founder, or early headman, such as Friso in the ancient bishops' town Freising, Echo in Eching, or Sentilo in Sendling, which is now part of Munich. The migrations, still mysterious and controversial, seem to have come in the sixth through eigth centuries from the areas later known as Bohemia and Moravia, and some farther to the south.[2] Later waves created settlements whose names often end in *-heim* or *-ham* (home), *-hausen* (house), *-feld* (field), or *-hofen* (farm), as in Franconian Ostheim, Babenshausen, Steinsfeld, or Lower Bavarian Vilshofen. The village settlements were usually under the wings of a clerical or secular power, a bishop, monastery, or nobleman. Many place names show the proximity of the overlord's castle on the hill (*-berg*), others the church (*-kirchen*). Some have the castle (*-burg*) itself in the name—such as Rothenburg (red castle) or Wasserburg, the "castle on the water" of the Inn River—or other important physical features, such as a brook (*-bach*), ford (*-furt*), bridge (*-bruck*), wood (*-wald*), or spring (*-brunn,* or *-bronn*). Ansbach is a simplified version of the old Onolzbach, one of the streams (now called Holzbach) on which it lies. Fürth is at the ford across the river Regnitz.

Some settlements grew into marketplaces or towns because of the power of their clerical or secular overlords, or because of their emerging economic importance in the caravan trade toward the eastern trade routes. Size had little to do with the difference between villages and the emerging medieval markets and towns. According to recent estimates, only about two hundred of the approximately four thousand towns and marketplaces of medieval Germany had over two thousand inhabitants, and three thousand were below five hundred. One account speaks of numerous "dwarf cities" of less than two hundred and small "small towns" of two to five hundred souls,[3] which must have been exceeded in size by many contemporary villages. Wilhelm Heinrich Riehl in 1853 spoke of *Dorfstädte* and *Stadtdörfer* (village towns and town villages) to indicate the difficulties of drawing the line.

The chief difference between the early towns and villages seems to have been a matter of the legal and actual domination of the villages by their respective clerical or secular overlords. The medieval towns, by way of contrast, had reached a state of relative autonomy after a period of early tutelage by an overlord, and this autonomy expressed itself in such things as having their own judicial authority, market rights with regard to their hinterland and trade routes, the often-cited right to fortify themselves with walls and gates against attackers, and their recognized corporate character.[4] The sociologist Max Weber also stresses the distinctive presence in the early villages of common grazing lands (*Allmende*). And, needless to add, the old villages never had their own judicial authority or a corporate character that could be represented in the general estates (*Landstände*), not to mention city walls. Their inhabitants, consequently, were exposed to such tribulations of "un-freedom," from taxation to serfdom,[5] as their overlords from time to time managed to impose on them and their property.

To sum up, then, it seems that a village is essentially a communal settlement of families that, like a patch of hardy grasses, somehow managed to endure under the heels of a succession of overlords and even under the hooves of conquering hordes, to sprout again and again in the fertile soil. A town, whatever may be its antecedents,[6] is a bundle of trade and exchange functions of mutual benefit that tie together the people inside its walls as well as the town with its hinterland and with distant trading partners. Towns could easily become the equal of any local potentate but were vulnerable not only to conquerors that forced their fortifications and put them to the torch, but also to changes in the social environment that nourished their trade and exchange functions beyond their walls, such as outbreaks of anarchy, war, piracy, or the rise of the robber barons in the fifteenth century.

Contemporary Social Change

All these village and small-town antecedents and many of the causes that gave rise to the difference between small towns and villages seemed like ancient history in the second half of the twentieth century. To be sure, today's small places in Bavaria still show their history—in particular their regional history—in many physical features such as the differences between Bavarian and Franconian small towns or villages. Small places in Franconia, with its history of political fragmentation, whether they were medieval or more modern towns or villages, often have more of a town-like center, a square complete with an ornate *Rathaus* (city hall), schoolhouse, church, and other seemingly representative buildings in a tight, irregular pattern. In Upper and Lower Bavaria, with its long history as a centralized duchy, the centers of larger towns are usually built along wide roads leading to the major trade routes. Most of the smaller places are likely to be dominated by scattered farmhouses or whole farms. Some of the smaller old Franconian towns, such as Ornbau, Merkendorf, or Wolframs-Eschenbach, still show their medieval origins. There is, for example, a cluster of three such recognized mini-towns and two market towns southeast of Ansbach that were all destined to be merged (along with a sixth small settlement) into one administrative union (VG) named Triesdorf in the late 1970s and early 1980s.

The name VG, meaning an administrative union of small communes, was used in the states of Bavaria, Baden-Württemberg, and, in East Germany, Thuringia, Saxony, and Saxony-Anhalt. In Lower Saxony, more or less the same thing came to be called *Samtgemeinde* and, in Rhineland Palatinate, *Verbandsgemeinde*. In Schleswig-Holstein, however, and in East German Mecklenburg-Vorpommern and Brandenburg, the name was *Amt* (plural *Ämter*). A good example of a current VG in our area of research is the VG Altmühltal, consisting of four small places: Dittenheim, with a 2007 population of 1731, Alesheim (1020), Markt Berolzheim (1362), and Meinheim (875). The long-established status of towns, such as a "town" (*Stadt*) or "market town" (*Markt*) is now merely part of their name. Let us describe three Franconian communities with the old title of *Stadt* in the VG Triesdorf I (see map 1.1a).

Ornbau (*Stadt*), one thousand years old (with a present population of 1627 and situated at the junction of the Altmühl and Wieseth rivers), has a semicircular, sometimes double wall around it that is completed with a straight wall along the Altmühl. An ancient bridge across the river enters the town through the old Lower Gate, which still shows the rollers where the drawbridge was attached. The eastern wall has a White Tower and a round Thief's Tower, the western wall three fortified battlements. The Upper Gate was destroyed by fire two hundred years ago but was rebuilt. The narrow streets appear not to have changed for centuries. Ornbau probably began in the ninth century as a village under the aegis of the Benedictine monastery of Herrieden and its present fortifications (built 1470–1490) were preceded by earlier walls, built in 1286 and 1317. Its town status was recognized in 1317 and by the middle of the fifteenth century it had some one hundred and fifty houses, a high court and a lower court, an episcopal administration, and a market. There are two very old churches on even older sites, St. Jakob and St. Jodokus, as well as a baroque *Rathaus* dating back to 1647.[7] Ornbau's current image also owes much to its being the location of the annual, international Mercedes-Benz automobile rally, which in 2009 drew over twenty thousand visitors.

Illustration 1.1. Ornbau bridge and walls.
Photo by Peter Merkl.

Merkendorf (*Stadt*), population 2,820 and near Ornbau, was a village founded around the year 1000 and, until centuries later, owned by the rich Cistercian monastery of Heilsbronn. It was granted market rights (*Markt*) status and the right to fortifications in the early 1400s. For thirty years, walls, towers, and moats were built and, in the 1470s, a *Bürgermeister* and city council for the first time sat as a court in the city hall (*Rathaus*). Before its partial destruction in the hostilities at the end of World War II, the town was considered a model of Franconian town centers. The city walls can still be seen although the town soon outgrew them.[8]

Wolframs-Eschenbach (*Stadt*) was long known simply as Eschenbach, or Obereschenbach, until in 1917 a local historian convinced authorities that it was the birthplace of Germany's greatest medieval poet, Wolfram von Eschenbach (1170–ca. 1220), known especially for his epic *Parzifal*. When I was going to school in Munich, I had to memorize and recite parts of this epic. Wolfram also authored two more epics, *Titurel* and *Willehalm*. The present name of the town was conferred by the Bavarian state in 1917. The settlement was known at least from the eleventh century when it was under the bishopric of Eichstätt. From the early thirteenth century on, it flourished as the seat of the Order of the Teutonic Knights. Hence

Illustration 1.2. Wolframs-Eschenbach gate with barbacane.
Photo courtesy of the city of Wolframs-Eschenbach.

it acquired the beginnings of walls, gates, and urban character long before Emperor Ludwig the Bavarian, in 1332, granted it the legal privileges of a town. In spite of the takeover of the local establishment by the Teutonic Order of Nuremberg in the fourteenth century, the city became rich and beautiful by being on the long-distance trade route between Nuremberg and Strassburg. The walled city still encloses Franconia's oldest (mid-thirteenth-century) large Gothic church, which now has a pointed, colorful cone. Among the historic attractions is the Renaissance palace of the Teutonic Knights (built in 1623, and used as *Rathaus* since 1859 in place of the older, Gothic one of 1471), and other splendid ancient and half-timbered buildings along its Main Street.[9] The high point of the medieval development of Wolframs-Eschenbach appeared to be around the year 1500 when it boasted 1,000 residents and 227 households, as compared to 451 households in Ansbach, and 217 in Gunzenhausen, 2 contemporary county seats nearby, and 68 in Merkendorf.

But in the following century, religious tensions between the Catholic Teutonic Order and the increasingly Protestant/Evangelical population dramatically reflected the coming of the Reformation, the Thirty Years'

Illustration 1.3. Ansbach: Orangerie of Margrave's Residence.
Photo by Peter Merkl.

War, and the rise of Prussian rule in Franconia. The war and epidemics decimated the population until, in 1636, only 65 of 177 houses still had living residents. After the war, the Teutonic Order once more rebuilt and beautified the city center and particularly the church in baroque style, adding a St. Mary's Chapel in which Wolfram is said to be buried. By the end of the eighteenth century, Prussian troops entered the town and put an end to the reign and possessions of the Order. But soon after (1806), the Holy Roman Empire of German Nation was dissolved and the Prussian parts of Franconia turned over to the new Kingdom of Bavaria. The dominant trade route, however, now ran from Nuremberg over Ansbach to Stuttgart, relegating Eschenbach to economic isolation and stagnation.

Today, after being freed from consignment to the status of a mere member commune of the VG Triesdorf I, the town has become the greatly enlarged center of a new VG Wolframs-Eschenbach, of which Mitteleschenbach is the only other member. The more rural community of Mitteleschenbach nearby recently celebrated the 950th anniversary of its ancient church. A new VG Triesdorf II was formed without these two communities, but with Weidenbach, taking its name again from the charming water castle (1454) and educational center of Triesdorf, which once was the summer residence of the Margraves of Ansbach. This VG Triesdorf/Weidenbach has 3,809 residents today, the VG Wolframs-Eschenbach 4,449 (2009).

Two towns with the title of *Markt,* Arberg and Weidenbach were also to be included originally in the VG Triesdorf I. Arberg can be traced back to the early thirteenth century and once boasted a castle, the Turnhügelburg, on a site at the edge of town where there is now a farmhouse. There is also an old church, St. Blasius, that dates from 1709. Arberg and Merkendorf regained their independence after the dissolution of the VG Triesdorf I in the 1980s.

In the second half of the twentieth century, all four of these venerable towns and marketplaces were in danger of losing the last shreds of their autonomy and dignity following long decades of population stagnation and relative economic decline even in the middle of the boom years of the Federal Republic. Their titles of *Stadt* or *Markt,* and even minor annexations, helped them as little as their remaining city walls against the impact of the economic realities of the 1970s. Ornbau had only 1,347 residents in 1975, Merkendorf 1,425, Wolframs-Eschenbach 1,774, Mitteleschenbach 1,285, Arberg 1,383, and Weidenbach 1,999, totaling less than 10,000. In the eyes of the state planning agencies, this made them practically indistinguishable from many newer small towns and ancient (and new) villages that became the target of local territorial reorganization and consolidation because of their marginal size. And even though some of these particular small town communes in the end seem to have beaten back once more the onslaught of the barbarian hordes upon their ramparts,[10] their predicament shall serve us as the peg on which to hang our tale of the impact of the last four decades of social change upon small places in Bavaria.

Social change, of course, has been going on all along in western, industrialized societies, and at the village level almost as much as in the urban centers. Nevertheless, it appears that the decades since World War II had brought about particularly dramatic changes to the village and small-town periphery of West German society, frequently also bringing earlier cumulative trends of the industrial age to a point that spelt the end of the old, self-contained identity and community—and underdeveloped condition—of these small places. Let us take a closer look at the secular changes that were said to have "hollowed out" their function and identity. Long before state planners decided to take away their *Rathaus,* their political and legal autonomy, and to force them to consolidate their entities into larger units, long-range changes had eroded their social autonomy and sense of cohesion as communities. The motorcycle and automobile broke down their physical isolation. Economic rationalization and market forces incorporated them into larger areas while at the same time changing the social functions of their village taverns, inns, retail stores, and, in some cases, even of their own separate post offices and railroad stations. The progressive separation of church parish from the village school and the final consolidation of schooling into large school districts united by school busses further eroded the primary community of these small places while radio and television brought the larger community life of state and nation into every living room.

As the winds of change completed the erosion of these small communities, an entire way of life, the stuff of an extensive and romantic ethnic home literature (*Heimatliteratur*), seems to be passing into the dustbin of history, nearly all more or less within the same generation. The nostalgic memories of older residents will soon pass away with them and, among the young, not even a sense of loss may remain as they live their busy modern lives amidst the ubiquitous signs of the urbanization of country life.

Fifteen Communities in Franconia

To observe more closely the fatal process of shrinkage and stagnation at the level of these small places, we decided to take a detailed look at this part of Bavaria that has been notable for its population decline and economic weakness over the last decades. Few American tourists who admire the medieval towers and city walls of Rothenburg on the Tauber are aware that this thriving tourist attraction lies in the middle of a declining region of similar if smaller old towns and villages that have not been able to keep up with the pace of German economic expansion. West Middle Franconia, west of Nuremberg, includes the city of Ansbach and the Landkreise (rural counties) Ansbach, Neustadt/Aisch-Bad Windsheim, and Weissenburg-Gunzenhausen.[11] This area in 1978 had the lowest population density (thirty-three inhabitants per square mile) of the sparsely settled state of Bavaria (averaging fifty-nine per square mile). See also table A1 in the Appendix. To be sure, this is not the only part of Bavaria that has been steadily losing population; the same is true of Lower Bavaria, Upper Franconia, and the Upper Palatinate, all the provinces along the eastern border of the nation. But West Middle Franconia's weakness has nothing to do with a border situation but rather with being in between the thriving conurbations of Nuremberg-Erlangen-Fürth, Augsburg, and Munich, which attract its population. The region also has lagged notably behind the per capita birthrate of the state and had a smaller percentage of people in the most active age cohorts between ages fifteen and sixty-five. Its average wage and salary level, moreover, was already about 14 percent lower than the state-wide average for Bavaria in 1969 before the reform, in fact in the areas of Rothenburg and Gunzenhausen as much as 20 percent lower.[12] In the meantime, the income differential has more than doubled.

In this predominantly agricultural and then poorly connected region, we selected fifteen communities to test several hypotheses that had been suggested by many of the mayors and Landräte (elected prefects) we had interviewed: that the territorial reorganization of Bavarian local governments of the late seventies was the logical result of decades of postwar social change that had "hollowed out" their sense of community and the social reality their town halls and councils were supposed to represent. The particulars of this process differed from statement to statement. But the gist of it was that the automobile and economic rationalization had ushered in a shrinking process in small communities, which led to the gradual disappearance of many of the social centers where people used to gather and of other indications and forms of community life. The major structural changes in Bavarian agriculture and the closing of many rural one- or two-room elementary schools in favor of larger school centers also helped to accelerate this process, and now many of these small towns and villages had lost their town halls as well.

The radical reduction of autonomous local governments in Bavaria suggests that, over the last four decades or more, most of the weaker ones have failed to achieve the critical size and economic strength needed to survive the planners' final selection of "small centers" among the new, unified communities (*Einheitsgemeinden*, EGs) and administrative unions (VGs) of micro-communes. As a result, they fell under the spell of such a new center nearby that, for one reason or another, had made the grade. In this chapter, we would like to examine in particular how some of the more obvious losers in this process of decline or stagnation seem to have failed to adjust sufficiently to (a) the population movement of the post-war decades; (b) the development impulses stemming from the impact of industrialization, urbanization, and the growth of the national economic market; (c) the development of supra-local social patterns; and (d) the transformation of agriculture since 1945 and earlier.

Population changes[13] and economic indicators are among the most meaningful symptoms of this adjustment, or the lack of it (see table A1 in the Appendix). The loss of agricultural jobs and the migration of persons once employed locally, and of many young people, to the more urbanized and developed areas of the country set off declining regions and communities from their more successful neighbors. Commuting patterns to jobs or schools outside a community are harbingers of the changing local economy[14] and of the raised expectations and future emigration of the young. But there are also changing patterns of social activity and of consumer habits that may or may not indicate the waning sense of community of a small town or village. As old community patterns are progressively replaced with more inclusive ones, we believe, the citizens also tend to lose more and more of their identification with the small places in which they have grown up and lived for a long time. Once they lose much of their local identity, the more mobile and especially the youngest citizens are quite likely to leave their village or small town for a larger place, where opportunity seems to beckon.

In contrast to successful and highly urbanized East Middle Franconia (the area around Nuremberg and Fürth/Erlangen) in 1978, West Middle Franconia had been in relative decline for some time. It was still off the existing *Autobahn* (freeway) net and poorly connected to the nearest metropolitan centers (Nuremberg-Fürth, Augsburg, Munich) and hence to markets and raw materials. To make matters even worse, the federal railroads had decided to discontinue many local lines that aggravated its marginal situation on the state boundary with Baden-Württemberg. According to the Bavarian state development program, it was rather rural—except for the vicinity of the "middle center" Ansbach—and needed

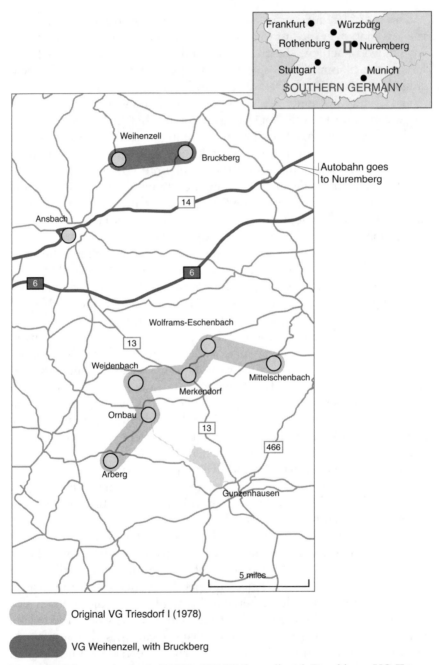

Map 1.1a. County Ansbach (1978): VG Weihenzell with Bruckberg; VG Tries-dorf I which included Wolframs-Eschenbach, Mitteleschenbach, Merkendorf, Ornbau, Weidenbach, and Arberg.

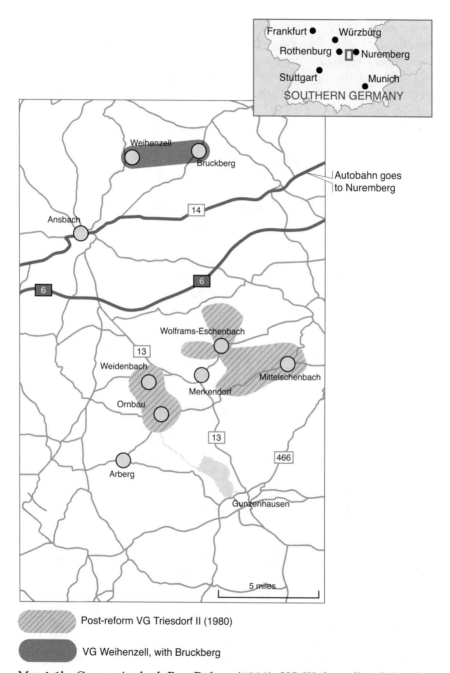

Map 1.1b. County Ansbach Post-Reform (1980): VG Weihenzell with Bruckberg; VG Wolframs-Eschenbach, with Mitteleschenbach; and VG Triesdorf II which included: Ornbau and Weidenbach, Merkendorf, Arberg again independent Note annexations of Wolframs-Eschenbach (VG): Selgenstadt, Biederbach, Adelmannsdorf, Reutern, Wöltendorf, Waizendorf, and others.

assistance both with its transport situation and with the further development of non-agricultural employment to counteract the emigration of population that had been going on for many decades.[15] Hence the territorial *Kreis* reform of 1972 reduced the number of rural counties (Landkreise) here from nine to three larger ones. The local territorial reform of 1978 reduced the 487 (1971) autonomous communes to 123 (1989), of which 86 were part of 22 newly created administrative unions (VG), leaving only 37 autonomous unified communes (EG). Generally speaking, the more administrative unions occur in a Landkreis, the more rural and scattered its population. Landkreis Ansbach has ten of them, more than most Landkreise.[16]

Our selection of the fifteen small West Middle Franconian communities—most of them now members of administrative unions—for a closer examination of this process of winnowing out deliberately chose some of the weaker units, as can be checked against the following indices: their population density in 1972 was only twenty-one persons per square mile (as compared to thirty-three for West Middle Franconia and fifty-nine for Bavaria). The average size of their agricultural holdings was below those of the state. More than 40 percent (versus 25 percent in the region and 29 percent in Bavaria) of their gainfully employed population commuted every working day to jobs outside the community. Their annual tax revenue per capita was DM 150 as compared to DM 262 for the region and DM 361 for the state.[17] We also gave preference to the administrative unions with the largest number of member communes, or with a center located outside the union, such as those found in Landkreis Ansbach. In this fashion we arrived at the following choice of communes (from the administrative unions named) for our interviews and examination of available records and statistics.[18] (See also tables A5–A7.) The fluctuating population numbers reflect, among other things, the annexations and other changes of the local territorial reform.

The interviews were conducted with mayors, teachers, and priests or ministers in these communes according to a list of questions regarding agricultural, other economic, social, and political changes since 1945. This list also included the changing roles of the mayors, teachers or principals, and priests/ministers in the life of their respective communities.[19] The long time span involved also made for a preference for older informants of long years of service and residence in the community in question, as well as for written chronicles or books about the region or its communes. In the case of the clergy, which customarily leaves the community upon retirement in order not to complicate the lives of their successors, two long-serving Protestant and one Catholic clergymen were consulted.

Table 1.1. List of communes selected for interviews

Name of Commune (1975–2008 Population)	Name of VG	Name of County
1. Weigenheim—(966–1,021)	VG Uffenheim	Neustadt/Aisch- Bad Windsheim
2. Ippesheim (Markt)—(877–1,095)	"	"
3. Ornbau (Stadt)—(1,347–1,627)	VG Triesdorf II	Ansbach
4. Markt Berolzheim (Markt)—(1,362–1,367)	VG Altmühltal	Weissenburg-Gunzenhausen
5. Meinheim—(785–877)	"	"
6. Ohrenbach—(766–627)	VG Rothenburg ob der Tauber	Ansbach
7. Steinsfeld—(1,179–1,245)	"	"
8. Adelshofen—(1,025–925)	"	"
9. Weihenzell—(1,754–2,819)	VG Weihenzell	Ansbach
10. Bruckberg—(1,249–1,337)	"	"
11. Mitteleschenbach—(1,322–1,579)	VG Wolframs-Eschenbach	Ansbach
12. Wolframs-Eschenbach (Stadt)—(2,019–2,870)	"	"
13. Burk—(1,019–1,168)	VG Dentlein am Forst	Ansbach
14. Dentlein am Forst (Markt) [not included]—(2,457–2,443)	"	"
15. Röckingen—(670–750)	VG Hesselberg	Ansbach
16. Langfurth—(1,886–2,148)	"	"

Population Trends

Like other industrialized countries of the West, Germany embarked on the great journey from its agrarian past in the nineteenth century. But urbanization and industrialization came rather late to Bavaria where, in 1871, 74 percent of the population still lived in nearly eight thousand hamlets with less than one thousand inhabitants each.[20] Aside from the capital, Munich, and such ancient urban centers as Nuremberg, Augsburg, and Würzburg,[21] the new urban-industrial centers had only just begun to draw away the rural population with jobs and the promise of a more interesting life. The whole country, of course, was still undergoing the gradual transition from its rural antecedents, which were character-

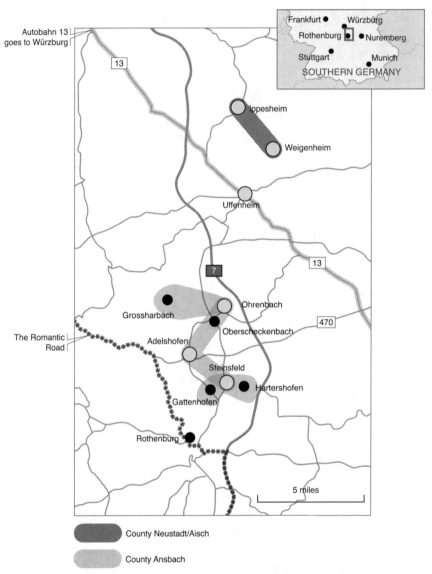

Map 1.2. County Neustadt/Aisch and County Ansbach: County Neustadt/Aisch includes VG Uffenheim with Ippesheim and Weigenheim; County Ansbach includes VG Rothenburg: Ohrenbach, Adelshofen and Steinsfeld. (Annexations mentioned: Hartershofen, Gattenhofen, Grossharbach, Oberscheckenbach.) The Romantic Road passes from Würzburg through Rothenburg and Dinkelsbühl to Augsburg

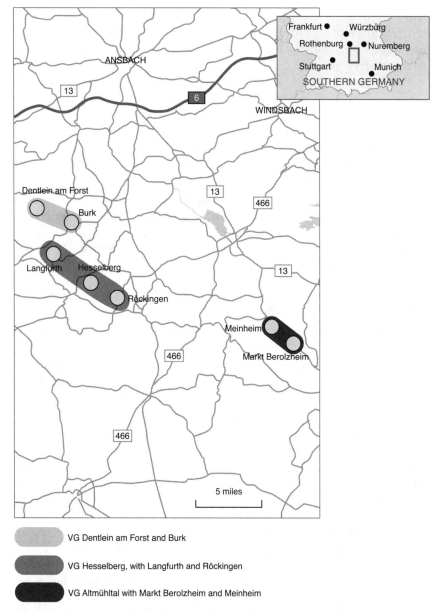

Map 1.3. County Ansbach: VG Dentlein am Forst; VG Hesselberg, with Langfurth and Röckingen; County Gunzenhausen/Weissenburg: VG Altmühltal with Markt Berolzheim and Meinheim.

ized by a large percentage (42.2 percent in 1882) of the German work force being employed in agriculture and forestry. By 1925, this percentage had shrunk to 30.3 percent and by 1950, to 22.1 percent, while the industrial and service sectors grew into leading positions.

But Bavaria lagged behind Germany by a quarter century. Here the percentage of the agriculturally employed still stood at 30.6 percent as recently as the 1950 census. It has since declined to 3.1 percent (2009) in Bavaria while it stands at 2.1 percent (2007) in the Federal Republic. These startling postwar changes occurred differently between the sexes. They are symptomatic also of the transformation of Bavarian agriculture,[22] and perhaps of agriculture in all European industrial societies. Because many farms have been operated by the farmers' wives and children while they have another job, for example, the males now only account for 3.5 percent in agricultural employment. Let us take a closer look at the changing population and employment patterns after 1945 in the fifteen communes under consideration.

The Arrival of the Refugees

World War II brought Bavaria its share of the casualties and disabled, about one tenth of those of the nation, and this predominantly among young males aged (in 1945) between eighteen and forty. But there was little damage from the Allied conquest itself, aside from the air raids on the larger cities. In the countryside, the war was felt only indirectly: there was neither the threat of death from bombs nor the acute food shortages of the urban areas, although food production was subject to wartime supply regulation. On the contrary, throughout the war and immediate postwar years, the village and small-town folks were the object of private foraging forays by many a hungry *Hamsterer* (hoarder) from the city who was ready to sell anything, from used fur coats to wedding rings, in exchange for food staples like chickens and eggs.

The air raids in the cities also brought the first homeless evacuees in droves into rural and small-town housing, which may have been the first hint of what was to come when the Red Army would advance toward Germany in 1945 and various once German-occupied Eastern European countries began to expel their German ethnic populations. While estimates vary, the Bavarian and Bonn governments insisted that, from the fall of 1944, over twelve million German refugees and expellees from beyond the Oder-Neisse (rivers) line, from Poland, Czechoslovakia, Hungary, and southeastern Europe, by mass transport or on their own, embarked on the great trek toward what was left of Germany after the collapse of the Third Reich. An estimated two million died along the way. By November 1946, refugee agencies in Bavaria had already issued 1.5 million refugee passes. Some moved on to other states. As late as 1950, 21.5 percent of the resident population of the state was considered of refugee origin.[23] Most of them had arrived destitute by rail or on foot and at a time when the big cities were hardly in a position to house and feed their own residents. So the refugees tended to spend their first years in rural and small-town areas of Germany not far from the boundaries of the Russian zone of occupation. Once they had settled down in villages and small towns after a transitional period in refugee camps, the natives frequently resented their presence and having to share food and shelter with people from different cultural backgrounds and, often, of different religion. The economic recovery of the early fifties finally enabled many of the refugees to move on to bigger towns and cities in search of jobs and social acceptance, while some remained behind.

In the meantime, one authority on refugee questions, aware of Germany's long earlier history of urban migration, had written in a newspaper article entitled "The End of Rural Flight?"[24]: "Since the beginning of the war the metropolitan population of Bavaria has dropped by 12 percent. In the flat country, that is in communes of less than 2,000 inhabitants, there is almost a million more people now and 775,000 more than in 1939. Country towns and markets nearly doubled their population … since 1939." There followed a statistical table showing the concentration of the increase in communes between two thousand and twenty thousand, and a 23 percent increase in those below that size, places like the fifteen under consideration in this chapter. The prospect of a reversal of the long-standing trend of a hundred years of industrialization and rural flight of population, of course, was not fulfilled. Nevertheless, this could have been a major opportunity for these stagnant communes to grow and prosper.

The population of our fifteen towns and villages, indeed, increased dramatically between 1939 and 1950, only to decline again during the 1950s, and in most cases to this day. The resistance to the presence of the refugees and expellees had expressed itself, among other things, by a reluctance of local authorities to make available residential lots on which they could have built houses. Only Burk and Markt Berolzheim distinguished themselves by supplying them with free or nearly free building acreage, which encouraged the permanent establishment of new trades and industry, thus creating additional jobs. We should emphasize that the refugees made major contributions to the Bavarian economy, adding 4,000 industrial enterprises (20 percent of the state's industry), 22,000 small trade enterprises, and 11,500 farms, and all this with a population of predominantly women, old men, and children. The old market town Markt Berolzheim, the location of archeological discoveries from Celtic times, picked up nearly 60 percent in population between 1939 and 1950, but lost half of this increment again in the next decades, in spite of becoming a bedroom community of the larger medieval towns of Treuchtlingen and Gunzenhausen. Burk, from similar agricultural antecedents, and with smaller gains, became predominantly a manufacturing town in the 1950s. The other communities evidently missed this opportunity for growth and economic expansion, although time soon appears to have healed the wounds of the first encounters between natives and refugees among those that remained.

The 1960s and 1970s, in most cases, witnessed a further slow decline or relative stagnation of the population in all but the communes of Burk and Weihenzell. The latter was close enough to the city of Ansbach to become something of a bedroom community without losing its agricultural character entirely (tables A2–A5).[25] Langfurth, Mitteleschenbach, and Ornbau grew in the 1960s, but slowed down in the 1970s. Among these, agrarian Langfurth actually turned into a predominantly manufacturing commune in the 1960s, while the other two only acquired a partially residential character without losing their agricultural basis. Others, like wine-growing Ippesheim, lost nearly a fourth of their small population over a period of twenty years, after having declined already by nearly one-half during the century preceding 1939.[26] Generally speaking, the losses of population were due more to out-migration rather than to an excess of deaths over the birth rate. In the 1970s, however, the declining birth rate became more noticeable in the statistics of such declining towns as Meinheim and Markt Berolzheim where it aggravated the migration losses. The four communes that grew in the seventies—Weihenzell, Burk, Ornbau, and Mitteleschenbach—are distinguished by the presence of substantial non-agricultural employment opportunities. In Langfurth and Burk, for example, there is a thriving brush-making industry. In Weihenzell, many people who work in Ansbach, in particular civil servants, have found lots for residential and even industrial sites. On the other hand, and with the exception of Markt Berolzheim, all the communes that lost population in the 1970s were predominantly agricultural. In recent years, the great recession further aggravated the population decline in many cases (save Bruckberg, Ornbau, Langfurth, Weihenzell and Wolframs-Eschenbach): In 2007–2008 Ippesheim lost eighty-five, Weigenheim sixty-three, Markt Berolzheim ninety-five, and Meinheim sixty-four residents.

Growth and Decline

Why did the population of some of these small places decline and others grow, aside from the temporary influx and exit of the refugees? Some of the change may indeed be a matter of local leadership (or its absence) that eagerly took on challenges such as the coming of the refugees and turned this temporary burden into opportunities for growth. Most of the change, however, must be accounted for with long-range trends that came from outside the small communities:

(1) The growth of non-agricultural employment opportunities as part of the rise of industrialization and of a regional, and national market for the goods produced by new industries, such as the brushes made in Langfurth, Ornbau, and Burk. To quote the mayor of Burk, a community with such a substantial non-agricultural sector should be considered "urban" rather than "rural."

(2) Changes in family size and composition: Like in other industrial societies, the Bavarian rural and small-town family has shrunk substantially, if not quite as much as in the big cities. The typical farm and small-town family now consists of the nuclear family, but with far fewer children than in an earlier age—one, two, or none is common—and a surprisingly high percentage of single-person households, young unmarrieds, widows, and many people who never intended to get married even though they may live together with a partner for a while. The percentage of one-person households has increased noticeably since 1950, though at that time there also must have been many war widows. The only difference from the city seems to be that the villagers and small-town folk, especially the farm families, like to have their elderly parents live with them rather than having them move into an old-folks home.

(3) Generational changes also distinguish today's rural and small-town society from that of 1939 when there was still a preponderance of the very young. In such declining agricultural hamlets as Meinheim, Adelshofen, Ohrenbach, and Ippesheim, in particular, the senior element now makes up well over 15 percent of the population, considerably more than the regional and state averages. As the younger people move away, the oldsters stay behind. The population of working age, fifteen to sixty-four, is under-represented in most of our communes, as compared to the regional and state averages. The Catholic religion of Wolframs-Eschenbach, and Ornbau—the others are predominantly Protestant—has not noticeably set off these communities by an abundance of children. Unlike some of the larger towns in the area, our fifteen communities were too small to have had significant Jewish populations before the war or Muslim (Turkish) minorities today.

(4) The character of agriculture itself and of the average farm has changed profoundly as we shall set forth in greater detail below. The impact

of the European Common Market, and of competition from such highly modernized overseas sources as the United States, has forced a shrinkage and rationalization upon Bavarian farming that clearly was not the choice of the farmers, or even of part-time farmers—as most of them had to become—in order to survive (see tables A2–A7).

(5) At the same time, the non-farming economy of these small places has undergone a process of rationalization of its own that affected especially the smaller businesses, Mom-and-Pop retail stores, taverns, bakeries, and similar trades, and in some locations made tourism and other services an attractive alternative for a declining local economy. Where the local economy was based on services to begin with, as in Bruckberg with its large children's clinic, there was no significant decline at all (tables A8 and A9).

(6) Culturally and socially, these small-town and rural places suffered perhaps their most severe blow with the consolidation of the village schools by the 1970s into large school centers, a change preceded by more than a century of retreat of the unifying, if heavy, hand of the church upon village education (see chapter 2). Finally, the coming of nearly universal automobile ownership since the 1950s and the rising patterns of commuting to school and to work broke up the relative physical isolation of most small places in Bavaria, bringing the outside world to their doorstep while television brought it into the living room (tables A5 and A11).

(7) The population figures on our list of the fifteen communities also suggest the impact of the local territorial reform, as distinct from the factors mentioned above. Really significant, reform-related changes occurred only in the cases of Wolframs-Eschenbach and Weihenzell, in the first case only after substantial annexations and the 1980 correction of the original reform. Most of our small communes remained more or less at their original level. The county of Ansbach is expected to lose another 5 percent of its population by 2028.

Stages of Community Development

Now we can plot the path of each of these fifteen Franconian communities from their agricultural antecedents to their present state. With the exception of Bruckberg, every one of them really began in 1950 as a predominantly agrarian place, including the medieval towns of Wolframs-Eschenbach and Ornbau. Only three of them did not change at all: Adelshofen, Ohrenbach, and Weigenheim. Röckingen and Ippesheim changed a little, but retained their predominantly agrarian character. We can apply the scheme underlying the macro-societal change from Bavaria's distant rural past to its current condition systematically to the changes evident in these communities over a period of six decades, 1950 to 2008. By using three variables—density of jobs per population; predominance of agriculture, industry, or services in employment; and the percentage of outward-bound job commuters per population—we obtain six types of communities.[27] While the first three types are consecutive, the fourth, fifth, and sixth should be considered more as alternative options. (See also table A2 in the Appendix.)

Table 1.2. Stages and types of community development

	Variable Thresholds		
Stages	Density of local jobs (percent)	Predominant Sector (percent)	Outward Commuters (percent)
1. Agrarian I	30 percent and over	2/3 and more agricultural	Low
2. Agrarian II	30 percent and over	Under 2/3 agricultural	Low
3. Agrarian-Residential	Below 30 percent	Predominantly agricultural	15 percent and over
4. Manufacturing	30 percent and over	Predominantly manufacture	Under 20 percent
5. Bedroom Community	Below 30 percent	Predominantly manufacture or services	15 percent and over
6. Services Community	30 percent and over	Predominantly services	Low

Our fifteen communities, whether growing, stagnating, or declining in population, can now be followed in their changes over the three decades prior to the local territorial reform. Of course, the tabulation is complicated somewhat by how in some cases (Langfurth, Meinheim, and Steinsfeld) places reversed the change by annexing neighboring rural communities. Bruckberg is a special case because of the large pediatric clinic facilities there that supplied about 450 service jobs. All the other communities, save the most declining (Adelshofen, Ohrenbach, and Weigenheim), show some change. Even declining Ippesheim has moved from Agrarian Phase One to Agrarian Phase Two, as has Röckingen.[28]

The declining density of jobs in agriculture, for example, and rising commuter patterns often ease the transition to the Agrarian-Residential (3) or Manufacturing and Trades (4) phase. Burk and Wolframs-Eschenbach arrived at Phase 4 in the 1950s, Langfurth in the 1960s, and Steinsfeld in the 1970s. Markt Berolzheim, with few jobs and many commuters, became a bedroom community for larger Weissenburg, although there is also a substantial service sector.

Changing Employment Patterns

It is axiomatic for the economic changes in these communities that, apart from the temporary impact of the refugees and expellees, the percentage employed in agriculture had declined while that in industry, commerce, and services had increased by the time of the reform. To be sure, they were nearly all still heavily agricultural in 1939–1950, except for Bruckberg, and were still behind the regional and state figures in this respect in 1970. Moreover, the communes that were most heavily agricultural in 1939 (over 80 percent in agriculture) were still the most agricultural (over 45 percent) among the fifteen in 1970: Adelshofen, Ohrenbach, Ippesheim, Weigenheim, Meinheim, Röckingen, Steinsfeld, and Weihenzell. By the same token, those with a good head start in manufacturing and trades in 1939 (24 percent and more) had by 1970 a majority in such employment: Langfurth, Burk, Ornbau, Wolframs-Eschenbach, and, with a slower start, Mitteleschenbach. They were ahead of the regional and state averages. In commerce and services, the pattern is less clear.

The increasing element of workers and service employees also raises the question of how well farmers and non-farmers get along in these communities. According to the mayors interviewed, their relations, by and large, have been good, as long as community planners have taken care not to locate new workers and white-collar subdivisions downwind from the noise and odor of farms. There have been tensions in the past between agricultural and workers' villages, and on occasion—for instance, upon the erection of May poles—brawls have barely been avoided. Farmers in a farm village like Ammelbruch used to look askance at a nearby workers' village like Langfurth that was once considered dirt poor and of an excessive birthrate. But World War II and rising prosperity have helped, at least among the young who now go to the same schools together, to break down the old contempt. Today, both form one community and only the older generation still recalls the old prejudices.

The perspective of the whole Bavarian economy since the mid nineteenth century when nearly 70 percent were employed in agriculture illuminates the character of these changes. In the first one hundred years, it was mostly the extraordinary increase of white-collar workers, pensioners, and workers in industry and the trades (independent businessmen declined somewhat). In agriculture, on the other hand, farmers and their family helpers dropped to one-third and agricultural laborers to one-seventh of the mid-nineteenth-century figures, and this development has continued to this day. In the last decade alone, the number of agriculturally employed persons dropped by 2.1 percent every year, to 192,000 in 2009. The number of farms now stands at 113,396, whereas it had still been 301,999 in 1970, before the reform. From 1950, on the other hand, only the white-collar and pensioner element appears to have grown a lot.

The 1987 census, moreover, revealed surprising age differences between those employed in agriculture and those in manufacturing and trades (see table A3). As many as 59.5 percent of those still in agriculture were forty-five years or older, as compared roughly to 33 percent of those in manufacturing and trades, and similar percentages in commerce and services. In a word, Bavarian agriculture began to face a critical problem of keeping its younger generation on the farm. We shall come back below to the reasons for this generational attrition.

A second dimension of economic change has been with respect to the position of each employed person. The long-range perspective of 125 years or so shows that in the hundred years from 1852 to 1950, the absolute number of independent farmers and business people, including their family helpers, has remained more or less at 2.5 million. But the size of the population more than doubled, from 3.9 million to 9.2 million, and the number of dependent workers, blue and white collar (agricultural labor declined drastically), grew to 5.1 million by 1950. In percentages, the changing composition of the work force from 1939 shows the recent changes in greater detail (see tables A3 and A5). In particular, an appreciable percentage drop occurred among the independents while the white collar employees have almost quadrupled. There has also been an extraordinary decrease in the number of family helpers who evidently now prefer to earn their money with strangers, another sign of the decline of the extended family in German life.

The corresponding changes in our fifteen communities are not quite as striking as the statewide figures, but noticeable. After a brief surge due to the presence of the refugees, the number of independents declined at rates varying from place to place, but very noticeably in every case. Farmers declined mostly in the 1960s, under the impact of the Common Market. Family help declined even more sharply in the 1960s and, according to official figures,[29] in the 1970s: by 1978, the total number of full-time family helpers in agriculture had dropped another 225 from 1970. On the other hand, civil servants and white-collar employees rose precipitately, especially if we compare the figures of 1939 and 1970. In Bruckberg, the large number of employees of the pediatric facility stands out. With blue-collar workers, again, the rates vary greatly, depending, among other things, on the arrival and the extent of the departure of the refugees. The residential-agrarian and bedroom communities had a disproportionately high percentage of workers among their gainfully employed (table A5). The high numbers of out-commuters and their balance over the inward-bound also tell a story about the daily lives of our fifteen small places (table A4). Finally, it should be mentioned that many of the white- and blue-collar households in these communities own and maintain rental housing on the side, and sometimes a small acreage for additional income.

This last-mentioned facet helps us to form a mental picture of economic life in these small places: With luck and some savings, thrifty small-town people could escape the discouraging labor market by acquiring rental property or engaging in a little production of fruit or vegetables on the side. Otherwise, they were fighting the odds of the long decline in agricultural ownership and the stagnation in manufacturing jobs in the wake of the energy crises of the 1970s and the current economic downturn. To take advantage of the expanding civil service and white-collar employee sector would have taken education and special skills, which, of course, explains the great emphasis on education and educational reform since the 1960s. But these opportunities were more likely to benefit the young: "What little Hans does not learn, big Hans never will," as the saying goes. Those over age fifty probably received all their education in one of the one- or two-room village schools that used to teach four or eight elementary grades simultaneously and were abolished in the 1970s. This may have been adequate for farming and good moral training, but even with the help of adult education, it greatly restricted their future options. The career of a small farmer hardly attracts even the farm children any more. And being a farmhand, male or female, has long gone out of style even though the wages of agricultural labor have risen impressively since the end of World War II.

The Transformation of Agriculture

Flying over Bavaria on a clear day—there are not many—one can distinguish the original settlement patterns as they vary from one historic region to another: The ancient peasant lands of Old Bavaria (and parts of Austria) with their scattered farms surrounded by the quilted patchwork of fields of hues of green or brown differ from the clusters of buildings of Franconian and Suebian villages, each of them a potential town. Some of the Old Bavarian farms, especially in Lower Bavaria, are arranged in a square of buildings like a circle of covered wagons to ward off a hostile world; some are so isolated in mountainous terrain they are called *Einödhof* (wilderness farm). Some of the villages in the Upper Palatinate, along the Franconian Main River, or in the reclaimed Danubian lowlands of Upper Bavaria (Karlshuld) are built along a main road, the navigable river, or the geometrically drawn drainage canals. The well-preserved patterns of the original settlements would make us believe that nothing really fundamental has changed in these farming villages from the days described in the romantic *Heimatliteratur*. Driving through the countryside can be just as deceptive, as one sees the lovingly preserved traditional houses, often half-timbered in Franconia and chalet-style in Upper Bavaria, with contrasting wooden balconies along the front, window boxes with trailing pink and red geraniums, and a religious mural or inscriptions under the vast, overhanging gables. The onion-shaped or pointed towers of large, baroque village churches press further the impression of an old and slow-changing peasant culture.

Appearances aside, nothing could be further from the truth than this picture of an essentially unchanging reality in the farm villages of Bavaria.[30] Behind many of the structural changes in employment lies a basic transformation that has been going on in Bavarian agriculture since the turn of the century, and especially from 1939. Spurred on by the rising prosperity among the non-farm population and the competitive pressure of the Common Market from the outside, the entire farm population, their farms, and their approach to agricultural production have undergone drastic changes. The rapidly rising wages and prices in agriculture of the 1950s, in particular, brought pressure to bear upon the farm operators to make their enterprises more cost-effective or to get out of farming altogether, or at least partially. The latter option was very real to the average Bavarian farmer, since this was a state of predominantly small farms.[31]

Work on the farm, once performed mostly by the *Knecht* or *Magd* (male and female farmhands) featured in the peasant fiction of Ludwig Ganghofer or Oskar Maria Graf, has changed its basic character. We have already seen the drop among the numbers of full-time family helpers and farm hands since 1950. In 1955, the federal government—where the Bavarian Farmers Association (*Bayerischer Bauernverband*, BBV) had an especially strong voice in the 1950s and 1960s—began to issue annual Green Plans, which pumped billions of marks in credits, through tax incentives, and via price policy into West German agriculture. This, in turn, facilitated agricultural mechanization and rationalization on an unheard-of scale. In the years from 1950 to 1968 alone, the number of tractors in Bavaria grew tenfold, not to mention the steep increases of other farm machinery, trucks, and passenger cars. There has also been a good deal of leasing and cooperative use of farm equipment.

Decreasing Numbers, Increasing Farm Size

Since 1968, Bavarian agricultural policy has centered on a "program of priorities" that underwent periodic adjustment. In the 1950s and 1960s, the number of farms over 1.2 acres decreased by one-fourth while their production rose by 60 percent, and the per capita productivity tripled. Yet despite all this agricultural rationalization, farm incomes still could not manage to catch up with the steeply rising prosperity in West German cities; they lagged behind by about 30 percent throughout that entire period and are still behind the urban level.

The social changes in the countryside are indeed of revolutionary proportions: Over the six decades from 1949 to 2007 (see table A7), the number of Bavarian farms has shrunk by about three-fourths while there has been a significant shift toward farms larger than 30 acres of arable land. Our 2007 figures show that this trend has continued unabated after the reform. The average farm size, in fact, grew from 21.5 acres to over 40 acres while the total area cultivated shrank by more than an eighth. More important still, by 1977, 78 percent of all Bavarian farms under 25 acres had become part-time operations[32] that were supported by outside jobs, frequently involving a commuting trip to another community. To be sure, that still left considerable numbers of small, seemingly marginal farms that were mostly self-sufficient—1.1 percent of all farms are under 2.5 acres, 2.2 percent between 2.5 and 5 acres, and under one-fifth (17.1) of them between 5 and 25 acres. There were also some (22.4 percent) of 25 to 50 acres that were part-time operations.

It is easy to understand the small farmers' motive: In 1977, most of the part-time farms (74.4 percent) had an annual farm-derived income below DM 15,000 (about $8,000). Most of the full-time farms (78.2 percent) had one above DM 15,000, which seems to have been the minimum for the more capital-intensive farms at the time of the territorial reform. By comparison, in 1977, a male industrial worker in Bavaria had an average annual income before taxes of DM 13,416, from which, of course, he still had to pay for housing and all the food for his family.[33] The Bavarian government encouraged part-time farming alongside the full-time farms as a course of action preferable to permitting limitless concentration of agricultural holdings as the market demanded. It hoped, furthermore, that part-time farming would increase the social and economic contacts between farming and industry for their mutual benefit. By 2009, however, after the world-wide recession had caused the value of Bavarian agriculture to drop by 9 percent, the official *Agrarbericht* warned that the "economic stability of part-time farming would really depend on the stability of the outside jobs."[34] To make matters worse, by then the average percentage of typical consumers' household budgets spent on agricultural produce had also dropped by about one-third to half of the percentage of 1980. Society needed farmers less.

Bavarian farmers, like other farmers, also used to have strong emotional attachments to their particular piece or pieces of land. The acreage of the larger full-time farms, as a result of centuries of successive ownership in the same family, often was scattered over a large area, which was an obstacle to cost-effective operation. The government program for consolidating such scattered holdings (*Flurbereinigung*) had been very slow in remedying this problem.[35] In recent decades, however, considerations of optimal conditions for farming have made such inroads into the sacrosanct relationship between a farm family and "its soil" that leasing additional acreage for profit now characterizes well over half of all Bavarian farms—up from one-fourth in 1949. Typically, full-time farm operations over twenty-five acres lease additional land from small part-time farmers. In many areas such as West Middle Franconia, however, there is still some community resistance to "outsiders" leasing or buying into local farm property, a leftover from the ancient communal way of life.[36] The reluctance of the younger generation of farm families to take on the farms of their parents, on the other hand, must have enhanced the attractiveness of leasing and sales regardless of ancient community taboos. The greatly expanded horizons and social contacts of farmers and their families resulting from the automobile, television, and all the social and economic changes we are describing here must also have narrowed the conception of what is "an outsider." Perhaps, today, to be an outsider requires being from a different region, or a non-farming background, rather than just from outside the village or town, although old local animosities and longstanding rivalries between some neighboring towns or villages still cast their spell.

Finally, there have been revealing structural changes in what is produced and how much land is used for this purpose. The number of draft animals such as horses per farm has steeply declined while that of meat-producing animals such as chickens and hogs has grown. The amount of land under the plough has declined in favor of pasture land. There has also been a tremendous expansion of agricultural exports, especially to Common Market countries and North America, but also to developing and Iron Curtain nations. Between 1960 and 1979 alone, the value of farm exports grew ninefold, making Bavaria (and the Federal Republic) a food surplus area on the world market. National and Common Market policies of subsidizing dairy production have also created unsalable surplus problems such as the "butter mountain," the "milk lake," and similar embarrassments of riches.

To sum up, competition with the rising incomes elsewhere has forced Bavarian farmers to treat farming more and more as a business and this explains most of the transformation of agriculture in the last quarter of a century before the reform. They have adjusted their acreage and staff, acquired training and equipment, and risen to the challenges of the market. Despite their seemingly successful adaptation, however, few farms seem to hold out much attraction for the next generation. However much farm incomes have managed to rise, the incomes of the non-farm sectors always seem to stay considerably ahead in the race. Even the unskilled farm workers' hourly wage rose from 70 Pfennig in 1950 to DM 7.94 in 1974 and DM 15 in 1989 (males only)[37]—DM 15.59 (2,881/mo.) for skilled farm workers—while the hours of work dropped from an average of 51 to 43.3 per week in 1989, which makes the hiring of farm help very expensive for the smaller farms. As a result of all these factors, three-fourths of all farms were now operated only on the side, and one out of every five farms in Bavaria—one out of three in West Germany—had been given up in the 1970s alone. When will it all end, and how? Will farming as a way of life die out altogether, as the farmers' sons and daughters shy away from a life of hard work and long hours—after rising before dawn—far from the cultural appeal and diversions of urban centers?

The Agricultural Periphery

Our fifteen communities in West Middle Franconia did not always follow the stagnant agricultural trends very closely, but were from the beginning more agrarian and also lost farms at a slower pace than the rest of the state. Precisely for that reason, and perhaps in a kind of delayed disaster, the planners expected this region to lose another one-third of the agricultural places of employment during the 1980s. Even thirty years later, the *Agrarbericht* declared all three counties of West Middle Franconia "disadvantaged agricultural zones." Between 1939 and 1970, the walled city of Ornbau had the highest rate of pre-reform loss (48 percent) of farms on the way from an agrarian to a residential-agrarian kind of community, a change also reflected in its high percentage of outward-bound commuters. The farms are, of course, all outside its semicircular city walls. The smallest farms (under 5 acres) were the first to go: from twenty-two in 1939 to fourteen in 1950, seven in 1961, to two in 1970. The next larger category (5–12.5 acres) followed from 1950: thirty-six in 1950, twenty-seven in 1961, and thirteen in 1970.[38] Farms 12.5 to 50 acres declined only from fifty-nine (1950) to forty-three (1970), and that decrease probably occurred only among those under 25 acres. There were still forty-three in 1989. Even in communities like Röckingen, Meinheim, Adelshofen, Steinsfeld, and Ippesheim, which remained agrarian, the overall decrease of farms was very considerable (see table A7) and again heavily concentrated among the smaller farms. This trend has continued to this day: In the last ten years (1999–2009), the loss of farms over 5 acres ranged from 25–28 percent throughout West Middle Franconia, below the state average. The percentage of gainfully employed in agriculture ranged from 6–8 percent in 2009. The average size of farm in the latter year was between 73 and 85 acres.

If we add up all the farms under five acres in the fifteen communes, their numbers have been exactly halved between 1939 and 1970, and most of the drop occurred in the 1960s, followed by a smaller decrease (7.3 percent) in the years from 1971 to 1979, with a much larger decrease (28.3 percent) between 1979 and 1987. The same drop (1939–1970) appears to have occurred in the whole district of (West and East) Middle Franconia, although in the entire state the reduction was more like by two-thirds. The next larger farms (5 to 12.5 acres) of our sample declined "only" 42.7 percent, again typical of the region, although statewide the drop was higher (53.8 percent) by 1970. From 1979 to 1987, however, the decline was much smaller (8.5 percent). The number of farms between 12.5 and 50 acres dropped by less than one-fifth (15–17 percent), and this was probably mostly among the smaller of this rather broad category, say below 25 acres. The statewide decline of farms of this size was 27.1 percent. For the period from 1979 to 1987, the figures were 20.8 percent and 18.1 percent, respectively.[39] Size appears to be crucial in the battle for economic survival among at least the full-time farms, even if we consider regional differences in climate and fertility. It goes without saying that in the economic crisis years since 2007, the more marginal, smaller farms went out of business at the fastest rate.

In the 1970s, the drop in the overall numbers of farms (see table A7) shows that Ornbau had stabilized while some of the other agrarian communities we named above, such as Meinheim, Ippesheim, or Weihenzell, were still experiencing an accelerated drop of agricultural holdings that approached the decline of the preceding two decades. Farmers in these parts do not believe in the sale of agricultural land, but leasing has grown tremendously as marginal farms were given up. For reasons of tradition, even leasing is kept strictly among the local farmers. In some communities, speculative reasons may have been reinforcing tradition: For instance areas affected by the 1991 plans for the completion of the *Autobahn* from Würzburg to Ulm (table A7) saw prices for agricultural land, and even for leasing it, that were far in excess of the normal level.

In West Middle Franconia, there is also the well-rooted tradition of not breaking up farm properties but giving house and land to one heir only, while the other heirs are compensated with payments if possible. Since it was not easy to find a younger person who would not rather move away to a larger town, anyway, the search often settled on one who would run the farm only on the side. According to one interviewee, the more educated the young people are, the less likely they want to stay and take over a farm. Not only is the work still hard and the hours long in spite of mechanization and rationalization, but now a farming couple has to do it alone, in most cases, in order to make a living. The days of farm hands and even of help from outside the nuclear family, with some variations in location, ended with the 1950s. Since farms do not "pay" any more below a certain size, a full-time farmer cannot hope to keep up with the rat race by reducing the acreage he has to work. It is possible, however, to reduce it and work it only on the side, while one or more family members hold outside jobs.[40] These "moonlight farmers," of course, have even less leisure hours to call their own as they carry out their farm chores in the evening and on weekends.

The total acreage used for farming has also decreased noticeably in two-thirds of our communities, but generally the pasture and other permanently green acreage decreased no less than the land under the plough. In a few heavily agrarian communities, the agricultural area has actually grown since 1950, owing to favorable circumstances for expansion. In two cases (Adelshofen and Steinsfeld), however, there are substantial areas of steeply sloping land where farming is no longer attempted.

A Different Kind of Farmer

Needless to stress, today's Bavarian farmer is rather different from his predecessors of seventy or a hundred years ago. An important aspect of today's farming in Bavaria lies in education. Compared to the old days when young farmers tended to learn their calling from direct observation and participation in the operation of the parental farm, there has been a veritable revolution in education. Typically, farm children rarely used to pursue secondary or vocational training, which meant that the old local one- or two-room schools were quite adequate for them. Today, the farm teenagers are very likely to attend at least a vocational school and to undergo an apprenticeship in agriculture. Some of the farmers in our sample of communities were themselves accredited trade masters (male and female) who could teach these apprentices on their own farms and could administer examinations and confer degrees in their calling. Many young farmers also take vocational training in additional areas appropriate to the maintenance of farm animals and equipment. Furthermore, many young farmers of both sexes go for specialized training in chemistry, biology, and farm management at the agricultural colleges and in adult education courses. The state government has been active in agricultural research and college-level training since 1803 when the first agricultural college was founded at Weihenstephan where they still brew beer and make cheese today. Modern agriculture makes great demands on a farmer's knowledge of fertilizers, insecticides, feed additives, of the botany and genetics of scientific agriculture, and a hundred other things. Given the character of farming today, farmers also need to learn business management and acquire a working knowledge of complex agricultural legislation and government programs. Adult education also serves the needs of older farmers and farm women and helps them master the challenge of major changes in farm management.

These educational self-help programs were already at an all-time high in Bavarian agriculture in the 1970s though they have declined somewhat: there were 10,000 agricultural apprenticeships involving a dozen specialties and producing about 5,000[41] journeymen and 700 master certificates (both male and female) a year. 3,173 young men and 1,400[42] women were attending agricultural college (*Landwirtschaftschule*) programs. In 1980, the Bavarian farm adviser network had been offering 1,610 adult education courses, 8,949 educational meetings, and 6,310 group advisory meetings, all of which were quite well attended.[43] Quite obviously, today's Bavarian farmers have become much smarter people than were their forebears of another generation, not to mention the cruel stereotypes of the *Dorfdepp* (village simpleton) coined by city folks anxious to demonstrate their own smartness.

Bavarian farmers also have long discovered the patent advantages of cooperative organization and collective action. Their farm cooperatives and associations have come a long way from the eighteenth century beginnings of various forms of farm organization[44] and the political divisions of agricultural politics in the 1920s. The foundation of the *Bayerischer Bauernverband* (BBV) in 1945 created the first unified farmers organization in Bavaria. The American occupation insisted at that time that its associational functions not be mingled with those of the official state chamber of agriculture, which has certain administrative functions.[45] As the BBV pointed out in a ten-year report in 1955, German agriculture at the time was overwhelmingly made up of small farms under twenty-five acres and the farmer felt as helpless vis-à-vis the forces of the marketplace "as the industrial worker did before the advent of trade unions." For this reason, the farmers believed they would always require some government intervention and aid.[46]

Farmers also hoped that cooperatives might make up for their critical lack in size and control of their market position while retaining the way of life of the family farm. Cooperatives to buy feed and fertilizer, or machinery, or to sell produce have been flourishing. In the years 1978 and 1979 alone, over 9,000 new farms had joined the 89 farm-equipment and mutual aid "rings" in Bavaria that brought their total membership to 63,870 farms. The mutual aid services rendered in 1978–1979 were the equivalent of 1,534 full-time working days. Membership in the producers and forest management cooperatives also had increased considerably.[47] Surveying opinions in our fifteen communities produced many positive references to the cooperatives, the most frequently mentioned being the one founded by F.W. Raiffeisen in 1864. There were branches of the Raiffeisen credit banking system in all but two of the fifteen. A majority of the communes belong to a milk cooperative located outside one of them. Until 1965, agrarian Röckingen even had its own milk cooperative. In some communities, there were also Forest Peasant Associations, one had a cooperative hunting society, and two belonged to producer co-ops. Most of them also belonged to a farm machinery ring. Over the years, some complained, certain cooperatives had become huge business corporations, however, that permitted their members little participation in their decisions beyond the vote in a general annual meeting.[48]

Long-term or lifelong residents of these small places often reflect with nostalgia and regret upon how their agrarian village has changed from the good old days. How did the mayors of these communities perceive the changes that have come over agriculture in their respective bailiwicks? Ten of them thought that mechanization was the biggest change that had overcome agriculture, usually including in this statement such phenomena as the decrease of agricultural help, the abandonment of draft animals, and the mechanized tilling of the soil. Four mentioned the evident specialization of modern farming, and three thought the consolidation of farm holdings was the most important change. Two each mentioned either the decrease in the number of farms, especially among the smallest units, or the trend toward part-time farming. There was some mention, also, of taking new pastures under the plough and of the heavier use of chemical fertilizers. Given the rapid rate of change within their lifetimes, few adults are at a loss to name obvious manifestations of the transformation of agriculture that left a profound impact on the nature of the traditional village community. In a word, even the farmers have long stopped seeing their world as unchanging, timeless, and subject only to the ebb and flow of the seasons.

The Social Net in the Countryside

This account of the role of farmers and agriculture in small towns and villages would not be complete without a sidelong glance at the extent to which they, too, have long been drawn into the national community of the West German welfare state. Far from the old stereotype of the agricultural periphery, where the individual farm person had to depend solely on local church welfare, family, and cooperative (*Berufsgenossenschaft*) arrangements—with all the implications of such dependence and of the vagaries of bad harvests and poor regions—West German farmers have been drawn progressively into the universal coverage of the "social net." At first, and still as recently as the Christian Democratic (CDU) Principles of Old Age Insurance of 1955, there were arguments to overcome to the effect that any public insurance program would take away the independence of one of the last major independent groups of society, the farm-owning families. Neo-Marxist critics, in rare agreement with the CDU, added "how can independent owners be among the exploited—they can only be exploiting themselves," an argument used also against the introduction of social insurance for small business operators.

In 1957, nevertheless, the federal parliament passed the Old Age Aid Act for Farmers to adjust the often meager family arrangements for a farmer in retirement, the traditional *Altenteil* (old farmer's share), to the increasing level of expectations placed on social insurance throughout the society. After several revisions, old-age aid soon also covered premature retirement, disability, widows, widowers, and former spouses, orphans, and helping farm family members. It has to be earned by age sixty-five, with fifteen years of contributions to a fund held by a farmers' cooperative society, and by turning over the farm to the heirs, or a buyer or lease-holder. Already in 1956 a disproportionate 16 percent of farmers were over sixty-five and another 59 percent between forty-five and sixty-five, and many small farmers had been unable to retire because they lacked sufficient retirement security.[49] Far from lucrative, the farmers' monthly pensions of DM 242 (for singles and DM 362 for married couples) at best only supplemented other retirement arrangements and, since 1975, have been indexed to rise with the level of all wages in West Germany.

Since 1971, there are also special subventions to enable younger farmers to quit farming and facilitate their entry into the non-agricultural pension system by means of back payments. Since 1972, there is a compulsory farmers health insurance.[50] There is no better way to gauge the extent to which the whole nation feels responsible for the well-being of its shrinking minority of farmers than to indicate the rising level of transfer payments for agricultural social insurance: In 1976, the federal government in Bonn was spending DM 2.7 billion for this purpose, as compared to a "'mere" DM 882 million in 1970 and next to nothing a dozen years earlier. When one recalls the centuries of exploitation and oppression of Central European village peasants by feudal lords, the church, cities, and merchants, not to mention conquering armies and empires that parasitically lived off the laboring peasants, this is a historic turning point: For once, the whole society is taking responsibility for every human being within its borders instead of one puissant part taking advantage of the other, more defenseless parts.

For the purposes of this book, we should also point out the parallels between the inclusion of the farm families of our small places in the social net of the welfare state and the other, more glaring interventions of the state into the autonomy and isolation of the village or small town. If the national welfare state concerned itself with the growing inadequacy of a farmer's *Altenteil* or health care funding, why shouldn't it also worry about whether the village or small-town school gave rural children an education and education-based social mobility adequate to a qualified career outside the small place, given talent and motivation? Why shouldn't it strive also to make other local government services, such as sanitation, road building, planning, and many others commensurate with what people in the urban areas could expect? At what point could a line be drawn to give all citizens, urban and rural, an even break and yet to protect the nostalgic village autonomy from such losses as villagers moving away in search of better jobs, elderly with cash pensions in hand seeking a more benign environment, or village culture remaining immune to the blandishments of the greater society?

There is plenty more evidence, as we will see in chapter 2, that the old village community romanticized in the *Heimatliteratur* of another age has been thoroughly transformed—regardless of how faithfully it may or may not have been reflected in that literature. There is at least some truth in the assertion that many of its communal functions and the old sense of small-town and village identity had been largely "hollowed out" by social changes long before the state decided to modernize the governance of these small places in the late 1970s. Agriculture in particular, the main livelihood of the vast majority of their residents for centuries had profoundly changed and shrunk to occupying only a tiny minority of them. It is the passing of their way of life that this book is about.

Notes

1. Ancient Regensburg had at first a Celtic name, *Radasbona*, then a Latin one, *Castra Regina*, and finally the germanicized Regensburg after the river Regen (Regina). Munich was named *Monachium* after an early settlement of monks, Augsburg after its founder, the Emperor Augustus, *Augusta Vindelicorum*. The Vindelici was the tribe in the area soon to be incorporated into the Raetho-Roman province, Raethia, whose name survives in -*ried*, as in Donauried.

2. See, for example, Karl Bosl on the formation of the German *Stämme* (tribes) of the Merovingian and Carolingian ages, "Was sind Stämme und welche Rolle spielen sie im modernen bayerischen Staat?" in *Freistaat Bayern*, Rainer Roth, ed., 3rd ed. (Bayreuth, 1983), 129–131; or Bosl, "Die historisch-politische Entwicklung des bayerischen Staates," in *Bayern, Handbuch der historischen Stätten*, Bosl, ed. (hereafter, Bosl, *Historic Bavaria*) 2nd ed., (Stuttgart, 1974), xix–xx.

3. See Hektor Ammann, "Wie gross war die mittelalterliche Stadt?" in *Die Stadt des Mittelalters*, Carl Haase, ed., 3 vols. (Darmstadt, 1969), I, 408–412, which reviews also the 1930 estimates of Heinrich Bechtel's *Wirtschaftsstil des deutschen Spätmittelalters*. Ammann concludes that far too many towns and markets were created in the twelfth through fourteenth centuries in Germany, which may explain the subsequent stagnation or decline of many of them. See also Fritz Rörig, *The Medieval Town* (Berkeley, 1967), 111–113.

4. See esp. Max Weber, "Die Stadt," in *Archiv für Sozialwissenschaft und Sozialpolitik* 47 (1921), 621 ff., reprinted also in Haase, *Die Stadt des Mittelalters*, I, 34–59. Many accounts agree that most medieval towns were still largely agrarian and that some, for example, the *Ackerbürgerstädte* (farmer-citizen towns) of Rhenisch winegrowers, even grew their own food rather than relying on trading their commercial and craft skills against food from surrounding villages.

5. On the varying conditions of their "unfreedom" over the centuries and in different parts of today's geographical extent of Bavaria, see esp. Friedrich Lütke, *Geschichte der deutschen Agrarverfassung* (Stuttgart, 1966), 22–29 and 163 ff. Bavaria never had estates and serfs comparable to East Elbian Prussia and Eastern Europe and, at the time of the emancipation of the peasants at the beginning of the nineteenth century, there was little to emancipate.

6. Unless their origins go back to Roman or even older antecedents, most of them went through a village stage, then were given market rights and, eventually, town privileges by the powers that be. Ansbach, for example, began in the eighth century as a "villa" next to an abbey, had a headman, *scultetus* (German *Schultheiss*), received market rights in the eleventh century and seems to have attained town status by 1195 when the inhabitants of the fortified settlement were referred to in documents as *cives* (citizens). In 1221 it was called a *civitas* (city).

7. See Bosl, *Historic Bavaria*, 561.

8. Five days of fighting in April 1945 destroyed the church, twenty-two houses, and a large number of sheds and barns. Ibid., 442–443. The town had already burned down once in 1634 and been rebuilt.

9. Ibid., 827–828. A modern new Rathaus now houses the city government. See also the account by Erwin Seitz, *Wolframs-Eschenbach wird Stadt* (Wolframs-Eschenbach, 2009) which describes the history and development of the town.

10. In a follow-up "reform of the reform," the state government decided to have only Ornbau and Weidenbach in the VG Triesdorf II, while Wolframs-Eschenbach was

permitted to form its own VG with Mitteleschenbach. Arberg and Merkendorf were allowed to remain autonomous communities.

11. Since 1972 it is Planning Region 8 of Bavaria, the western half of the *Regierungsbezirk* (province) Middle Franconia. The eastern half of this district comprises four large cities, Nuremberg, Fürth, Erlangen, and Schwabach. It is among the more developed regions of the state and a major destination of emigrants from the western half.

12. See also Bayerisches Staatsministerium für Landesentwicklung und Umweltfragen, *Landesentwicklungsprogramm Bayern*, Teil C. (Munich 1976), 751–758 (hereafter, *Landesentwicklungsprogramm*).

13. We can easily follow the population changes of most communities of Bavaria with the help of official statistics, published as a result of the territorial reform, back to the years 1840, 1871, 1900, and 1925. See Die Gemeinden Bayerns, Änderung in Bestand und Gebiet von 1840 bis 1975. *Beiträge zur Statistik Bayerns*, Heft 350 (1976).

14. As of 2010, the Autobahn 6 is about five kilometers south of Ansbach, a freeway extending right below Roth (not too far from Weissenburg) and A7 runs perpendicular to A6. These connections are actually more favorable than, for example, in prosperous, Upper Bavarian Rosenheim County, and environs. There is an area of roughly thirty-five square miles not touched by freeways as opposed to one of twenty-seven square miles in West Middle Franconia.

15. See *Landesentwicklungsprogramm*, 759, where the stress of structural planning is on securing and augmenting the number of jobs near the places of residence of the rural and small town population. Industrial and service sector employment, including the development of tourism, is the most likely source of additional jobs to make up for the loss of agricultural employment. West Middle Franconia has also developed two major reservoirs as tourist attractions as well as for water management and energy that were then under construction.

16. Of eighty-six communes, which were member communities of twenty-two administrative unions, fifteen were selected for further study, including some that eventually succeeded in bettering their status as a result of the "reform of the reform." Most (seventy-seven) of the eighty-six were lacking in one or more essential features indicating adequacy for surviving the reform, such as local schools (some lost them as a result of the school reform of the late 1960s or early 1970s), pre-schools or kindergartens, hospitals, pharmacies, specialized doctors, senior citizen homes, and other signs of socioeconomic development during the 1960s.

17. See Bayerisches Staatsministerium für Landesentwicklung und Umweltfragen, *Region Westmittelfranken*, Kartenbeilagen (Marktheidenreid, 1975).

18. One of these sixteen, Dentlein am Forst, had to be dropped from the list when its mayor failed to make himself available for comparable interviews. The statistics are for 1939, 1950, 1960, 1970, 1980–1981, 1999, and 2009 and cover population changes, the gainfully employed by sector and position, commuters, non-agricultural employment, size and number of farms, and distance to railroad stations.

19. Most of the interviews were done by Elfriede Offergelt of the Lehrstuhl für Soziologie, Professor Peter Atteslander of the University of Augsburg, and with the help and supervision of Dr. Walter Zingg of the same Institute, who also interviewed several of the mayors. I interviewed some mayors, communal councilors, *Landräte*, other state officials and representatives of some of the communal associations and protest groups and analyzed the state and local statistics.

20. See *Statistisches Jahrbuch für das Deutsche Reich*, 1880, (hereafter, *Jahrbuch 1880*), 6. Even in 1920, there were 6,925 Bavarian communes with a population under 1,000 and another 727 communes between 1,000 and 2,000, though the population had

grown from 5 to 7 million and most of this in towns and cities above 2,000. *Jahrbuch 1914*, 4–5. In 2009, the state had a population of 12.5 million, including 1.2 million foreigners.

21. According to the urban census of 1882, Munich then had 234,129; Nuremberg, 102,874; Augsburg, 61,331; and Würzburg, 51,397 residents. *Jahrbuch 1890*, 38–39.

22. See *Jahrbuch 1971*, 121, *Bayerischer Agrarbericht 1980, 2006, 2008 and 2010* (Kurzfassung), and *Jahrbuch 1987*, 436; *Statistisches Jahrbuch für Bayern, 1990*, and *2009* (hereafter, *Jahrbuch Bayern* with year). Also *Statistisches Jahrbuch für die Bundesrepublik Deutschland 2007* (hereafter, *Jahrbuch BRD*, with year).

23. According to Allied wartime sources, the evacuees were estimated at 3 million for the whole country. There was also a sizable problem of released German prisoners of war who could not return to areas of their birth because these were now under native governments. See Martin Kornrumpf, *In Bayern Angekommen* (Munich, 1979), 960, 973–979.

24. Kornrumpf, "Das Ende der Landflucht?" *Neue Zeitung*, May 1947.

25. The territorial reform of 1978 makes the later data difficult to compare to the earlier figures since many boundaries have changed.

26. In 1840, Ippesheim had 1,052, Weigenheim 1,313, Adelshofen 1,153, and Weihenzell 1,481 inhabitants. *Die Gemeinden Bayerns* (1976), 98–108.

27. This scheme was successfully used by University of Augsburg sociologists to study the changing environs of Augsburg over the decades. It is not a scheme of unilinear development, but permits considerable diversification and specialization at its lower end (stages 4, 5, and 6). See also the survey of classifications in Ulrich Planck, *Die Landgemeinde* (Linz, 1978), 12–32.

28. Considering the last four decades, Dentlein am Forst, Ippesheim, and Weigenheim are declining. Burk has experienced no change; Adelshofen and Röckingen have been stagnating and Weihenzell, Ornbau, Markt Berolzheim, Meinheim, Ohrenbach, Steinsfeld, Bruckberg, Mitteleschenbach, Langfurth, and Wolframs-Eschenbach are growing. The latter annexed substantial farming areas but their small populations did not change its stage of development. Bayerisches Landesamt für Statistik und Datenverarbeitung, *Gemeindedaten 2009*.

29. See *Bayerns Wirtschaft, Gestern und Heute* (1980), 54. On the shrinking of Bavarian agriculture, see esp. *Agrarbericht, Kurzfassung 2009* and the earlier editions for 2006 (covering 2004 and 2005) and 2008.

30. See also Ernst Klein, *Geschichte der deutschen Landwirtschaft im Industriezeitalter* (Wiesbaden, 1973), 1 ff, who stresses the "agrarian revolution" that had to precede and accompany the industrial revolution to make the latter possible. Klein also gives telling descriptions of German rural poverty and overpopulation around 1800. Ibid., 45–49.

31. In some ways, the adjustment of German agriculture to the pressures of the international market can be compared to the agrarian crisis of the 1870s when agricultural imports overwhelmed farm production and, as a result, a large proportion of the farm population either began to migrate to the new industrial centers or to the New World.

32. These *Nebenerwerbsbetriebe* (part-time farms) were defined simply as households that derive more than 50 percent of their income from other sources. There may be additional part-time farms with less outside income. The average size of the part-time farms at the time of the reform was 13.3 acres, while full-time farms averaged out at 44.2 acres.

33. *Agrarbericht 1980*, Tabellenband, 17. One-third of all farms and 62 percent of the part-time farms had an annual farm-derived income below DM 5,000 (less than

$2,000 at the then-current exchange rate). Nearly half of all Bavarian farms produced less than DM 10,000, and this was true also of 61.3 percent of the full-time farms. See also the critical discussion of this aspect by Onno Poppinga, "Gebrauchsanleitung zum Agrarbericht," in *Produktion und Lebensverhältnisse auf dem Land*, Poppinga, ed., special issue of *Leviathan*, no. 2 (1979), 72–111, esp. 87–96, where a minimal farm size of 50–75 acres is deemed necessary for a farmer to approximate industrial wages.

34. See *Agrarbericht 2009*, Kurzfassung, 22. See also Helmut Hoffman, *Bayern, Handbuch zur staatspolitischen Landeskunde der Gegenwart*, 2nd rev. ed. (Munich, 1974), 162–165. The total share of part-time farms in Bavaria was already 41.7 percent at the time of the 1971 census and 52.6 percent in 1987, after the reform.

35. Hoffmann, 165–168. Recent efforts at acreage consolidation concentrated, among other regions, on the southeast and west of West Middle Franconia.

36. The Weimar Settlement Law (1919) also set up cooperative settlement societies with the right of first option in sales of agricultural property.

37. This corresponds to annual salaries of DM 1,855 and 17,341, respectively. Since 1965 alone wages have tripled. *Agrarbericht 1980*, I, 26.

38. The information for the years after the reform has to be analyzed on the basis of the results of the territorial reform. For example, after the reform Ornbau had twelve farms under 5 acres, nineteen between 5 and 12.5, sixty-one between 12.5 and 50, and ten over 50 acres. *Gemeindedaten 1980*, 223 and *Gemeindedaten 2009*.

39. Holdings larger than 50 acres and especially over 125 acres appear to have declined sharply between 1939 and 1950, but to have reappeared in some of the more agrarian communities of our sample in larger numbers (all with more than 67 percent agriculturally employed). *Gemeindedaten 1980, 1988*, and *2009*. At the national level where Bavaria has almost a fourth of the 400,000 farms, the largest (over 125 acres) are only 14 percent in Bavaria, but more than one in five are in the Federal Republic. *Jahrbuch BRD 2007*.

40. The economic mechanism at work here can also be gathered from the official indices of income gained from dependent labor or from property and entrepreneurial activity. From 1960 to 1978 alone, income from dependent labor increased by a factor of 5.5 in Bavaria while the latter rose only by a factor of 3.6. Independence bears an increasingly higher price. See *Bayerns Wirtschaft. Gestern und Heute* (1980), 224.

41. *Jahrbuch Bayern 1990*. This figure represents a 54.2 percent decline from the 13,000 apprentices of about thirteen years earlier. In 2009, 2,245 persons began programs of agricultural education. *Agrarbericht 2009*. The number had declined, slightly, to 4,676 for the school year 1986–1987.

42. Again, these figures represent a reduction of 623 (19.2 percent) and 476 (32.8 percent) respectively from eleven years earlier. *Agrarbericht 2009*.

43. *Agrarbericht 1980*, 13.

44. The first *Landwirtschaftlicher Verein* (1810) was in response to the abolition of serfdom (1806) and an association of members of the Royal Academy of Sciences that broadened its base only in 1839. The real origins of farmers' associations in Bavaria occurred in the 1880s and 1890s following the agricultural crisis in the 1870s and 1880s, beginning with the *Fränkischer Bauernverein* (1880) and including the political *Christlicher Bauernverein* (1893) that sponsored the growth of cooperatives on a large scale in the years before and after World War One. Elsewhere in Germany, the first farming societies date back even farther and enjoyed state promotion in the early nineteenth century, although their expansion similarly took place only in the 1880s. See Klein, *Geschichte der deutschen Landwirtschaft* (1973), 132–142.

45. See the account of Klaus Schreyer, *Bayern—ein Industriestaat* (Munich, 1969), 142–151, and Bayerischer Bauernverband, *Zehn Jahre Bayerischer Bauernverband* (Munich, 1955), 1–75.
46. *Bauernverband* (1955), 285–292.
47. *Agrarbericht 1980*, 13.
48. See also Onno Poppinga, "Bauern in der Bundesrepublik Deutschland," in *Landleben*, Anna D. Brockmann, ed., (Reinbek/Hamburg, 1977), 300 ff., especially 307. Also Willem Grünemann, "Konzentration und Zentralisation in der Agrarindustrie und in den Genossenschaften," in Poppinga, *Leviathan* (1979), 30–71.
49. See Ernst Bendixen and Helmut Harbeck, "Zur sozialen Sicherung in der Landwirtschaft," in Poppinga, *Leviathan* (1979), 112–115, and the sources cited there. The farmers themselves seem to have welcomed the inclusion in the social net.
50. Accident insurance for farmers dates back much farther, to 1886 and 1942. See Ibid., 120–122.

Chapter 2

THE SMALL-TOWN OR VILLAGE COMMUNITY

The social changes of the small-town and rural scene that we have explored so far, of course, are not unique to Middle Franconia or Bavaria, but have been occurring throughout Western industrialized countries. Striking effects have been caused by such mechanisms as motorization and economic development, particularly international competition (such as in the European Common Market) and the rising curve of national wages and consumer expectations. Their most significant impact, however, is sociocultural: The widening of horizons of individuals and community, powerful if not always very explicit, and the loosening of community ties, a kind of urbanization of the minds of the small-town and village residents. What unmade the small community? In our fifteen communes and probably in similar settings elsewhere as well, it was particularly the unity of church and school within their narrow geographic confines that had to break up first. Their cultural and social (or associational) life first reflected the integrated past and then the new mobility and the possibility of larger communities and their identities. The economic insights and activities of individuals and firms then began to reach out for larger boundaries and, perhaps, new markets.

From earliest living memory, each of the small places, even the scattered villages of old Bavaria, has had one or more social centers around which the social life of the small town or village congregated at regular intervals. One such center had always been the village church and village school, whose activities were once intimately connected, as we shall show below. The church or churches—Catholic, Protestant, or both—were not just communities of the faithful, as in the United States. They were the heirs of their medieval power when they were the dominant part, with rare lapses, of the united clerical-aristocratic hierarchy that held the Holy Roman Empire of German Nation and its tribal monarchies together. The rise of cities and their trading leagues in the fourteenth and fifteenth centuries foreshadowed the decline of the church's power from this high mark. But even in the last two centuries, at the municipal level, the churches were not only the scene of community services, mass, and community celebrations on Sundays, high holidays, and frequently during the week. They also ministered to the ill and the troubled and figured prominently at many of the most important moments of the villagers and townspeople's lives: They could hardly be born, christened, marry, or die and get buried without the solemn sanction of their priest, and in the presence of their community. The village school and school teacher, as long as each small place still had one, were constantly and intimately involved in these and other church celebrations. The school children sang and the teacher was organist or violinist, and choir director for all church and secular communal festivities—weddings, funerals, religious processions, and so forth.

But the relation especially of the Catholic church and the village and small-town community really requires further historical clarification from the vantage point of the profound changes of the Napoleonic era when, among other Enlightenment and French Revolution aspects, the secularization of monastic orders and their possessions—the church owned about half of all Bavarian farms—transferred such rights of ownership to the monarchic state. The Bavarian state mostly wanted to extract taxes and the "freed" farmers, large and small, no longer had to render many other services as to their clerical-feudal lords. The new monarch even offered them the option of buying complete ownership of their farms for 600 gulden (then about twice the annual income of a farm in Bavaria), an offer most of them never took. The state also sold them and landless peasants monastery land and forests in small parcels. In a typical village or small agrarian town of the early nineteenth century, two-thirds consisted of small or medium-sized farms. Their owners were mostly illiterate and unable to follow to any great lengths the bold new ideas or even all the technical innovations that the Enlightenment brought to agriculture. Only the largest farms and their educated owners were likely to run their farms in the quasi-agribusiness fashion that is now again in vogue.[1]

Secularization and Community Life

In religious affiliation, West Middle Franconia is a mixed Protestant-Catholic area where the Protestants predominate[2] in all but two of our fifteen towns. During the Reformation and Counter-Reformation eras, this mixture of the two faiths was, of course, a cause of continual conflict and also of accommodation within and among communities, and between them and their regional or state authorities. Before the mediatization of ecclesiastical and Imperial territories and before the addition of Franconia, Suebia, and other territories, Old Bavaria, the Electoral Princedom, was a Catholic princedom[3] in which the ecclesiastical authorities down to the local priests of small communities dominated community life and education. The unity of village and parish was a major feature of that characteristic Bavarian rural culture we mentioned earlier. Of course, there was some dilution of the priestly influence over the last one hundred years: Where in 1820, there was a ratio of one priest for every 422 parishioners—a communal closeness that held the Enlightenment at bay and kept it from penetrating the communal order—in 1978, at the time of the reform, it was one to 2,090. The addition of Protestant and mixed areas of Franconia meant, among other things, the presence of two and more different churches,[4] officially decreed religious toleration (1803), and the eventual assumption by the Bavarian monarch of the Protestant summepiscopate[5] until 1918. Although Catholics still outnumber Protestants in the state by 67 percent to 23 percent, they are in the minority in Middle (36 percent Catholics, 54 percent Protestants) and Upper Franconia (46 percent Catholics, 49 percent Protestants). Before World War II and the holocaust, there had been a Jewish minority in some of the larger towns of Middle Franconia, in particular in Fürth, but no significant presence in such small communes as ours.

The addition of various territories in the early 1800s had brought 752,000 Evangelic-Lutherans to join the 3.2 million Bavarians, along with official toleration (1803) and promises of equality with the Catholics. The Evangelical Churches came in three different varieties but were united more or less under the Bavarian crown. Both Catholics and Evangelicals experienced powerful religious revivals after the assaults and triumph of the Enlightenment, feeling similar depths of resentment of the Enlightenment campaigns of the government, but they were also shaped by their conflicts and by the great tensions of nineteenth century politics, such as the 1848–1849 revolution and the reaction to follow. Of particular importance for the local level in both Catholic and Protestant communities were the continued principles of clerical supervision of elementary education and the denominational school (*Bekenntnisschule*):

Each school and its teachers had to be either Catholic or Protestant and church authorities were in control. The end of the monarchy and its summepiscopate over the Evangelic-Lutheran church in 1918 freed the latter from its dependence on the state, but it also ended its rights of clerical supervision over the schools, without abolishing the denominational character of the latter.

At the start of the nineteenth century, as the Bavarian state recognized Evangelic-Lutheranism in the Edict of Tolerance of 1803, there were at least three different Protestant churches that were united, more or less, under the Crown although their equality at times was in question in Catholic areas. Their conception of rationalism was curiously bifurcated from that of the French Enlightenment: While to their monarchic antagonists, rationalism was that of the enlightened (if extremely greedy) absolutist state that desired centralization and simplification of government, Protestants were haunted by their specter of rationalism in religion, represented by various groups and movements. Bavarian Protestants, moreover, henceforth followed a very different political path from the Catholics who from the days of the Bismarckian *Kulturkampf* (struggle against Catholic privileges) had mostly rallied to their own Catholic monarchy and the Catholic Center (*Zentrum*) party. The Center party became one of the pillars of the Weimar republic and, in arch-conservative mode and under the name Bavarian People's party (BVP) dominated Bavarian politics until the Third Reich.

The Protestants and their clergy, by way of contrast, took the defeat of the German army and fatherland in 1918 very hard and tended to gravitate to anti-republican groups such as the militant Free Corps, *völkisch* (crypto-Nazi) groups and the arch-conservative German National People's party (DNVP). With the coming of the Third Reich, many of them were swayed by the Movement of German Christians (*Glaubensbewegung deutscher Christen*) and its efforts to take over the church: By 1935, the German Christians had no fewer than thirteen thousand members and had established seventy-three locals in Germany. The brazenness of the Nazi takeover attempts eventually provoked a strong reaction among the faithful and their clergy which saved the church but exposed it to further harassment. In 1937, the Third Reich also abolished denominational schools of both religions. During the war, half of the Protestant clergy was drafted; 144 died. Most church bells, of both faiths, were confiscated and any ringing of bells *verboten*. The church press was denied paper. Many churches were destroyed in air raids and no funds given to the clergy.

In the years immediately after World War II, both churches and their flocks benefitted from a religious revival that reflected their moral—if not untainted—images as victims of Nazi totalitarianism. It was not to last though this time, at least, the Protestants were included in the revived Center party, now called the Christian Democrats (CDU or, in Bavaria, the Christian Social Union, CSU). Their restored status brought them new influence and a restoration of the denominational school, at least until 1968. The flood of ethnic German refugees added over seven hundred thousand Protestants to their numbers and required the establishment of new deaconries (*Dekanate*) in Regensburg and Augsburg to accommodate them. Other reforms strove to bring the Evangelic-Lutheran church into the twentieth century, such as the new Church Community Statute (*Kirchengemeindeordnung*) of 1964 and revised Church Constitution of 1972 by which time a new ecumenical trend was emerging to keep the secularization of society at bay.

To appreciate the significance of today's local church as the center of community life and local identity, we can also look at the venerable age and history of particular churches and observe the parishioners in our fifteen communes. The *Simultankirche* (Protestant-Catholic church) of Weigenheim, for example, had its ecumenical character recognized by the King of Bavaria in 1834 after centuries of embattled existence going back to the Reformation and subsequent appropriation by the Catholic church in the 1600s. In the 1700s, as a local chronicle by a Protestant minister discloses, the Catholic priests on their weekly visits had made the local inn their headquarters with a regular expense allowance to be paid by the parish. After the incorporation of Franconia into Bavaria, a new church was built (1828–1832) with considerable help from the townspeople. In 1945, under fire from the invading American troops,[6] the church burnt down and the services had to be held for several years in Jordan's Tavern. The new church took five years to build, beginning naturally with a bell tower and new bells, and has been owned and maintained by the town. To old Weigenheimers, this is the center pole of their community.[7]

Parish, School, and Social Life

The traditional community life of small places in Bavaria used to revolve around certain key institutions and figures. Especially among the town-like Franconian villages, from a visual point of view alone, the church, the school, and the communal hall (*Gemeindehaus*) or *Rathaus* were at the center of the small community.[8] The local priest or minister, the teacher, almost always a male,[9] and the honorary mayor were the key notables who, together with the better-off farmers, dominated its public and much of its private life.[10] Under the pre-1789 regime, the priest or minister was clearly the dominant figure among the three, controlling the very limited elementary education received by the village or small-town children. With a population at least half illiterate, public awareness of the desir-

Illustration 2.1. Wolframs-Eschenbach: Main Street with church.
Source: J.B. Kurz, *Wolframs-Eschenbach: Kulturbilder aus einer deutschen Kleinstadt* (1919).

Illustration 2.2. Wolframs-Eschenbach: Tower of St. Mary's Ascension church.
Photo courtesy of the city of Wolframs-Eschenbach.

Illustration 2.3. Gothic altar of 1490.
Photo courtesy of the city of Wolframs-Eschenbach.

ability of mass education was shallow and most of its prerequisites were absent: good schoolhouses, textbooks, and teacher training outside the church. In 1802, nevertheless, Old Bavaria (and the Upper Palatinate it had acquired in the Thirty Years War) decreed compulsory education from age six to twelve. But it took years of overcoming inadequate facilities and unqualified teachers to arrive at the status we are describing here. Much of this retardation resulted from the deep resentment by the villagers and small bourgeoisie of the brutal secularization of church property—which often involved violence, destruction, and plundering of monasteries and churches—and the royal Enlightenment campaigns that actually tended to restore the authority of the church. Unbowed by Bismarck's later *Kulturkampf* and even Nazi *Kirchenkampf* against all organized religion, Bavarian Catholics remained in their own world and experienced their religious revivals. Their rich associational life particularly drew the ire of the Nazis who pressured members to drop out, barred them from enlisting in the German Labor Front (*Deutsche Arbeitsfront*), a refuge for the unemployed of the great depression, and eventually shut down all Catholic clubs. Fifty-seven thousand Catholics were persuaded to leave their church. The Third Reich also focused on church-associated teachers and, during the war, on monasteries as religious centers, taking them over instead as hospitals and for other purposes.

As a result, the local priest regained and retained much of his pre-revolutionary aura in the village and small town. Linked to the supra-local and international hierarchy, he reflected the splendor and mystique of the religion. A man of superior education and tastes, he also stood out in small poor places with his stately dwelling or *Pfarrhof* (large priestly farm) and its acreage and personnel, all potent symbols of status in an agrarian community. The mayor and the notables of the commune defied the church only at their peril, and it rarely failed to back up its express will. The priest or minister also dominated the social life of the community that consisted almost exclusively of church festivals, christenings, weddings, and funerals staged by the church with the help of faithful parishioners, the teacher, and his school children.

The role of the village priest as a figure of unquestionable—if not always unquestioned—authority is a popular staple in Bavarian literature about the village life of the past. The priest was the public guardian of family life and individual morality, enjoying universal deference as Your Worship (*Hochwürden*) wherever he went. He could also appear as an avenging angel, publicly denouncing sin and confronting sinners personally with their trespasses. Villagers would remove their hats and bow their heads and rowdy children would quiet down the moment they saw the village priest. The village teacher, always male, was hired only if the church approved of him. Among other things, he had to conduct the church choir, accompany it on the organ, or with a violin, and perhaps also keep the church clean and heated in the winter. His training naturally had to include the appropriate musical skills and he had to be prepared to spend many a weekend and evening rehearsing with the choir or with school children. His choir members or the children in his one- or two-room village school were the mainstay of all church and public festivities. His classroom teaching likewise had to reflect the pastor's moral concerns, sometimes even including sanctions for non-attendance of the church on Sunday. The priest in any case knew his village children well both from church and school and from house calls in the community.

The Role of the Pastor Today

As a result of the communal reorganization, many of our small communities in West Middle Franconia have both a Catholic and a Protestant church and some, like Steinsfeld, inherited several churches of the same kind. However, both churches, and especially the Catholic church, have long embarked on programs of rationalization and economy.[11] Steinsfeld for this reason was not permitted to continue its four separate churches and priests inherited from its antecedent communities, but now has only one clergyman who ministers to all the flocks of the new community.

In many cases, the clergymen have been given additional communities to take care of since the communal reform that, of course, loosens the close personal ties between parishioners and their shepherd, especially if the minister lives in another village. Such mergers also increase the administrative workload and compel the priest to schedule several services at different times in his several communities. The Catholic town of Wolframs-Eschenbach is a rare example to the contrary with both a priest and a chaplain. Weigenheim since the communal reorganization has two clergymen for three of the original parishes and churches. Ippesheim's original priest also serves the old Bullenheim district of the town and there is a new pastor for the newly annexed area of Herrnberchtheim. Reorganized Ohrenbach near Rothenburg o. T. now has one pastor for three parishes. Adelshofen's priest was given three additional parishes. Markt Berolzheim's two Protestant churches had already been reduced to one minister in the 1950s and its Catholic church has lacked a priest for years. Langfurth has had two Protestant parishes with only one minister and a vacancy since 1973. Only Bruckberg, which had been a part of the parish of Großhaslach, now received its own parish and priest.[12] On balance, the fifteen communities appear to have lost considerably in the quality and density of spiritual solace, just as they have lost other personal services and supplies.

For the Catholic church, according to the well-known if controversial theologian Hans Küng, the loss and sharing of priests among parishes had long reached catastrophic proportions. It was no longer rare for a priest to have to celebrate the Eucharist five times in one weekend alone. Children and teenagers could no longer expect to be prepared for first communion by the regular pastoral staff. Couples about to be married, the troubled, the sick, and the dying no longer received all the pastoral attention they deserved. Pastors were often not permitted to retire at the normal age limit, even if they should be infirm.[13] A prominent critic of Vatican policies, Küng blamed this "breakdown of the church's mission" on the resistance of the Roman church to a long list of popular reforms.[14] The injunction to celibacy alone, the theologian wrote, kept large numbers of theology students from the priesthood.

By the time of the reform, the welfare functions once performed by the churches were largely supplied by secular public or private institutions that still used the religious title *Schwester* (sister) to connote a nurse or social worker. Social services in this area are mostly organized into so-called "social stations" that can dispatch a multipurpose communal nurse (*Gemeindeschwester*) on request. These communal nurses can take on health functions, minister to the elderly and to preschool children, and at times will run the entire household if the farm wife and mother is ill or temporarily unable to take care of her flock. Markt Berolzheim and Wolframs-Eschenbach had their own communal nurses. Burk had a branch of the Feuchtwangen Deaconate with a nurse. Since 1980, Steinsfeld had a Protestant Association (*Diakonieverein*) with nurses who often have to fill the gap for the absence of a medical practice. Bruckberg, Weihenzell, and Mitteleschenbach, on the other hand, have neither a nurse[15] nor a connection with a social station. The elderly are generally taken care of by the family and live there, an example of the survival of the extended family. But there are several old-folks homes in the vicinity of our communities, including a private one for twenty-four persons in Burk. Their clientele are elderly people from elsewhere and those without a home and family.

The shortage of money and recruits to the priesthood in both churches produced responses of significance for community life. Following the Second Vatican Council (1962–1965), the Catholic church began to explore parish mergers and cooperative arrangements at the diocesan and regional levels. The steeply declining numbers of members of religious orders and their increasing age also meant a significant decline in the education and health care functions they used to perform in society.[16] In the early 1970s, the church also tackled its problems in a common synod of West German bishoprics devoted to the development of lay participation in parish councils, diocesan committees, and diocesan councils. The presence of a network of large Catholic lay associations must have been very useful for this democratization of religious life.[17]

The Protestants also broadened the already considerable lay participation with their Church Community Constitution (*Kirchengemeindeordnung*) in 1964 and took to training many more teachers of Protestant religion for the post-1968 common elementary schools. Their Evangelical-Lutheran church also developed a special plan, the Wassertrüdingen Model, for coping with the shortages of funds and personnel.[18] Developed in West Middle Franconia in 1972, this plan provided for an association of several parish councils in areas where there was only one minister available and for the substitution of deacons and qualified laypersons "deputized" for functions other than conducting the services. These helpers and lay volunteers were to serve as youth counselors, Sunday school and schoolteachers, for home visits, and for health care. Ideally, there might be weekly visits to the sick and troubled, and a lay counselor for every twelve to fifteen families. These measures of organized lay participation all served to renew the integrating function of the religious village community in an age of changing loyalties and preoccupations.

Let us turn to the remaining role of the clergymen of our small communities in Franconia. They vary considerably in length of term in office, mostly dating from no more than three years ago. A few had been there for a long time: the Catholic priest of Mitteleschenbach for twenty-eight and the Protestant minister of Ippesheim for twenty-seven years. Some had been in their community a decade. Their ages averaged between forty and sixty with occasional exceptions, such as the young Protestant minister of Meinheim at thirty and the priest of Mitteleschenbach at seventy years. Their predecessors used to stay in office for several decades until their retirement. It is customary for a retired clergyman not to remain in the community so as not to get in the way of his successor's efforts to win the trust of the parishioners. Unlike the other key figures, clergymen thus served as an integrating factor only while in office. Their changing roles in certain respects permitted them to concentrate more exclusively on such things as church ceremonies, sacraments, and counseling parishioners when their counsel was sought. At the same time, they had been losing the wholistic functions of a community leader and moral guide, especially in elementary education, along with the specific functions and services now performed by the lay helpers.

Some local priests and ministers also enjoyed more respect than others, often depending on the local memories of church struggles in the Nazi era. Some of these conflicts still rankled in the minds of survivors and may even have manifested themselves in the relationship to and attendance at the respective churches. Other factors of change come from the transformation of agriculture and the motorization of the villagers. Urban influences have overcome typical village patterns or thinking in matters of everyday life. A clergyman's sermons and moral advice have to take into account urbanized morals and frequent contact with the world outside the small community, from school bussing to commuting to places of work. Mixed marriages and marriage to outsiders of more or less urbanized background are much more frequent than they used to be.[19] Premarital and extramarital sex, as well as living together without benefit of marriage, are no longer less common now in the countryside than they are in the city. Clergymen are no longer expected to intervene in such things and any attempt to do so may be counterproductive in that it might "reduce the clergy's moral authority." Illegitimacy of birth, on the other hand, once a very common phenomenon in the countryside because of the legal and financial obstacles to getting married, has declined.[20] Clergymen today concentrate instead on awakening the conscience of the young and giving their thinking a religious foundation. But the parishioners no longer look up to the priest or minister as an authoritarian stand-in for God, with the possible exception of the elderly, and the clergy show little interest in maintaining social control. Only in Mitteleschenbach, as a holdover from the past, there was still a custom that called for the priest to tell his flock from the pulpit on New Year's Eve what he considered morally wrong in the community, though not necessarily by naming names.

Territorial and social changes have also affected the outcome in unexpected ways. Before the school reform, the priests or ministers usually got to know the local children also during religious instruction in the local school. Now, the youngsters were more likely to attend elementary school outside of their community. The Ippesheim pastor used to have a Sunday school service for the children following the regular service, but now he had to hold a second adult service in the parish of Bullenheim instead. Many clergymen no longer have the time for home visits. Most young adults and those between the ages of thirty and fifty are likely to be off commuting during the week anyway. And the "moonlight farmers" and other holders of part-time employment cannot be expected to have time in the evening either for church social or cultural events. Frequently, the church has to compete with such communal Sunday morning pastimes as soccer games or other sports or festivities. Even voluntary fire drills are no longer scheduled so as not to conflict with Sunday services. In this fashion, the church has become a marginal factor in the lives of most villagers save the elderly. It has "lost its authority," as Germans like to put it, although on both sides[21] there has been some regret and efforts to make up for the erosion of functions.

There has also been a noticeable shift in the activities of the clergy from the purely spiritual to the social gospel, particularly in their involvement in organized youth activity, family counseling, and senior citizen care in these parts. In the vestibules of many churches, visitors can see a plethora of announcements and solicitations for humanitarian aid organizations in developing countries and at home. There is a Protestant Rural Youth (*Evangelische Landjugend*) and a Catholic Young Men's Association; some even supply a youth center or a church kindergarten. Many have senior citizen clubs or senior afternoons. Although clergymen still define their own role in the community, the demands and expectations of their parishioners help to fashion what they actually do and, at times, may add to what they originally intended to perform.

In communities without a schoolteacher, for example, priests often render all kinds of new services. The pastor of Reusch, a part of Weigenheim, for example, contributes a local chronicle to commemorative books on festive occasions. Many secular local clubs and associations, not just the church-associated groups, now expect the pastor to show up at some of their meetings. Clergymen also have to assemble and direct their own choir, a task that had always belonged to the school teachers.[22] Some have a brass wind orchestra for the church. Since the 1950s, the wives of Protestant pastors have taken on many of the social tasks of their husband's ministry, including also the organization of Protestant women's circles. The wife of the pastor of Ippesheim, for example, helped old women without a family to find a place in a suitable senior home or assisted handicapped persons with the time-consuming red tape associated with obtaining handicap certificates. The wife of the pastor of Meinheim conducts the choir and plays the church organ. Unless their own families are too large or demanding of the mother's time, the Protestant ministry appears to be well on the path toward marital job sharing.[23]

Comparing this predominantly Protestant area of Bavaria with heavily Catholic (80–92 percent) Rosenheim County, southeast of Munich, reveals a similar shortage: Only two priests—one seriously ill—and one assistant "covered" the eight Catholic churches of the consolidated town of Wasserburg, the local hospital, and the home for the elderly. The 120-year-old Wasserburg girls' *Realschule* was closed because there weren't enough nuns to teach there.[24] In the county seat of Rosenheim, the city pays salaries to priests and sisters of religious orders who work in the public schools and the hospitals.[25] City and state helped to finance the construction of the Catholic Educational Center of the Archdiocese in Rosenheim, which provides day care facilities, inexpensive musical training, craft and cooking classes, and space for adult education programs run by the state. The Catholic *Caritas* and Protestant Inner Mission offer charitable services. The overwhelming presence of Catholicism is reflected in numerous wayside shrines, murals, crucifixes, and at public processions and services, all contributing to the traditional ambiance. But the attendance of the faithful at Sunday mass and other services is rarely higher than about 20–25 percent of the registered church members, although it often reaches 50 percent in Wasserburg.[26]

The Elementary School and the Community

Before the French Revolution, compulsory public education was introduced in the Old Bavarian Electoral Princedom only in 1771, a reform followed by many other encroachments upon the privileges and responsibilities of the Catholic church.

The Emergence of Secular Education

There is perhaps no better way to measure the retreat of the church from village life than to chronicle the gradual emancipation of German rural elementary education from church control. Until the eighteenth century and, in Old Bavaria, until the 1770s, rural elementary education was entirely dominated by the churches. The Enlightenment led to progressive attempts by the secular state to regulate and spread formal education, especially through the so-called "trivial schools" for the masses. But when the state decreed mass education in 1802, it mandated only that children of school age "should," not that they "must enroll." It imposed a weekly tuition of two *kreuzer* and assembled teacher training for a pathetic collection of recruits and facilities. By 1820, there were 5,400 schooling locales, about 5,000 schoolhouses, and 7,114 teachers for half a million pupils.[27] Schools were organizationally separated from the church without however denying the local priest supervisory authority over "his" school. It was not until after the upheaval of 1848–1849, in which secular teachers played a prominent role, that teacher education (1866) and remuneration (1861) were liberalized. The progress of secularization of Bavarian elementary schools, however, was halted at the threshold of entry into the Bismarckian empire, at the same time that it proceeded apace in the rest of Germany. The schools remained "confessional schools" in conformity with the local parish and under the supervision of the church authorities until the 1950s. Rural schooling, moreover, had to accommodate the priorities of agricultural life by confining much of its instruction to the winter, holidays, and other slack periods of farm work. From the planting to the harvest season, the children were not free to receive schooling.

The three decades before 1900, nevertheless, were not years of stagnation, as the numbers of elementary schools rose, the number of full-time teachers increased from ten to fifteen thousand, and the average teacher-student ratio was improved. The compulsory school age also was eventually raised to fourteen upon local option, a path which all larger cities soon adopted. But it took a Socialist state government (1919) to end the supervisory authority of the clergy over the schools, to introduce parent advisory councils, and to give the elementary school teachers the security of civil service status.[28] So, how much were Bavarian villagers and small-town folk really alienated from the church in these two hundred years? If we would measure religiosity by the sales of devotionals like saints' pictures and the like, there was only a slight drop in the peak years of secularization, 1795–1815, and almost none after that. But a gradual alienation really began after 1820, or perhaps from the severe economic recession of

1816, between the faithful and the clergy, foreshadowed by resentment, disobedience, and downright rebellion in the lower clergy.

In rural areas such as the fifteen communities under consideration, an eighth-grade education with three years of limited vocational training—two for agricultural specialties—became compulsory only in 1938. Moreover, as recently as in 1964–1965, 62.5 percent of Bavarian elementary schools were one- or two-room "village dwarf schools," a prime target of educational critics and reformers who spoke of an "educational catastrophe" and expressed particular concern about the denial of educational opportunities to the rural population. The Bavarian government finally tackled the dwarf school problem by creating larger school districts (1961) and launching a major school reform bill (1966). This was followed by a plebiscite abolishing the confessional schools (1968), and the introduction of a compulsory ninth grade (1969).[29] Throughout the Federal Republic, such school reforms reduced the number of elementary schools drastically, even though the numbers of students changed little. Between 1966 and 1978, the number of elementary schools (*Grundschule* and *Hauptschule*) declined from 29,217 to 17,797.[30] This must have included the replacement of many of these small rural schools with school centers involving various consolidated grades and ultimately all grades for the newly created school districts. In the rather agrarian state of Bavaria, and especially among the Landkreise only, the reduction in the number of elementary schools between, say, 1961 and 1981, is even more striking: the remaining schools numbered only a third of what they used to be twenty years earlier.

Before this school reform, the prevailing form of elementary school in the fifteen communities was a one- or two-room school in which one or two teachers taught up to eight grades simultaneously. Elementary school teachers were still likely to have lived in the same community for many years and constituted key persons of communal life. These village teachers had until then been also a major instrument of the social control of the church over the community: Selected to suit the church, they served as organists, choir directors, festival organizers, and most of all as the long arm of the church over the school children who were likewise drawn in as participants and audience into the festivals, weddings, and funerals at little or no expense to the church.

The new elementary school districts also appear to have anticipated the communal territorial reform in general if not everywhere in detail. They were certainly a major institutional step down the road to larger local units. There was of course some resistance to the details of the school reform here and there among the fifteen communities. But the loss of indirect social control by the church was not something greatly lamented by the populace, with the possible exception of older people who might have looked back with nostalgia to the primordial days of the village united around steeple and school house.

The Role of the Teacher

The changing role of the elementary teachers since the 1950s alone mirrors the slipping grip of the church over the village ever since the teachers were the principal, classroom teacher, and specialized teacher all in one, frequently making up personally whatever educational materials seemed to be desirable. The village teacher also used to have to be a counselor and nurse to some of the children. Teachers were expected to maintain and, in winter, to heat the school house, and, if we go back far enough, the local church as well. Now the teaching personnel of the new district schools became highly differentiated and specialized, and there were even professional teachers' aides for various auxiliary tasks short of secretarial duties, for which again there now was specialized personnel. But the village teacher also had several other significant functions for the community, the loss of which is perhaps more important to the life of the community than it may have been to the individual teacher.

In the old days, when a vacancy occurred, communities typically would specify certain extracurricular skills the successor should have to possess to be satisfactory. Frequently, the municipality had a little house and garden to offer the teacher though the pay was small. Bavarian village fiction, as in the plays of Ludwig Thoma, liked to depict the teacher as always hungry and eager to accept free meals and gifts from the villagers. In most cases, the teacher also had to be a passable organist for the church and a competent director for the local singing society (*Gesangverein*), as well as the town secretary and archivist. Further cultural initiatives relevant to community life, such as organizing festivities or plays, were warmly appreciated in a teacher candidate. The teachers and their students generally were expected, with adult assistance when available, to provide the musical entertainment at such festivities as Christmas, Easter, and memorial occasions. They had to decorate the altar of the local church for harvest festivals, and frequently to sing at funerals and sometimes at weddings. Sometimes they rose to prodigious challenges. At Wolframs-Eschenbach in the mid 1950s, for example, the local teacher staged the Parzival epic of the town's most famous son, the medieval poet Wolfram von Eschenbach. All the acting and the theatrical support was supplied by residents, some of whom grew beards for the occasion. Only the orchestra had to be brought in from Nuremberg. The play was performed twice, in 1954 and 1956, before local enthusiasm died down and some actors moved away.

This nurturing role of the local teacher of cultural activities for his town began to change toward the end of the 1960s. Some of the role change was due to the school reform and the lapsing of the residence requirement which had insisted that teachers live in their respective communities. Not only were there many teachers at the new school centers and no one in particular responsible to that community or any other, but now teachers could live anywhere. Particularly the younger teachers and teaching interns (*Lehramtsanwärter*) tended to prefer the personal freedom and anonymity of larger cities to the public and social character of a teacher's role in a small community. Some even commuted every day from the metropolitan Nuremberg/Fürth area to their schools in West Middle Franconia. Young female teachers were even less willing to commit their leisure time any more to community activities. The gender difference has been particularly evident, for example, in Weihenzell and Bruckberg where only two of nine female teachers were still actively involved in the 1980s, one as an organist, and the other as an athletic club director.[31] Of the male teachers, half or more were likely to serve the community as members of the communal council or parish council, church deacon, president or member of clubs, choir or band director, etc. Retired teachers in the communities and some of their wives also liked to remain active in community life.

Where the local schools were closed, by the same token, teacher-directed cultural activities threatened to atrophy. In the VG Rothenburg o.T., for example, there used to be four bands, Gattenhofen (Steinsfeld), Grossharbach (now part of Adelshofen), Adelshofen, and Ohrenbach, each directed by their local teacher. With the school reform, only the Ohrenbach band director remained in the community since he became the superintendent of the school district. Grossharbach still received some services from the former band director who now lived and taught in Uffenheim. The Gattenhofen band had to hire a new director from Rothenburg. Adelshofen gave up the band.

Finally, the school reform also replaced the old requirement that teacher candidates had to learn to play the organ, the piano, or the violin and required only "an instrument of their choice." Hence many young teachers now only play the guitar or other "less useful" instruments for the musical needs of a small community. The whole teacher-training curriculum, in fact, has shifted noticeably from encouraging cultural and social skills toward specialization in hard academic subjects that often require also far more of the non-teaching hours to prepare and to keep up with them. Again, the villagers did not always appreciate the quality of the new curriculum and of teacher education, as compared to what the old village teacher knew and what he could teach under the circumstances of a one-

or two-room school. The new teachers were generally unable as well as unwilling to follow the example, say, of the old village band director of Ohrenbach who, for thirty years, volunteered all his Sundays playing the organ and rehearsing or directing the band for weddings, funerals, and other festivities. The villagers, of course, cannot understand why the new teachers will not devote "all that free time" to their cultural life. They tend to blame the teachers rather than the system.

The role of the old teacher in the village was also marked by a close and mutual relationship with the villagers. On the one hand, the teacher was a *Gschtudierter* (educated person) whose knowledge and wisdom put him or her on a pedestal shared only by the village priest. He enjoyed general respect and deference, and his advice was sought at his home, in the tavern, and in the street as well as at school. His door was always open to callers and he made frequent home visits with his students' families who were very likely to invite him for Sunday dinner, or when they had one of their recurring slaughter days, or other feast days. The teacher knew everyone and everyone knew him and his generally impecunious circumstances. Gradually, the character of these close contacts changed and so did the economic situation of the teacher, who received fewer presents and was invited less and less. Perhaps the villagers felt that their gifts and food were no longer needed or appropriate.

The teachers also no longer wield their old authority in or out of the classroom. In class they were no longer feared nor did they still wield the cane of yesterday. Outside, adults no longer addressed them as "Herr Lehrer," or "Frau Lehrer", by their title,[32] nor were they expected to intervene when, while walking through town, they came across unruly children. Even their school authority has diminished, as parents try to influence the grading or ignore the teacher's judgment regarding whether their child may be gifted enough to apply for transfer to a *Gymnasium* (secondary school).[33]

The most incisive change, however, has been the destruction of the close relationship between the village teacher and the community by the school reform, the bussing, and the distant school centers. The village parents often do not even know the teachers of their children any more, and there rarely is a particular teacher that "belongs" to their community. In place of the home visits, there is now a regular parent-teacher consultation period at the school, which can hardly make up for the growing distance and the loss of personal contact in the village.

Parents rarely go to the consultation hour unless their child is in real trouble at school. The schools have not been unaware of the changes and have attempted to overcome the gap with recurrent school festivals. The school in Oberscheckenbach (Ohrenbach), for example, holds a public

Christmas celebration and an annual summer festival, as well as a biennial arts and crafts show. The schools are always careful to involve all the classes and individuals in order to motivate the parents to attend. This may provide better contacts for parents and schools, but it hardly contributes to the autonomous life of the original small communities. In fact, it may reinforce a competing, larger community pattern as do the other patterns we have discussed.

But Bavarians do not devote all of their energy to the serious side of life—they enjoy as well the associational life with the social meetings, activities, parties, and celebrations such organizations provide.

Social Groups and Festivals in West Middle Franconia

Since the nineteenth century, and in different forms before, German associational life has been very rich and forms a densely interwoven net of the most varied associations. In larger towns or cities, we would expect to find also trade unions and workers associations devoted to pursuits ranging from early childhood education to funeral societies. During the heyday of the presence of refugees in our fifteen communities in West Middle Franconia, the various ethnic *Landsmannschaften* (e.g., the Silesians) and other refugee groups must also have been present in force as was their party, the BHE (Party of Expellees and the Dispossessed).

There is a revealing historical perspective on the emergence of associations in Germany that relates different kinds of groups to historical eras or events: Veterans associations usually reflect war generations, such as those of the Napoleonic wars early in the nineteenth century, the Franco-Prussian War of 1870, or the two world wars of the last century. Some Masonic lodges were revived in 1840 (Bayreuth) and in the 1870s, after being suppressed earlier. The 1840s also saw the growth of the bourgeois and nationalist *Schützenvereine* (rifle clubs), *Turnvereine* (gymnasts), and *Gesangvereine* (singing clubs), which were in the forefront of the liberal revolution of 1848 and subsequent patriotic festivals in the 1860s and the 1920s. The 1860s witnessed the beginnings of associational growth among the working classes and, eventually, under the umbrella of the Social Democratic party (SPD). Popular educational societies then addressed their efforts also to bourgeois sponsors and audiences to bring German culture "to the people," a task frequently and self-consciously taken on by local governments as well. From about the 1890s, politics became a matter of mass organizations, ranging from the socialist and other unions to the Catholic *Sozialverein*. From this time on, also, many soccer and sporting clubs were founded, as well as popular bowling, and dog or other pet clubs.[34] Since the turn of the century, historical preservation and cultural appreciation societies, especially the *Trachtenvereine* (rural costume and dance groups) have gradually gone from the big cities into even the small communities, a measure of the spreading nostalgia for the passing of a rustic way of life.

Even though Bavaria has become increasingly secularized over the last two hundred years, it enjoyed, until recently, the dubious distinction of having fourteen mandatory, paid religious holidays, exceeding any other German state. Many of these holidays are, in fact, religious holidays from the Roman Catholic Church calendar or, in the north, Evangelic-Lutheran holy days, or both. A number of other religious festivals occur locally, often on weekends, but also during the week to honor such figures as the patron of the parish church, and saints receiving special devotion. Pilgrimages to religious shrines occur frequently, as do masses in honor of the saint-patrons of special market days that persist from medieval times. The local church will often schedule additional celebrations throughout the year, sometimes in conjunction with the Church calendar—such as specific religious rites of passage like first communion and confirmation. Sometimes it will sponsor a purely secular cultural or social event for the community.

Associations Build Community

Voluntary associations, which we will discuss more completely below, schedule *Fests* and other activities, usually as fundraisers. Anything from a simple barbecue or dance to a week-long beer festival might be on the agenda. Events are advertised in the local or regional papers since associations rely heavily on visitors from outside the local community (from other Bavarian counties, other parts of Germany, and even Austria) to help support these local events. Most celebrations occur in summertime to take full advantage of good weather and tourism; however, except for the Lenten season, festivals and celebrations occur throughout the year in much of Bavaria.

In Protestant Middle Franconia, there is no lack of festivals or of the clubs and associations that organize them. Although the parochial unity of old may have broken apart and the church and school play a far smaller role in putting on community celebrations, their place has increasingly been taken by the fabric of voluntary associations that now constitute the heart of its remaining community life in an age of otherwise urban lifestyles. "In Steinsfeld," as the local chronicler put it succinctly, "the following societies are active for the well-being and benefit of the people." There follows a list that includes the Volunteer Fire Brigade, founded in

1890, a fraternal organization named *Burschenverein Fortuna* (dating from 1899), a garden and horticulture club, founded in 1929, and the veterans' *Militärverein*, which was established as recently as 1970. The list is very likely incomplete, for we look in vain for the ubiquitous *Gesangverein*, *Gartenverein*, agricultural associations and cooperatives, including the Raiffeisen bank, sporting clubs, and religious associations, not to mention political parties and their affiliates such as the CSU youth organization, the Young Union (JU).

These associations at the local level can play a major role in focusing and supporting community life in a modern egalitarian, participational setting. The more socially oriented clubs, whatever may be their ostensible purpose, are a significant agent of socialization and resocialization. Young people practically grow up within their age-heterogeneous atmosphere. Aspiring politicians do well to join and hold office in the more important local clubs before daring to face the voters at large. The clubs and societies also become very active in organizing recurrent local festivities and celebrations, thus making up for the declining roles of the local teacher and even the churches who originated most of the festivities in the first place. Historic festivals as in Rothenburg, Dinkelsbühl, or Wolframs-Eschenbach, moreover, show how organized efforts can develop a popular sense of local identity from events of the distant past. A fair number of our fifteen communities have a historical background that can be dramatized in this fashion. In many cases, the distant past and late nineteenth century "cultural ambitions" of a town could be brought together by local boosters in the form of concert or theatrical festivals with historical costumes and parades. The local trades and retail stores stood to gain from such activities no less than did the local taverns and inns.

A brief survey of our fifteen hamlets shows that local associations, unlike other manifestations of community life, hardly ever die. To be sure, in Bruckberg the soccer club was dissolved in the 1950s—hence no more soccer field; in Mitteleschenbach it was the Bicycle Club, and in Ohrenbach, in 1969, the *Gesangverein* died for lack of eager members. In Ippesheim, a veterans association went to sleep in the 1960s. In Steinsfeld and Meinheim, on the other hand, after a temporary slackening of interest, the organized club activities were revived in the 1970s.[35]

Sports and Music

Music looms large in all our hamlets. They all have at least one and often several musical associations and, in addition, church choirs and brass groups. Twelve of the towns have sports clubs, often with diverse sections that show what games are popular here—soccer, table tennis, or women's gymnastics. Röckingen was even planning a tennis club, a sport still rather limited to the upper classes. There are a number of *Krieger* (warrior clubs) or *Militärvereine* (veterans clubs) that generally date from the First World War or the late nineteenth century. Such an organization existed in Wolframs-Eschenbach, but it was moribund—and so are most of them—unless it could recruit current army reservists. In Bruckberg and Röckingen there are relatively new reservist clubs. The traditional and ubiquitous local *Schützenvereine* (rifle clubs) and the garden and horticulture societies are all of very long standing and their emphasis is more social than focused on bullets and geraniums. The *Schützenverein* is rarely absent in a festival parade, often in historic or rural costumes and with old muskets and flags.[36] More singular associations here and there are a hiking club, tourism association, carnival society, carrier pigeon club, horseback-riding club, Young Red Cross group, Sudeten German ethnic *Landsmannschaft* (in Markt Berolzheim), the Protestant *Landjugend* (Rural Youth), the *Kolping-Verein* (Catholic Workingmen's Club), and the Young Men's Christian Association.

Women have been less involved in associational life, although they have become more active since the mid-1960s. Gender stereotypes among the villagers tend to limit them to traditional social roles. but they do play a modest role now in *Schützenvereine* and, probably for lack of competent and willing male recruits, in groups like the very active, 50-year-old Ohrenbach brass band. The Meinheim *Trachtenverein*, the Bruckberg table tennis club, the horseback-riding club, and the hiking society have many female members, as do the mixed choirs. For the most part, though, women are in their own gymnastic groups and in garden and horticulture societies. In Catholic Wolframs-Eschenbach, there is also a Catholic Women's Association in which traditional Catholic notions of a woman's role are dominant.[37]

The activities of these clubs and societies, after a temporary lapse sometimes attributed to the spread of television in the 1960s, are fairly intense considering the size of these hamlets. In Weigenheim, for example, there are fifteen clubs and the facilities for meetings available to them are often inadequate to meet their needs.[38] The rather new *Trachten* (rural costume and dance) group of the Meinheim tourism association has performed throughout the whole county of Gunzenhausen-Weissenburg. The Hiking Club of Burk every Sunday schedules hikes that attract an average of 25 participants. It has also organized at least five popular long-distance "runs." The communal reform has not affected these organized activities very much except that now, frequently, there may be several clubs of the same kind in the same consolidated community because the incorporated additions each continue to maintain their own clubs.

Clubs, churches, and local governments often cooperate in staging important communal festivities, such as club jubilees or *Kermis* (*Kirchweih*), which is celebrated somewhat differently in Protestant than in Catholic areas. Formerly, the patron saint and/or the dedication of each church was honored by festivals (variously called *Kirchweih*, *Kirmes*, *Kermis*, or *Kirta* in different Bavarian regions) which often lasted several days. Gradually, day laborers and even farmers spent more and more time celebrating not only their own church festivals but those of neighboring villages. During the original period of secularization, around 1800, Count Montgelas changed all this by consolidating all such church celebrations and having them fall on the same day.[39]

Kermis can be quite riotous—"inviting someone" for it can signify a physical threat—and it takes place in all fifteen communities, and often in their parts as well. It is organized mostly by the innkeepers or the commune, or both, with minimal participation by the church. *Kermis* is a popular occasion for annual family reunions and other such meetings. In four of our hamlets, it is customary to erect a *Kirchweih* pole. In twelve of them, the young people or a club also put up the traditional Maypole[40]—Mitteleschenbach does both—and in some cases, each part of a town may have a separate one around which dances and festivities can be staged. Overlapping club memberships in a town make for greater social cohesion and may help to prevent physical conflicts among clubs, though not always among different communities, on such occasions as *Kirchweih* or May Pole raisings.[41]

When an old custom lapses or dies out, a willing local club often has the opportunity to continue it. In Weigenheim and Ohrenbach they still use the customary town crier, using a bell, to call out communal news. In most communities, however, a printed news sheet has taken the place of the town crier. Some mayors called the town crier custom "out of date" and in one case, none of the young communal officials was willing to do it. Clubs could, of course, take it up as they have done with many other activities. They have also developed prodigious efforts on the occasion of the popular annual national contest "Our Village Must Become More Beautiful" which was already won at various levels—nationwide by Gattenhofen (Steinsfeld) in 1961 and at the county level by Langfurth in 1979—and at different times. The requirements go beyond esthetics into expensive infrastructural criteria that are often beyond the organized efforts of the clubs. Still, nothing binds a community together better than a common, all-out effort.

Some of the communes also have their own local festival which involves appropriate local clubs and associations. Ippesheim, for example, has an annual wine festival, the *Bremserfest,* for sampling its new vintage.

Bullenheim which was incorporated in Ippesheim has its own wine festival. The Ohrenbach Gardening and Horticulture Society has annual "garden festivals" that are not by any means limited to exhibiting gardening triumphs. Adelshofen has a communal festival every year. Wolframs-Eschenbach celebrates summer solstice and Mitteleschenbach has a solemn consecration of old flags and club banners. Since 1975 Röckingen has celebrated the Hesselberg Mountain Mass with appropriate flourishes in a beer tent.[42] In Weihenzell, there is a *Schützenfest* (shooting meet) and an annual to-do of the Aero-Club Ansbach which has a small flying field within the communal territory. Weigenheim's clubs, finally, have theater performances and the kindergarten puts on a summer fest for the adults. Nearly all of these communal occasions, of course, involve social evenings at which there is music, dancing, and beer—or wine, women, and song.

In our survey of Bavarian small-town mayors, we asked the mayors and other informants whether they felt that there had been much change in the social life of the community. The answer was frequently that there had been a noticeable drop in the sense of common concerns (*Gemeinschaftssinn*) over the years which most of them attributed to changing agriculture. In the old days, the argument went, people were much more dependent upon each other and forced to cooperate, for example, in bringing in the harvest or in threshing the grain together. Nowadays, farmers and their grown children have become so independent in income and in their work, each pursuing their own self-interest and often commuting to a job outside the village, that the close neighborly patterns of mutual aid, social contacts, and cooperation have also declined. Some claimed that the villagers, and especially village youth, were too busy to attend to communal life. Others thought that many actually had more time now, especially the farm women who once used to labor so hard from morning till night.

Frequent festivals and get-togethers today also were said to counteract the modern trend toward withdrawal into the life of the family. On the other hand, there has also been some decline in the popular skills for communal life. The widespread cultivation of musical skills for *Hausmusik,* for example, has died down since 1945 to the point where few young people seriously learn to play an instrument any more. The once ubiquitous *Hausmusik* groups have become rare and the easy availability of canned music on radio, in records, and on tape probably discourages musical efforts among the young.[43] In some communities, such as rural Adelshofen and Weigenheim, by the way, respondents said emphatically that communal life had not changed at all. In Ohrenbach and Bruckberg, furthermore, neighborly cooperation still plays an important role. It is not easy to arrive at an objective judgment in such subjective matters.

This survey of the changing fabric of social life in small and medium-sized communities has clearly shown the retreat of the church from what was once a quasi-totalitarian monopoly over the social life of these rural and urban places to a partial, supportive role in a pluralistic society. Even the receding numbers of church attendance—around 29 percent in the national average and perhaps twice as high in Catholic areas—would overstate what is left of the role of the church in social life, but it can hardly be said that there is not still a rich community life with or without the church.

Economic Enterprises and the Community

Taverns and Inns

Churches and schools were not the only meeting places of the small community. As irreverent Bavarians have rephrased the biblical words: "In the beginning, there was the great thirst. And the good Lord decided to have mercy upon the thirsty sinners and he gave them the noble barley [and hops] juice and a local tavern to drink it in good company." Even the smaller places in Bavaria always had at least one tavern (*Wirtshaus*) and restaurant, often several and perhaps an inn as well. The tavern, usually paneled in dark wood and decorated with deer antlers and memorial plaques, had been the other major center of community life where people would gather after church on Sunday and on many other nights as well. In the old days, the local tavern was the daily meeting and drinking place for the well-to-do local farmers who from about 4 PM on a work day would repair to their regular tavern table (*Stammtisch*) to talk politics, gossip, drink beer, and, perhaps, play cards. Their favorite games were Sheepshead or Tarok. The farmers would leave their farmhands and family members in charge of their farms until suppertime or even later, and sometimes they had to be brought home by friends.

The gradual disappearance of farm hands and family helpers since 1945 and the reduction of the typical farm family to just a very busy couple and its children alone suggests that the clientele of the local tavern must have shrunk. But as recently as 1960, as our table A8 shows, even villages of less than five hundred inhabitants still had, on the average, one-and-a-half taverns or restaurants. Places between five hundred and one thousand had two-and-a-half, and those between one and two thousand nearly four such establishments each. Larger towns, of course, had more. Today, one typically sees older men making up the clientele of the *Stammtisch* and downing vast amounts of beer. Every third or fourth one of even the

**Illustration 2.6.
Beer coaster: Dorn
Bräu Bruckberg.**
Author's collection.

smallest places in 1960 had an inn or similar place to stay overnight, and towns between five hundred and two thousand averaged one apiece.[44]

To be sure, the typical inn of the smallest communities (below five hundred) involved less than three gainfully employed people, frequently a couple and their half-grown child or a relative, less than five beds, and less than DM 30,000 a year in turnover. The typical tavern in the same community involved, on average, barely over two gainfully employed people and just under DM 20,000; some of them also offered beds. The total of all such tavern and inn establishments in Bavarian communities of varying size added up to 36,766 in 1960, and their numbers even rose to 38,507 in 1968, only to drop again to 36,220 in 1979[45] while their personnel has not changed very markedly in absolute numbers. By 1996, the number of beds had risen to 541 and 71,011 overnight stays (per DM 1.000 turnover) a year, a hefty increase from the 391 beds and 56,000 stays of 1980. There is a problem with these figures because they include urban areas and even big cities and were not broken down further. There may also be a substantial increase in tourism in small places hidden in these figures, possibly making up for a substantial decline among those catering mainly to the locals. In the 1970s, just before the reform, increasing numbers of the smaller taverns began to fail—1,400 between 1970 and 1974

alone—at the same time that the average cash turnover of all guest establishments rose from DM 129,000 (1970) to 180,000 (1974). It nearly
doubled between 1970 and 1980. But, many of them became part-time
operations or switched from full-time to part-time personnel. In 2008,
Bavaria had 9,418 hotels, inns and the like, of which Middle Franconia
had 1,097. The number of guest beds was 46,670 for Middle Franconia
(6.6 million for Bavaria) and 6.6 million tourists stayed there, including
1.3 million near the newly developed *Altmühltal* reservoirs, not far from
our communes.[46]

Tourism and travelers, of course, have always been reflected in the clientele of taverns and inns. There still are numerous old inns with the
word *Post* in their names, as in *Gasthof zur Post*, evidently leftovers from
the days of the postal coach and often connected to a butcher shop or
horse stables. The coming and relative decline of the railroad age are similarly represented in many a railroad station tavern (*Bahnhofswirtschaft*)
that sometimes stays on even though the train no longer stops in a small
town or village.

What, indeed, separates a small town from all kinds of diverse settlements of comparable size? One of the smallest surviving Franconian cities is the town of Rothenfels, between Lohr and Wertheim on the Main
River, and evidently named after a twelfth century castle by the same
name (red rock). Huddled between the foot of the cliff and the river, it
only has about six hundred residents in its core. Its inhabitants and those
on the plateau at the other side of the castle today are mostly part-time
farmers who commute to larger towns nearby. Farming and fishing as callings are nearly extinct. A youth hostel and convention site in the castle,
ten taverns and restaurants, a small brewery, and a few tradesmen and
artisans make up the economy of Rothenfels.

Is this rather typical Franconian "dwarf town" so different from many a
thriving village? The development of tourism in the sixties and seventies
has benefited community life as well as the economic health in many a
declining region. The number of overnight stays from 1952 to 1980 has
quadrupled, both in Bavaria and in the Federal Republic until it slowed
down again.[47] In our fifteen small communities, however, the volume of
tourism had been so low as to not appear in the official statistics until
1990 when Steinsfeld (near Rothenburg o.T.), with 114 beds and 15,489
overnight stays, and Wolframs-Eschenbach, with 123 beds and 13,650
overnight stays, did appear in the communal statistics.[48] Most of them
have not even made the attempt, in part because they would like to preserve the rural character of their hamlets. Others are trying hard, as in the
case of Bruckberg or even Mitteleschenbach, where inns and vacation
homes began to be made available in the 1970s.

In recent years there was also a revival of the old custom of offering vacations on a farm, "*Urlaub auf dem Bauernhof.*" Such services are economically beneficial, but they also add to the farmers' workload, especially to that of the farm women. In Ornbau and Ohrenbach, there were two such vacation farms each and in Weigenheim, where the town developed a system of the popular hiking trails, there were at least three. Ippesheim, which shares the cultivation of wine with neighboring Lower Franconia, hoped to make its wine festivals an attraction to tourists.

Oddly enough, the communities in the vicinity of Rothenburg on the Tauber receive little benefit from the international crowds of tourists. Only when Rothenburg is overbooked, some tourists may find their way to Ohrenbach or to Steinsfeld, where some facilities are available. In the Ohrenbach area there are some ancient towers built by one of the powerholders in Rothenburg's varied history. The medieval town of Wolframs-Eschenbach with its double walls, towers, and gates is perhaps the greatest tourist attraction among the fifteen—we shall return to it below—although the well-preserved fifteenth-century city walls and gates of Ornbau should attract attention as well. This partly walled town has also installed hiking paths to enhance its attraction to German and foreign tourists. Yet even rising tourist statistics still do not rate publication in the official *Gemeindedaten* of the state statistical office. The latter only begins to count when a place reaches a total of four thousand overnight stays a year.

Are there new patterns of community life that are taking the place of the older use of the village taverns today? For one thing, the gregarious life of the villagers has shifted from the older adult company to the young, which, in the seventies, led to the popularity of discotheques. Since only two of our communities developed such facilities, the motorized young went elsewhere. In the meantime, the trend has long turned again and one of the discos, in Wolframs-Eschenbach, had to close. Some communities have maintained their leisure time patterns quite well, thanks to soccer fields and club activities in the taverns. In Markt Berolzheim, special community efforts have shown the desired results. In half of the communities, youth meeting rooms have been available, which are often maintained by a local church. Röckingen just completed such facilities, and in Langfurth, where the church already had a youth center, there is an additional "youth meeting room," but it has gone unused for lack of a volunteer to take the responsibility for maintenance. All communities had established sports fields, sometimes several in different parts of the town, and most have the so-called *Bolzplätze*, unkempt soccer fields for teenagers, and playgrounds for the children. Wolframs-Eschenbach has a sports center with several playing fields and a spectacular children's park.

Adelshofen is building a soccer field. In Bruckberg, there was only a *Bolz-platz*, but interest centers on table tennis, anyway. All but four of the communities also have indoor facilities. For the summer, most have either communal swimming pools or ponds.

The local tavern—there still is at least one in each of the fifteen hamlets—in some towns has become a meeting place for youth, but this development is not always viewed with favor by the adults. Otherwise, its importance as a community center varies from town to town. Especially in the more agrarian communities, the tavern is still a meeting point for club activities, communal festivities, dances, and rare political or theatrical evenings. In Steinsfeld, near Rothenburg, Friday night has been the time for social get-togethers at the taverns of the several original parts of the consolidated town. Since the communal functions of these patterns seem to serve the incorporated original parts rather than the enlarged community of Steinsfeld, we cannot exactly call them a factor of communal integration. Other community taverns have lost their central importance: fewer people go there and their "regular tables" have declined. The traditional, after-church Sunday *Frühschoppen* (mid-morning drink and snack) has been separated from the antecedent church attendance: churchgoers no longer socialize afterward in the tavern. And, except in Catholic Ornbau where the *Frühschoppen* without church service caught on big in the 1960s, this social custom now has also been in decline.

Economic Enterprises

As the old patterns of agricultural village solidarity fade, there may well be new social or economic patterns that hold a small community together. Germany does not have the exact equivalent of the old cracker barrel and general store of old small-town America for people to gather around. Nevertheless, certain food retail stores have always been social centers, even in urban neighborhoods. The green-grocer, milk and bread store, or butcher shop where shopping housewives would meet and chat daily was such a social center, at least until freezers, supermarkets, and discount stores with lower prices and greater variety weaned them away from the old Tante Emma (mom-and-pop) shops. The erosion of the small food retail business in Germany's smaller communities has followed the decline of the Tante Emma (literally Aunt Emma) stores in the city where steep competition, hard work, long hours, and meager returns discourage the owners and, even more, their sons and daughters. In some small communities that lost their food retail outlets, in fact, a kind of foodmobile comes around two or three times a week to sell groceries to the remaining clientele. This foodmobile solution seems particularly handy for senior citizens who can find even public transportation to distant retail centers a burden. Some scattered tourist meccas, for example ski resorts during the off-season, also find the foodmobile idea attractive.

In our fifteen communities, by way of contrast, each still has at least one grocery store. Ten of them also have bakeries, seven butcher shops. Since many of the farmers still slaughter some of their own livestock, half the communities never maintained a butcher shop. Where there is no baker, the grocery store often sells fresh baked goods. Some of the bakeries also carry dairy products and some canned goods. Communities without bakers or butchers receive weekly deliveries by a van that stops with clamorous announcements in all parts of town—so the customers can walk there—and takes orders. One town is visited by the "fish man" every other week. In this respect, as with the dying Tante Emma stores, the small places now resemble urban neighborhoods in Munich where vegetables, especially potatoes, are often sold from a truck and orders are taken for eggs and cases of beer. The distribution of durable consumer goods is less adequate though there are a few shops here and there selling textiles, shoes, or bicycles. In Burk, there has been a modestly successful department store since 1910 that has established a faithful clientele.

The automobile has revolutionized shopping habits, taking most of the regular trade to supermarkets and discount centers in larger towns of the vicinity. The local greengrocer thus became a mere stopgap for whatever shoppers forgot or what they ran out of prematurely. A look at the shelves shows the wide range and yet very selective list of items that will sell. Even the unmotorized elderly clientele is not much help because most of the seniors live with a family that can provide transportation. The steep drop in earnings forced many small shops to close. Others can survive only to the extent that they have outside income. In Steinsfeld, for example, each of the three shop-owners could rely on additional income: one has an inn and a farm on the side, another one has a pension, and the third had a son living there who is a full-time master electrician. There also used to be a *Spezereilädle*, a kind of spice and delicatessen store, which closed because the welter of new government regulations for this kind of retail store would have required a prohibitive level of remodeling and restructuring of the facilities. Many owners try very hard to meet the challenge by expanding or diversifying their supplies, especially of convenience foods, but also of magazines, tobacco products, toys and so forth. Some try to enhance their appeal by introducing self-service and special bargains. But these efforts further burden their declining profit margin.

The 1979 Bavarian census of both retail stores and guest establishments revealed the full extent of the concentration that had taken place before the reform: the taverns and inns had declined 5 percent in nine

years (table A8), the retail stores by 15 percent by the time of the reform. It is a reasonable assumption that most of the 2,100 fewer taverns
and inns and 13,000 fewer retail stores in Bavaria had been lost by small
communities such as the fifteen in West Middle Franconia. Even of the
remaining numbers, three-fifths (61 percent) involved only two persons,
frequently "mom" and "pop," though the cash volume generated per person gainfully employed had quadrupled among the retail stores and tripled
among the guest establishments since 1969.[49] The new part-time operator
or employee of many of these firms may well have been a part-time farmer
in his remaining hours of work, thus also accounting for the increasing
frequency of part-time farmers in the 1970s. After 1976, the numbers employed in such small firms, after a decade of growth, began to drop and has
been dropping ever since.

What had been true of West German retail trends in general had an
inevitable impact also on the stores of these small communities. While
the retail volume in DM grew more than tenfold to DM 342 billion in
1978, the number of West German stores declined by nearly one-half.[50]
The typical neighborhood Tante Emma shop is practically extinct and the
surviving grocery stores rarely fulfill their traditional social get-together
function any more. The shoppers no longer represent the neighborhood
but merely a random collection of the lazy and forgetful. And their future
is as doubtful as is that of the family farm: Who will take over the shop
when the aging shop owners no longer can or desire to go on fighting the
odds of survival? What will take its place as a social center for housewives
and other neighborhood shoppers?

If it is not their buying and consumption habits, perhaps the inhabitants might be brought together by daily work in the gradually growing
sector of nonagricultural enterprises? Next to the taverns and local retail shops, larger places of employment have always had a major social
function, which is sorely missed if they should fail and be replaced by
equivalent social centers in the next larger town. A typical example of
such local enterprises is contained in a recent list for the community of
Steinsfeld. Even though Steinsfeld is only three miles from Rothenburg
and little more than a mile from the railroad station of the once separate
commune of Hartershofen,[51] it had its own brewery and inn—there were
still some 788 (1986) mostly small local breweries in the whole state,
down from 1,022 in 1977 and over 3,000 in the fifties—two other inns,
a sawmill and carpentry firm, a construction company, a hardware and
crafts shop, an electronic repairs and sales business, two blacksmiths, and
a veterinarian. All these offered employment to those Steinsfelders who
were not in agriculture and not commuting elsewhere but coming in daily
from elsewhere. The official count for Steinsfeld in 1977, at the last such

census before the reform, was sixteen handicraft enterprises, down from twenty-five in 1968, and thirty-six in 1956, when the presence of ethnic German refugees may still have swelled the ranks of both customers and proprietors.[52] German statistics call most traditional trades and services "handicraft" (*Handwerk*). The three local construction firms shrank to two, while their employees rose from twenty-nine to thirty-four. The total number of gainfully employed in local handicraft—132 in 1956, 133 in 1968, 121 in 1977, and 148 employees in 1989—suggests a process of considerable concentration. It also shows the limited significance of such employment in a place that is still predominantly agricultural.

This dovetails with developments in the region but can be contrasted somewhat with the development of the whole West German Republic where the number of handicraft enterprises had dropped by nearly one-half, from 1949 to 1977, while the number of gainfully employed in handicraft rose somewhat and the monetary volume of their work grew by a factor of fifteen. In the building industry, after 1980, the number of firms rose by nearly one-third by 1996 while the numbers employed sank by one-fifth. In the state of Bavaria, the handicraft enterprises also dropped from 174,000 in 1956 to 106,000 in 1977, while the number of gainfully employed rose slightly. Some callings, such as tailor, shoemaker, or blacksmith, have clearly declined, while others, such as cleaning services, auto mechanics, and electricians, but also butchers, barbers, and locksmiths, have increased their numbers and their personnel. Most significantly, handicraft shops still train 38 percent of the nation's ubiquitous apprentices—where the overwhelming majority of German youth learn a trade. They also offered one-fifth of West Germany's independents a livelihood, even though handicraft only produced 11 percent of the country's wealth and employed only 15 percent of its labor force. It is easy to see that the social and political importance of handicraft exceeds its economic significance.

This too becomes more meaningful in the historical context: Just as part-time farming is hardly new—as many as one-fourth of small farmers in the eighteenth and early nineteenth centuries bettered their lives with handicraft and non-agricultural production activities, for example weaving and making wooden implements—the reported 17 percent of handicraft workers frequently carried on some agricultural work on the side. Many of them, in fact, never belonged to a trade guild but hired out to churches and monasteries, which, with the secularization of the latter and the termination of their welfare functions (pensions, healthcare), precipitated an economic catastrophe among some of them in the 1810s. In a local setting, the lines are fluid and economic activities not as sharply delineated as our statistics suggest. Rural poverty also is not easily separated from marginal farming and pre-industrial cottage industries of various kinds. Their biggest problem was the sale and distribution of their goods and services, which they often addressed by travelling and selling from their "backpacks," or bringing their skills to customers' houses (*Stör*), both activities not unknown today.

To come back to our other small communes, there was the same overall shrinkage of the numbers of non-agricultural enterprises, with some notable exceptions (table A9): Langfurth and Wolframs-Eschenbach became manufacturing-and-trades communities, and Bruckberg's pediatric clinic may well support additional services and enterprises. The totals for the region West Middle Franconia and its three Landkreise have conformed to the same trend as Steinsfeld, and this was a more reliable measuring rod than the figures for the individual communes, many of which have incorporated substantial additional areas and populations between 1968 and 1980. The attrition factor may be considerably larger than it appears to be.

Most handicraft firms here are small and locally owned. There is also an unusual industry in Burk and Langfurth, the brush-making trade, which, including various suppliers, has employed some 250 persons in each of these communes. Most of the brush-making enterprises are locally owned also, except for that in Ornbau, which is a branch of a company in Fürth. Other branch settlements are a sheetrock (*Gyproc*) company, an asphalt mixing plant, and a power plant of forty employees in Markt Berolzheim. There are two breweries in Bruckberg and one each in Röckingen and Steinsfeld. Until 1920, there were two more in Burk, which were bought up and closed down by a large regional brewery concern, a fate shared by most small breweries in Bavaria. Building contractors with up to forty employees and related trades make up the bulk of the rest of the enterprises. The former blacksmith shops usually have switched from horseshoes and farm wagons to repairing agricultural machinery.

Two blacksmiths in Burk even became plumbers. Locksmiths are relatively rare in our communities, except in Weigenheim, but there are a number of sawmills and carpentry shops. Cobbler shops, on the other hand, used to be a frequent sight in the old days—often several to a community—but have nearly all been put out of business by the shoe factories. Today, most communes have either none or, at best, one surviving shoe repair shop that is likely to be operated by a retired cobbler to supplement a meager pension. A few other handicraft shops have also closed down here and there, mostly one-man businesses lacking a young person to take them over upon the retirement or demise of the owner. On the other hand, there has been a critical shortage of traditional apprenticeships in our small communities—in line with the national shortage—which has forced about half of the young villagers to seek their apprenticeships outside their community.

Markets and Services

Our survey of agriculture already hinted at the many ways that the changing character of agriculture may act to reinforce or supersede the communal patterns of the small town or village. For example, community-centered economic and associational cooperation among farmers may help to bring together the people from their scattered farms more often than before, although the same factors and more wide-flung markets could just as easily have oriented the population away from the established community and toward a larger area. We need to examine other changing patterns of community life such as the agricultural and non-agricultural markets and services. Villagers, of course, have always raised some of their produce for people outside the community, such as their feudal overlords, monasteries, and cities in whose hinterland they were. In exchange, they took money, manufactured items, or services rendered by the artisans and professionals of urban centers. If today the farmers produce for ever-distant markets in far-off regions, for countries of the European Union, or even for overseas, the change may merely lie in the volume and method of their production and in the distances involved.

This is less true of non-agricultural enterprises that not only produce almost exclusively for distant markets, but also supply a concentrated piece of the local labor market that usually brings together people from a wide circle of different communes, including part-time farmers who thereby, indeed, may associate almost daily with industrial coworkers from other small towns and villages. We shall come back to these commuting patterns later. Local services, too, have the dual character of being important for the relative self-sufficiency of an isolated community and, on the other hand, serving a much larger constituency. Their local seat may well attract customers and give prestige to the commune where they are located.

As compared to the state and national trends,[53] services play a negligible role among our fifteen small communities, regardless of whether they are public or private services. Down into the 1960s, some small places here still boasted the legendary village gendarme whose functions have long been taken over by state Police Inspections (offices) in county seats like Ansbach, Dinkelsbühl, Heilsbronn, Rothenburg, Gunzenhausen, and Uffenheim, with varying jurisdictional boundaries.

These police stations are at an average distance of six miles from our hamlets. Another protective service, fire protection, has changed a lot less. Each community still has a volunteer fire brigade that often fulfills some social functions as well as that of suppressing conflagrations: In 1964, at the time of its ninetieth anniversary of foundation, the *Freiwillige Feuerwehr Mitteleschenbach*, for example, had a membership of 260, including 76 active firemen, which made it the largest association in town. Its members were likely to form a network encompassing most other local activities. Its anniversaries naturally turned into two-day festive occasions involving the local *Gesangverein Heimat* (singing club homeland), luncheons, bands, a dance, speeches by local officials, and a big parade.[54]

Health care is spotty in comparison to the big city. Mitteleschenbach, Wolframs-Eschenbach, Bruckberg, where the pediatric clinic is, and Markt Berolzheim each have had a general physician. Ornbau used to have one but he left in 1968, and after that the county medical association closed this position. Wolframs-Eschenbach had a dentist but this position was vacant at the time of the reform. None of the other communities had a medical practitioner. There is an average of 3.6 miles from most of our communities—in one case six miles—to the nearest doctor or dentist, not to mention specialist. This may not seem very far to many Americans, but in Germany it is considered very inadequate. Pharmacies, often present in the same community as the doctor, exist only in Mark Berolzheim and Wolframs-Eschenbach and, until 1970, there was one in Bruckberg. Hospitals, like the Police Inspections, can be found only in places of higher centrality, which usually involves a one-way trip of about six miles from any of our communities. Childbirth, once performed only at home with the help of the local midwife,[55] has almost completely moved into hospitals. By 1978, only Langfurth, Ornbau, and Mitteleschenbach still had a resident midwife. All the others once had midwives, but dropping demand and retirement all but put an end to the profession.

Since many of these services are located outside the communities in question, we should also take a look at the availability of bus and railroad connections. The services of buses (not counting school buses) vary considerably from town to town. Some towns get a bus four to six times a day, others only twice. Ornbau, for example, has had six buses leaving daily for Ansbach, eight miles to the north, but no public transportation at all to Gunzenhausen, seven miles to the south. Ansbach, to be sure, is the seat of the *Landratsamt* (county prefecture) for Ornbau. In many communities in their present boundaries, the busses that run do not stop in all the scattered parts of town, which can pose a problem for the elderly who do not drive a car, and may have to walk for miles to a bus stop.

Except for Hartershofen near Steinsfeld and Rothenburg, none of the communities have a railroad connection in town any more. Even the Hartershofen station is not exactly within walking distance for most parts of consolidated Steinsfeld. The station of Markt Berolzheim was closed in 1978. Ippesheim, which annexed Herrnberchtheim with a railroad station, saw this station close down in 1977. Table A10 shows the distance of each of our communities to the nearest railroad station in 1950 and 1981, before and after the reform. The periodic rationalization campaigns of the Federal Railroads have shut down many less traveled lines and stations. Along with the other such losses, this was bitterly resented by the communes affected by these economy campaigns. The most recent drive, in 1982, touched off a protest collection of eight hundred thousand signatures of citizens and the endorsement of some seven hundred elected officials at all levels. The protest petition was organized by the Railroadmen's Union (GdED) under the slogan "The Railroad Must Remain." In pleas that must have sounded familiar to many Americans, the organizers were urging the railroad administration to resolve its financial straits by increasing the transportation of freight rather than reducing the passenger trade.

All the communities save Ippesheim still had post offices after the reform, although some were open only part of the day. Ippesheim lost its post office—another economy drive—in 1978. The mayor of the town claimed that there were no complaints, however, since the mail carrier, a woman, also picked up the people's mail at their homes, which is not customary otherwise in West German postal practice. In Steinsfeld, the communal reorganization brought incisive changes in the number of post offices and public mailboxes. Before the reorganization, every one of the original four parts of Steinsfeld had one post office and two mailboxes. Now there was only one part-time office for the whole town and one box in each part of it. This, again, may still not seem inadequate to many Americans in rural areas, but it is obviously less than what was available earlier.

The availability of veterinarians is rather adequate, as we would expect it to be in agricultural areas with emphasis on livestock and dairy production. Steinsfeld had a resident veterinarian. From the other communities, the average distance is about four miles to the nearest veterinarian practice. There are bank branches in all the communities, especially the farm cooperative Raiffeisen banks, and savings institutions. In some communities, however, the savings banks only have weekly customer services.

The elderly are generally taken care of by the family and live there, an example of the survival of the extended family. For the older folks who remember how confined and confining life used to be in these small places, nostalgia for the slow pace of the good old days may come easy. Their needs at this point in their lives can usually be satisfied without going very far from where they reside. As long as basic health care and consumer supplies are available in or near their community of residence, they can take all further modernization or leave it. Theirs is an eagle's eye view over the decades that can perceive the change without worrying about it one way or the other.

Commuting Patterns

Few other indicators are as obvious a sign of the weakening of the geographic isolation of small communities as the massive rise of daily traffic and commuting during the period in question. The significance of motorization was easy to see from the start in 1945, when personal travel was limited more or less to public transportation and riding on the scarce trucks and utility vehicles: there was a 1946 court case before a Bavarian country judge involving a young defendant who had promised matrimony to more than twenty village lasses throughout a large rural area. When the judge in Roman Law fashion admonished the culprit and asked him how he could possibly do such a dastardly thing, the defendant replied: "Well, you see, *Herr Richter*, I have a motor cycle ..." This is a true story that illustrates how a lack of transport and frequent contact among villages could have kept village and small-town youth in different places ignorant of the duplicity of this young swain.

A certain amount of routine commuter traffic, of course, has always been present, although no official statistics appear to have been kept on this with regard to any but the largest Bavarian centers before 1945. In the postwar years, it became truly a non-metropolitan mass phenomenon thanks to the explosive growth in motor vehicle ownership. This growth occurred in two waves of which the first began in the late 1940s, involving motorcycles, and leveled off in the mid fifties. By this time the second and bigger wave had established itself with passenger cars and vans, and it has continued to this day (table A11). In a little more than three decades, the personal mobility of Bavarians thus had increased a hundredfold[56] and the rural areas very likely were ahead of the metropolitan centers in this respect. The upward trend continued with nearly half a million motorcycles and 6.4 million cars by 1996. During the same years, the number of passengers transported by public transportation also doubled, the number of telephone conversations grew to twenty-four times their initial numbers—and the Bavarian road network grew over one-fourth in length, not to mention the improvements in road quality, road width, and the removal of some of the bottlenecks in the roads that were once so frequent in German small towns and villages.[57] Between 1956 and 1961 alone, community-owned highways in communities under five thousand inhabitants saw a significant reduction in the percentage of roads that had no tar or bituminous topping and therefore were not suitable for heavy motor traffic or in very bad weather; 86.4 percent of the internal communal road net and 96 percent of the communal roads outside the communes proper were originally of this description. Five years later inadequate roads only made up 73.7 percent and 86.7 percent, respectively. The *autobahn* in Bavaria alone grew by about 50 percent in length between 1980 and 1996. To be sure, there were still one-way bridges and gates entering small places and their town squares but, in most cases, bypass roads have been arranged or built to take the through traffic around the cores of these villages and towns.

Against this background, the commuting patterns are quite revealing, even though the statistics leave something to be desired.[58] 1970 is the last year for which there was a reliable database, although there are some data for comparison that go back to 1939 and others that go up to 2003. The number of outward-bound commuters in the rural Landkreise (not counting independent cities) in Bavaria had quintupled from 1939 to 1970, and in Middle Franconia even more. The increase in the smaller communes for the years from 1950 to 1970 remained somewhat lower unless they were in the path of a growing metropolitan area or the like. By the year 2008, in any case, the number of gainfully employed out-commuters (not schoolchildren) in our fifteen communes was extraordinary (table A4), leaving most of them with a negative balance of in- versus out-commuters.

We also know a good deal about the profile of the typical Bavarian commuter of 1970, though without being able to qualify this profile by community size: males outnumbered females three to two, commuters on their way to work were three times as many as those on their way to school. Outward-bound commuters also tended to be under forty-five years of age, and workers or employees rather than independents. Disproportionate numbers of those with an agricultural activity on the side, or in construction, mining, every kind of production, and in the processing industry were commuters. In 1987, two-thirds of the outward-bound commuters drove their own cars, another 8 percent rode with them, while 3.9 percent used a bicycle, a motorcycle, or walked; 24.2 percent were picked up by a company, school bus, or streetcar, and 5.7 percent went by train.

We also know that the bulk of commuters (two-thirds) could make it to work or school in less than half an hour and that in small communes under two thousand inhabitants, the commuting generally took less than fifteen minutes. The smaller the community, at least below five thousand, the more the commuters favored a car, van, or motorcycle over the means of public transportation. In communes below two thousand, of course, the absence or closing down of the railroad or convenient bus connections may not have left them much choice. In communes over five thousand, the way to work or school more often took thirty minutes to an hour or more. The differences seem to reflect a different sense of distance and may well be another expression of what keeps some people living in a small community rather than a more urban environment. On the other hand, the percentage of commuters among the gainfully employed of communities of varying size has always been disproportionately high in communities below ten thousand and especially in those between two and five thousand. This is the measure of the motorization and social mobilization of the once-isolated small towns and villages, and it seems particularly true of Franconia.

What about the commuting patterns of our fifteen small communes? Except for two, they seemed unlikely as destinations of commuting from elsewhere. With the exception of Burk, which already had a positive balance between in- and out-commuters in 1939 and 1950, and Steinsfeld, which attained such a balance in 1961 and 1970, their patterns tended to go outward. Steinsfeld draws commuters from Rothenburg, Ohrenbach, and Hartershofen to its manufacturing industries. The number and percentage of out-commuters among the gainfully employed of each community has risen consistently since 1939, when it still lagged noticeably behind the state average. But by 2008, the balance of commuters (in versus out) was well into the negative hundreds as well over 85 percent of the gainfully employed of most communes were drawn to outside employment sites. We should add that nearly all of them also lost population in the economic crisis years of 2007–2008: Weihenzell 275, Wolframs-Eschenbach 269, Ornbau 149, Bruckberg 146, and Steinsfeld 105.

There is no mistaking the rising patterns of mobilization of the Bavarian periphery. By 1961, four of the fifteen were ahead of and, by 1970, ten topped the percentage of out-commuters of the region and the state, leaving behind only such less developed agrarian communes as Adelshofen, Ippesheim, and Ohrenbach, and also such relatively strong importers of commuters as Bruckberg and Steinsfeld, which probably absorbed most of their own labor force. The highest out-commuting rates in 1970 were found in the bedroom community Markt Berolzheim and the residential-agrarian Mitteleschenbach—from where an estimated two-thirds of the commuters went as far as Nuremberg, Schwabach, or Gunzenhausen, a distance of ten to twenty miles or more. Next came Ornbau, increasingly a bedroom community for Ansbach, eight miles away. The commuters from Markt Berolzheim were most often headed for Gunzenhausen, nine miles away. The availability of jobs within a radius of twelve miles determines the structure of most of our communes today.

In contrast to the job commuters, the student commuters chiefly reflect the availability of elementary and junior high schools (*Hauptschule*), or more advanced school facilities in or outside the communities. Since

the school reforms of the early 1970s, there are very few of the old one-
or two-class schools left anywhere in Bavaria that would leave the way
to school a mere walk within the community. Bruckberg had 50 nursery
school places and a small vocational school with 24 places to bring in
student commuters of sorts. Burk also had nursery school facilities (50
places) and so did Langfurth (100), along with an elementary school with
a capacity of 264, enough to attract 101 student commuters. Ohrenbach,
Ornbau, and Röckingen also have elementary schools, but the latter two
were rather small in capacity (93 and 54 places, respectively). Weihenzell, (like Ohrenbach), on the other hand, had an elementary school for
296, which explains the 147 student commuters. Wolframs-Eschenbach
had one for 476 students, evidently including 121 commuters. Markt
Berolzheim also had a nursery school (25) and an elementary school for
295, which attracted 101 student commuters every school day. It goes
without saying that student commuting, at least from a traditional farmer's perspective, may open a Pandora's box in the receptive minds of the
youngsters. Once they have gotten to know a larger urban center where
the school center is, why should they want to live in their confining old
village when they are grown? Worse yet, a more sophisticated education
than the old village school ever offered is likely to leave them "overquali-
fied" for operating the parental farm some day, and may awaken their ap-
petite for other careers.

The Future of Small Places

Village and small-town residents old enough to remember must be acutely
conscious of the dramatic social changes that have overcome their small
communities during their lifetime. We have gone over various facets of
the grand transformation in agriculture and of the shrinking economic
and social bases of their respective communes since 1945—the shrinkage
and changed function of village taverns, grocery stores, and the widening
role of nonagricultural enterprises and employment beyond their communal boundaries. We have also described how the automotive revolution
and the commuting habit have mobilized the population of isolated small
places and put them in quasi-urban context with each other. By now, the
dimensions of the great change that has overcome life in the Bavarian
countryside have become clear, and there is no mistaking the direction
of the change.

Now the question arises what the future may be like for small places
like our fifteen communities in West Middle Franconia. Will they continue to have a life of their own or will it all merge into one great ho-

mogenized pudding, indistinguishable from living in an urban area? Will these small towns and villages continue to lose population to Nuremberg and other conurbations, or will they be able to generate an ample supply of new jobs to keep people at home? Will the bootstrap operation of forcing the smaller communes to merge and form larger unified EGs (*Einheitsgemeinden*), or quasi-federally joined administrative unions (Verwaltungsgemeinschaften, VGs), and the implied bureaucratization really breathe new life into these seemingly weak and declining communities? Did the Bavarian state government bite off too large a piece, raising unrealistic hopes for a more democratic, integrated life? There was bound to be a considerable disconnect between the planners' visions and what was likely to be achieved. The long-range answer to these questions may have to await the passage of another generation or more. We shall leave the institutional changes undertaken in the seventies and eighties to the next chapters and attempt to answer the rest.

The Visions of the Planners

First, let us review the state planners' estimates for the region with regard to population changes and employment up until 1990 and beyond. The planners projected, back in the seventies, rather optimistically, a modest population increase of 4 percent for West Middle Franconia for the 1980s, after three decades of decline. As we have seen, the long-range trend has gone in the opposite direction. The population increase between 1989 and 2009 barely exceeded 12 percent while agricultural employment in the region now only accounts for 6–8 percent.[59] Even the planners expected the number of persons employed in agriculture to drop another third by 1990 because of the continuing impact of structural changes in agriculture. In manufacturing and service jobs, on the other hand, the planners hoped for a 13–14 percent increase by 1990,[60] which would have more than made up for the shrinkage in agriculture and given the region a balance between the three sectors that would resemble the statewide averages.

To achieve this ambitious goal, they proposed to a) improve the quality and quantity of the job market in the region's biggest city, Ansbach (37,893 inhabitants in 1990), and b) to enhance its attractiveness over and against the mighty conurbation of Nuremberg-Erlangen-Fürth. Until 1989, Ansbach too had been losing population. They also suggested retraining programs for the farmers that quit farming and to promote tourism where conditions seemed favorable. Ansbach was to be boosted to the centrality level of a Large Center (*Oberzentrum*), while the Medium Centers (*Mittelzentren*) Neustadt (11,199) on the Aisch, Dinkelsbühl

(10,849), Gunzenhausen (15,795), Weissenburg (17,596), and Rothenburg (11,350)—all medieval cities—were to receive whatever structural supports they required to serve their respective hinterlands better. The competing "potential medium centers" Bad Windsheim (11,390) and Feuchtwangen (10,836) also were to be strengthened to the extent that this did not conflict with the existing Middle Centers. The planners also proposed to build up the Lower Centers (*Unterzentren*) Heilsbronn (7,734), Neuendettelsau (6,829), Scheinfeld (4,337), Uffenheim (5,720), and Wassertrüdingen (5,701), but there was no mention of smaller places such as the fifteen communes of our study whose modernization had been a long-range goal of the reform. At best, these structural changes would create an urban-industrial counterweight to the pull of Nuremberg-Erlangen-Fürth. Considering the fiscal crisis ever since the second oil shock of 1979, the continuing economic recession before and after German unification, and the world-wide crisis of 2007–2010, however, it is difficult to see where the state would have found the funds for all of the structural improvements that were thought up during more affluent days.[61] The great reform simply outran the available resources.

The planners had some advice for farmers, too, namely: full-time farms "capable of development" were to be maintained and those not so capable to be helped in becoming part-time farms. Cooperative arrangements, the planners hoped, might serve the needs of the part-time farmers as well as they served full-time farms, to produce and market their goods. The planning authorities also promised other structural improvements to benefit agriculture, including promoting the "vacations on the farm."[62]

The development of recreational areas, along with building dams and reservoirs, was expected to attract more tourists to the area. The building of *Autobahns* and of some new train services throughout this poorly connected area also was to create opportunities and to fill the needs of small-town and village residents along the east-west development axes Nuremberg-Ansbach-Heilbronn and Nuremberg-Neustadt-Würzburg, and the north-south axis Würzburg-Rothenburg-Nördlingen. Again, the critical shortage of public funds has delayed and frustrated such plans although the A7 was completed in the end. New or improved railroad connections from Würzburg to Donauwörth, Nuremberg to Stuttgart, and the electrification of the rails between Ansbach and Crailsheim followed. Finally, better water management and treatment facilities would have benefited farms and residences in a region lacking in water supply and modern facilities to husband the available streams. Some of our small places have joined special districts to assure adequate water supplies. Five belong to the Aqueduct System of Franconia (*Fernwasserversorgung Franken*). In some cases, annexed parts of the new communes have their own, if not necessarily satisfactory, water supply (Weihenzell), while Ohrenbach and Meinheim have their own well water.

Anticipations of Local Leaders

Planners and administrators may see a future different from what small communes and their political leaders can perceive. How did the mayors of our small places view their future, disregarding for the moment their reactions to the local territorial reforms of 1978–1979 and anticipation of a corresponding functional reform of local government? What future development did they anticipate? The expectations appeared to follow three different routes, depending on the character of the community involved:

In predominantly agricultural communes, which preferred to maintain their character, plans for expansion were limited to gaps in the cores and construction at the edge of the original parts of the community, and all this only for the existing population. There were few plans for preempting fertile farmland for commercial or industrial uses. The resident tradespeople were to occupy a small area for mixed use and there was little intention of inviting branch settlements of outside companies because, at that time, there was no excess labor available and, as was already mentioned, most people wanted to maintain the agrarian character of the community. Thus, they expected the loss of population to continue and that people would be leaving the farms for other occupations. Communes of this description are Röckingen, Adelshofen, Ohrenbach, Ippesheim, and much of Steinsfeld.

There were communes of agrarian character that did expect an influx of population. Meinheim, for example, expected people from Gunzenhausen and Treuchtlingen to buy land and build houses there. In Weigenheim, all interested outsiders were screened and land sales contracts contained clauses requiring the buyer to build within three years so that speculation would be discouraged. Bruckberg, in about 1980, adopted a land use plan which assigned forty acres to new housing for approximately five to six hundred residents, most of which were expected to come from the city of Ansbach, a mere six miles away.

In communes that were no longer predominantly agricultural, areas had been set aside not only for the construction of housing but also for commercial and industrial development. These communities already had substantial numbers of outward commuters in the 1980s who promised to supply the labor force for new companies. Among them were Weihenzell, Langfurth, Burk, Markt Berolzheim, Mitteleschenbach, and Wolframs-Eschenbach. The latter two also set their hopes on tourism, which might allow them to maintain their present character better. Ornbau also hoped to gain from the tourist traffic generated eventually by the Altmühlsee and Brombachsee reservoirs, although this required some effort by local tourist enterprises. Weihenzell's proximity to Ansbach assured its future growth, but there was some sentiment in favor of curbing the influx and to maintain the present character of the community. However, efforts were also being made to integrate new residents in Weihenzell—the commune with the highest numbers of both out-commuters and out-migrants—and it became customary to introduce new citizens at the town meeting.

The continued health and stability of the member communes of our sample, of course, also determined if their administrative unions (VGs) could be expected to last in the long run. If many of the member communes atrophied, then the whole VG system may have to revert to the formation of unified communes (EGs) from the leftovers of the present member communes. Thus, we have to account also for the likely demographic, economic, and cultural trends that may or may not have assured the survival of these communities: the outward commuting patterns in themselves were an ambiguous factor that, at worst, could be an antecedent to emigration altogether from these areas. Thus, it was imperative that the communes make it attractive for the commuters to reside there and pay taxes. A continued drain of population toward more urbanized areas can be fatal to any community.

The changing fabric of agriculture was no less ambivalent, since the trend toward part-time farming and a generational turning away from farming may well tend toward large-scale agribusiness enterprises buying out or pushing out the remaining farmers, part-time and full-time. The local trades may, by now, have stabilized more or less after decades of attrition, but they could hardly be expected to do more than maintain the status quo. New industries were likely to wax and wane with the business cycle and were, therefore, no panacea of economic stability. Retail and other services already had become rather concentrated in towns larger than our fifteen communes. Thus, the economic future of the communes was not likely to be influenced one way or the other by the presence of VGs, except in the long-range sense of better infrastructural development affecting the conditions for optimal economic development.

Notes

1. Among the innovations for better farming were such tools as the Palatinatian plow, three-field rotation, and new crops for uncultivated land like the potato and clover. On the agrarian underclass, see also Dietmar Stutzer, "Unterbäuerliche gemischte

Sozialgruppen Bayerns um 1800 und ihre Arbeits- und Sozialverhältnisse im Spiegel der Statistik," in *Krone und Verfassung: König Max I. Joseph und der neue Staat*, 3 vols. (Munich, 1980), I, 290–299. "Lower peasant" is defined as families with an annual income below 300 gulden. Stutzer estimated the population at 52.2 percent peasants and 17.3 percent handicraft trades, with plenty of shared part-time activities and an underclass of 10–20 percent. Also, *König Max I. Joseph*, II, 367 ff.

2. In contrast, in Old Bavaria (Upper and Lower Bavaria) and Suebia (*Schwaben*), Catholics predominate as they always have, and as do Protestants in Franconia. Catholics also boast a much higher rate of church attendance and involvement in church activities than the Protestants.

3. There had been some Protestant additions as early as 1740 and 1777.

4. There were three Protestant and two Catholic strains in the new kingdom, not to mention the small Judaic communities, which received official recognition in the Emancipation Acts of 1813. At the time of the great religious survey of 1987, there were 5,282 Jews and 215,288 Muslims in Bavaria, and 553 Jews and 38,495 Muslims in Middle Franconia, which includes urban Nuremberg/Fürth/Erlangen and Schwabach. *Jahrbuch Bayern 2009*.

5. For details, see Gerhard Hirschmann, "Die evangelische Kirche seit 1800," in *Bayerische Geschichte im 19. und 20. Jahrhundert, 1800 bis 1970*, 2 vols., Max Spindler, ed. (Munich, 1978), II, 883–912 (hereafter, Spindler, *Bavarian History*).

6. A nest of armed resistance of German troops had established itself nearby and stray shots from the resultant shelling hit the church that had just been refurbished. Its bells had already been requisitioned and presumably melted down for the German war effort in World War II.

7. From an unprinted chronicle by the retired pastor, August Kollert, *Weigenheim unter den Bergen*, which also contains a list of all the names of Protestant pastors back to 1558.

8. There is a striking difference in the appearance of Franconian as compared to Old Bavarian or Suebian villages. The former present a town-like picture with closely grouped buildings and, not infrequently, remainders of a wall with gates or small towers. Old Bavarian villages more often look like a group of scattered big farmhouses, with small cottages in between, and isolated farms on the fringes. Churches or old manorial estates may lend them a focus but the communal hall is rarely part of the seemingly oligarchic core. There is more of a cooperative-egalitarian, even democratic, look to the old hamlets of Franconia and Upper Palatinate.

9. It was only in 1871 that women teachers in Bavaria were recognized as communal officials. Two years later women were first admitted to Bavarian universities. It was not until the academic year of 1903–1904 that all academic limitations were removed from women's attendance at the university. See Zorn, Wolfgang, "Die Sozialentwicklung der nichtagrarischen Welt," in Spindler, *Bavarian History*, II, 869.

10. See Christel Kohler-Hezinger, "Lokale Honoratioren," in *Dorfpolitik*, Hans-Georg Wehling, ed. (Opladen, 1978), 54 ff. See also Helmut Witetschek, "Die katholische Kirche seit 1800," in Spindler, *Bavarian History*, II, 914–949. This author emphasizes the reluctance of the church to accept the realities of industrial and, more recently, of consumer society, which has shown less and less commitment to religious loyalties and values.

11. There have been both financial and personnel problems in both churches that resulted in the reduction of the number of clergy and parishes. On the nineteenth-century Catholic church, see *König Max I. Joseph*, II, 411 ff. Some of the shut-down monasteries were reopened after their secularization, if without their lands and forests.

12. The reason for this change was that the Bruckberg pediatrics home used to be run by a priest who was replaced in 1981 by a secular administrator. This made the establishment of a new parish with a separate priest more feasible.

13. Küng cited a circular of the Bishop of Rottenburg-Stuttgart, Georg Moser, and explained that the number of communities there without a pastor of their own was already 95 in 1960 and had risen to 185 in 1978, and an estimated 350 by 1984. In the entire Federal Republic the number of diocesan priests was expected to drop from 12,165 in 1979 to 7,624 by the 1990s and this in spite of the large-scale recruitment of foreign priests. To remedy this situation at least in part, the bishop proposed in his circular to (1) reduce the number of Sunday services, (2) combine services for foreigners and natives, (3) hold some percentage of Sunday services without a priest, especially in parishes without one of their own, (4) arrange collective weddings, christenings, and funerals, (5) find lay helpers for many functions, and (6) a reduction of outside commitments of priests, such as on communal or parish boards.

14. Among the reforms for which there are public opinion polls of German Catholics are birth control (81 percent are for it), marriage of priests (72 percent), ecumenical services (67 percent), and female ordination (57 percent). "Als Deutsche im Missionsland," *Süddeutsche Zeitung*, 12–13 February 1983.

15. A more encompassing network of social stations has been advocated in the party programs of the Bavarian Christian Social Union (CSU) and the national CDU. The church involvement in the current services probably requires substantial public subsidies to expand.

16. The state increased some of the educational functions in 1968 when it replaced the prevalent "confessional" public elementary schools with the *Simultanschule* (common schools).

17. See Helmut Witetchek in Spindler, *Bavarian History*, II, 914–945, esp. 937–938 and 944–945.

18. See Karl Grunwald, "Das 'Wassertrüdinger Modell,'" in *Unser Auftrag*, No. 1 (1976), 13 f., and Grunwald, "Unsere Landgemeinden sind seelsorgerliches Notstandsgebiet," in *Korrespondenzblatt*, 96, No. 2 (1981), 14 ff., and No. 2 (1977), 13 ff.

19. In 1985, 45 percent of Protestant and 17.5 percent of Catholic weddings in Bavaria were mixed marriages. *Jahrbuch Bayern, 1987*, 684.

20. This is not the first time different Catholic social policies have been in conflict.

21. Voluntary contributions of cash and services for church renovation in Meinheim have actually increased since the reform.

22. Sometimes, a pastor may have to upset tradition to maintain his choir: in Meinheim, the church choir had always had its rehearsals in a back room of the local inn. The female choir singers consequently would drop out of the choir upon getting married because their husbands thought it unseemly to let them go to the tavern. Eventually, the pastor succeeded in overcoming this barrier to having a well-staffed church choir.

23. A news release of *The Week in Germany*, 13 (24 November 1982) carried the story of a husband-and-wife team of ministers at the Church of the Trinity in Bremen who, with the consent of their congregation, shared Sunday services, funerals, confirmation instruction, and other pastoral duties, including a kindergarten (his) and other children's services (hers). This was a three-year experiment in job sharing and joint ministry. None of our fifteen communities, however, has a female pastor now.

24. There is no critical shortage of funds as long as the state continues to levy the church tax from all persons identified with either one of the established religions. It is made

quite difficult to drop the denominational label at the civil registry, which would be the only way to get out of paying the tax.

25. Two orders of Franciscan nuns, the Poor School Sisters and the Schönstett Sisters provide nursing care and day care for children. They also serve in an orphanage and a home for the elderly. The bulk of the charitable work is done by lay people.

26. The information in this paragraph has been supplied by Dr. Pat Heck from her research in Rosenheim County.

27. Compulsory public education was decreed early in the eighteenth century in Northern and Central Germany—1715 in Prussia—and 1771 in Old Bavaria. See Albert Reble, "Das Schulwesen," in Spindler, *Bavarian History*, II, 950–958. The requirements of religious toleration in a multi-religious kingdom evidently encouraged the growth of a "neutral," if not secular, educational state administration. By 1802, a compulsory period of schooling from age six to twelve was established, at least on paper. Elementary school teachers' education lagged behind these bold departures. Many teachers were grizzled army veterans and the curriculum of the first half of the nineteenth century emphatically stressed patriarchal traditions and conservatism with strong religious overtones.

28. Most of them had to depend on some outside income as recently as 1900. The Hoffmann (SPD) cabinet also freed the schoolteachers from the auxiliary and custodial duties they had to render to the local churches. But even the Socialists were unable to put an end to the "confessional" character of the schools—only 3 percent of Bavarian elementary schools were *Simultan* schools in 1920—until the Third Reich abolished them (1938) by a policy of harassment and dictatorial fiat; until they rose again after World War II.

29. In 1964–1965, no more than 3.7 percent of the elementary schools were *Simultan* schools, even though only one-third of the prevailing confessional schools could point to a religiously homogeneous student body. Most other states of the Federal Republic by this time were much farther ahead in the elimination of their rural "dwarf schools." See Reble, "Das Schulwesen," in Spindler, *Bavarian History*, II, 978–980 and 984–988. The school reforms of the 1960s also stressed questions of equal opportunity and long-range objectives of economic growth for which undereducated rural children were considered a reserve that ought to be developed to the level long offered by urban education.

30. *Tatsachen über Deutschland* (1979), 302. The number of students only changed from 5.7 million in 1966 to 3.7 million in 1986. *Jahrbuch Bayern, 1987*, 434. In 1954, there were about 31,000 schools and 5.6 million students.

31. In Langfurth-Burk, on the other hand, four out of six women teachers have taken on community roles.

32. They are more likely to use his name and, in a tavern or club, may even lapse into the familiar "Du."

33. In the old days, it was one of the functions of the village teacher to identify gifted students and to talk the parents into the expense of a secondary education. Today, most parents would like to push their children into more prestigious tracks regardless of their real intellectual ability.

34. New celebration days, of course, had been added to the old Christian holidays, such as the Kaiser's birthday and first name-day (on the Christian calendar), or the anniversary of the German victory at Sedan in the Franco-Prussian war.

35. In Meinheim, for example, the sporting club and the garden and horticulture society declined but both came back to life in 1968.

36. German rifle clubs, unlike their US equivalent, have no quarrel with their country's regulation of firearms or access to gun ownership. Their emphasis was political and patriotic in the beginning and now is mostly social and tradition-minded, even though critics sometimes accuse some *Schützenverein* of harboring unreconstructed old Nazis and their attitudes.

37. The Bavarian CSU, like the national CDU with which it is affiliated, has a very active women's organization as old as the party and its predecessor (the Bavarian People's Party, BVP), in which conservative ideals of family life and the role of women are carefully juxtaposed to the more emancipatory notions of the SPD and FDP.

38. The local taverns and inns probably owe their survival to the meetings of these clubs that, in marks and pfennige (or now euros), may be a way of gauging how far the newer patterns of community life make up for the decline of older patterns of village life. Taverns have also inherited some family festivities, such as weddings, christenings, and wakes that used to take place exclusively at home and in churches.

39. See Hubensteiner, *Bayerische Geschichte: Staat und Volk, Kunst und Kultur* (Munich, 1977), 347. Also Eberhard Weis, "Das neue Bayern—Max I Joseph, Montgelas und die Entstehung und Ausgestaltung des Königreiches 1799 bis 1825," in *König Max I Joseph und der neue Staat*, I, 49–64.

40. Ornbau let the custom lapse between 1972 and 1978 until a group, the Friends of the Maypole, revived it. In Burk the Maypole was replaced for twenty years by a "Walpurgis night" that seemed to involve carrying to the marketplace all objects that were not firmly tied or nailed down, until the town fathers persuaded the young in 1975—with the help of ample free beer—to return to the Maypole custom instead.

41. Brawls are not uncommon, as is suggested by the phrase "inviting someone to *Kirchweih*" as a euphemism for challenging a person to a fight. With Maypoles, some areas in Bavaria have traditions whereby the young of one community attempt to steal another community's pole, either before it is even raised or before it has been inaugurated with the traditional dance.

42. The nearby Hesselberg Mountain has considerable historic significance as, among other things, the corner where Franconia, Suebia, and Bavaria have met since olden times. It is also a fine lookout point.

43. See Hans Schmid, "Musik," in Spindler, *Bavarian History*, II, 1212–1233. Also Karl Horak, "Volkslied und Volksmusik in Altbayern," in *Bayerische Symphonie* (Munich, 1968), 2 vols., Herbert Schindler, ed., II, 279–287.

44. Unfortunately, the censuses of 1968, 1979, and 1987 were not broken down by community size. The numbers include all eating establishments including ice cream parlors and cafes. The 1968 census indicates the 21,164 of the 38,507 still averaged only two persons. Half of them had a cash turnover of less than DM 20,000 each, and the rest had DM 20–50,000.

45. The percentage of the number of such enterprises under DM 20,000 turnover per year dropped from 10.7 percent in 1970 to 4.6 percent of the total in 1974, after which date there were several poor years reflecting the impact of the energy crises. Rudolf Kern, "Das Gaststätten- und Beherbergungsgewerbe in Bayern," *Bayern in Zahlen* 31, no. 9 (September 1977), 327–329. See also Kern, "Bayerns Gastgewerbe" (May 1971), 144 ff. on the 1968 census.

46. Bayerisches Landesamt für Statistik und Datenverarbeitung, *Bayern Daten 1997/1998*, 11; and Rudolf Kern, "Struktur und Entwicklung der Unternehmen des Handels und Gastgewerbes in Bayern," *Bayern in Zahlen* 35, no. 1 (January 1981), 12–16.

47. *Jahrbuch Bayern 1978* and *1987*.

48. *Gemeindedaten 1990.* The guest arrivals in Steinsfeld and Wolframs-Eschenbach, respectively, were 12,180 and 4,913, then.
49. Kern, "Gaststätten- und Beherbergungsgewerbe ... ," 329. Also *Bayern Daten 1997/1998.*
50. From 445,000 in 1962, to 233,000 in 1978. *Tatsachen über Deutschland,* 188. Also *Bayern Daten 1997/1998.* In Bavaria, the decline may have been slowed down because of the relatively less urbanized character of the state.
51. It is also situated on a federal highway, No. 25, and a good country road, AN 8, not to mention bus connections to Rothenburg and Ansbach. *Geschichtlicher Überblick,* by Ortsteilsprecher E. Klinger, Steinsfeld, mimeogr., no date.
52. *Gemeindedaten 1980,* 226. The 1950 census disclosed 493 inhabitants for Steinsfeld as compared to 344 in 1939, 373 in 1961, 345 in 1970, and, after communal reform and enlargement, 1179 in 1979. *Bayerische Gemeindestatistik 1970,* vol. 4 (*Beiträge zur Statistik Bayerns,* Heft 305), 238.
53. The tertiary sector in Bavaria has grown from 16.4 percent of the population in 1882 to 28 percent in 1950, and slightly above 50 percent in 1987. *Jahrbuch Bayern 1981,* 111, and 2009. Public and private white collar employees increased from 40 percent in 1980 to 50 percent in 1996. *Bayern Daten 1997–1998.*
54. *Festschrift 90 Jahre Freiwillige Feuerwehr Mitteleschenbach,* broch. (1964).
55. See also Gerd Berkenbrink, *Wandlungsprozesse einer dörflichen Kultur* (Göttingen 1974), 50 ff. In critical cases, a doctor was brought in, too.
56. Indeed, by 1989 personal automobile ownership had increased by 707 percent over 1947. *Kreisdaten 1989.*
57. Rudolf Kern, "Die Gemeindestrassen in Bayern," *Bayern in Zahlen 17* (May 1963), 171–174. Also *Bayern Daten 1997/1998.*
58. Not only are the findings of the censuses of 1950, 1961, and 1970 not comparable in all respects, but the changing communal and *Kreis* boundaries resulting from the territorial reform play havoc with comparisons in the 1970s.
59. If one looks at population growth ending in 1988, and compares that with the population on 31 December 1979, however, the population of West Middle Franconia had only increased by 2.15 percent, less than half the projected population growth.
60. Again, if one makes a preliminary comparison of those individuals who are obliged to pay social insurance in industry, trade and transportation, and services between 1978 and 1988, one sees an increase of 7,977 jobs in all, for a 10 percent increase, somewhat below the planners' expectations.
61. *Landesentwicklungsprogramm,* Teil C, 747–749.
62. Ibid., 764–765 and 775–777.

Chapter 3

PLANNING LOCAL
TERRITORIAL REFORM

How do large organizations such as a multi-tiered state bring about large, sweeping changes? Whether from the top or the bottom, the time has to be right. The desire for change must be in the air. But there also has to be a body of theories to guide the reformers.

The Era of Reforms

The 1960s and early 1970s in West Germany witnessed an era of internal reforms. There was a pervasive feeling that the arduous task of rebuilding the country after the destruction and deprivations of World War II and the postwar years had been completed. The hungry postwar years were over and now it was time to go on and think of the future. The economic recovery of the 1950s, in fact, had turned into an "economic miracle" of sustained growth and unprecedented prosperity for West Germany. The time was ripe to take a second look at many of the structures handed down by German history and, if it seemed desirable, to improve or correct them.[1] It was a time also to remember such basic principles and promises of the constitution as that of equality and equal opportunity for all and to check whether they were indeed nearing realization. It was also high time to think ahead toward the expanding opportunities of the future and to make sure that the structures of the past would not restrict the hopes of the future. The West German and later all-German Basic Law (constitution) promised its citizens equality of many sorts (Article 3 and elsewhere), which the status quo before the reform of 1978 did not always provide. With regard to rural-urban differences, in particular, there was a large and painful gap to fill.

In this mood of reform there could be little doubt but that what little remained to distinguish urban and country living had led to invidious comparisons between the advantages and opportunities of urban life and living in small communities such as we have described in chapters one and two. Throughout the 1960s and earlier, for example, various studies had shown the extent to which persons of rural or small town origin were less likely to enjoy the educational and training opportunities of their urban cousins.[2] Not only was the diversity of available career paths lacking, but there were popular calculations that showed how much less the very same occupation and amount of work earned in small town and rural areas as compared to the big city.

The Rural-Urban Migration

If there had been any more need to demonstrate the glaring disparities, there was the continued and massive migration of farmers and small-town people to bigger cities, to the edge of metropolitan areas, and to the burgeoning metropoles themselves. Munich had grown from 840,000 inhabitants in 1939 to 1.3 million in 1980. The three cities complex of Nuremberg, Erlangen, and Fürth had increased from 558,000 to 685,000, and ancient Augsburg from 200,000 to 250,000, all in the same period. More significantly, the population in communities below 2,000 inhabitants had dropped from 47.2 percent of Germans in 1939—it had been 61.7 percent in 1900—to 21.4 percent in 1975 and 9.9 percent in 1989,[3] after the local territorial reforms. As different-sized communities grew over these four decades (1939–1980), the percentage shares of those between 10,000 and 100,000 also grew in the most dramatic fashion, namely from 14.3 percent in 1939 to 30.1 in 1989, after the local territorial reforms and before the German reunification.[4] There was no mistaking the phenomenon of rural and small-town flight, even if we grant that the decision to move from a smaller to a larger place was not always a rational individual choice based on all the relative advantages and disadvantages of either one.

Public opinion surveys confirmed the impression that many of the people living in the smaller places would prefer to move to a larger place. At the height of the planning for the local territorial reforms throughout the Federal Republic, some 20 percent of rural and small-town residents indicated that they would rather move to a larger town or into the vicinity of a great urban center.[5] Another survey in five Bavarian rural counties in 1980 revealed that as many as 28 percent of the remaining rural and small-town population would prefer to live in or especially at the edge of a metropolis, that is, in a suburb or smaller city near the big one. Forty percent of the respondents under the age of twenty-five thought so while above the age of fifty this view was shared only by 16 percent of the respondents. Between the ages of twenty-five and fifty about 25–30 percent opted for a more urban environment. Among the youngest cohort, women and the better-educated particularly favored an urban environment. Curiously, an analogous survey among big-city dwellers brought out a proportion of 36 percent—and this especially among those over fifty and under thirty, and among men and the less-educated—who said they preferred living in a village or small town.[6] As particular advantages of country living the respondents named housing (presumably ownership of single-family houses), the environment, the social atmosphere, and the cost of living. The urban setting, on the other hand, was praised for practically all occupational aspects, educational opportunities, the availability of cultural attractions and of consumer goods, and of good health care. If we leave aside for the moment the human propensity for desiring whatever people don't have, there still remains a consensus on the respective attractions of urban and rural settings and perhaps a greater likelihood that many rural people would follow the better alternative they evidently perceive.

The perception of the relentless rise of urban prosperity and the relative lagging behind of the rural and small-town population may have spread with the nearly universal acquisition of television sets by farm families in the remotest village by the 1970s. If television could make the world a village, as Marshall McLuhan has said, surely it could also integrate the village with the rest of the world. For one thing, the television screen brought High German language and big city ways into family living rooms hitherto dominated by Bavarian dialect and traditional folkways, thus breaking through one of the barriers with which village society usually insulated itself against strangers. In all probability, the older generation must have felt exceedingly quaint and conspicuous in the eyes of their own youngsters who were sure to pick up the invading waves of the national culture upon its regional shores: "Why do we speak funny around here, Papa? And why do you and Mutti, in particular?" A tell-tale vignette on these defensive reactions was the abortive attempt of Bavarian politicians in the late 1960s to introduce Bavarian dialect as a compulsory subject in the public schools. National television in other countries may have played a similar role in stirring up ethnic minorities to assert themselves politically.

This is not the place to go into the history and terminology of regional planning or planning in general for which interested readers can find a copious contemporary literature elsewhere.[7] But the story of how the initiative for territorially reorganizing local governments came from the West German federal government and then was taken up by the individual *Länder* (states) is worth telling at this point.

Federal Initiatives Toward *Raumordnung*

Even while West Germany was still preoccupied with overcoming wartime devastation and dislocations, in the early fifties, the first attempts were made in the Federal Ministry of Housing and Urban Affairs to draw up a comprehensive Federal Construction Law (*Bundesbaugesetz*). This seemingly innocuous undertaking for the immediate purpose of clearing away the legal thicket of different *Länder* laws regarding planning, land use, and real estate transactions so that the federal government could help to rebuild bombed-out cities and smaller towns had far-flung ramifications. First of all, both houses of parliament and the cabinet had to ask the Federal Constitutional Court for an advisory opinion on the constitutional limits that federalism might impose upon such a federal initiative. The court ruled that the Basic Law (art. 75) indeed gave the federal government the right to legislate on this subject,[8] and the Federal Ministry of the Interior proceeded to explore the intergovernmental prerequisites for such action with *Land* planning agencies and other federal ministries (see chapter 5).

The New Concern with Spatial Order

By the second half of the fifties, the various related undertakings—the Federal Construction Law was not passed until 1960—had taken on broad overtones of a concern with spatial order (*Raumordnung*)[9] and long-range planning, and this in spite of the well-known resistance of the Adenauer administration to planning: A commission of experts was told to work out a "*Raumordnung* concept" and submit proposals for its realization while federal and *Land* administrators negotiated an administrative federal-state compact (*Verwaltungsabkommen*) to facilitate future cooperation on *Raumordnung* throughout the country. By 1957, Federal Housing Minister Paul Lücke also announced that[10] "Federal housing programs needed to be distributed more deliberately among the regions in order to disperse settlement patterns and thus to equalize the structural differences [among the regions]. Small and medium-sized communes that are capable of development and rural areas should be strengthened economically through subventions for the creation of jobs and federal housing."

This policy not only had the express support of the *Deutscher Land-kreistag* (Association of Rural Counties), and the *Deutscher Städtebund* (League of Small Towns), but also played a role in federally subsidizing housing construction in areas along the border with East Germany and with impact grants to communes where the new federal army was to be garrisoned.

By 1959, a conference on *Raumordnung* began to explore how federal *Raumordnung* policies could best be coordinated with regional planning by the *Länder* and local planning by the communes that were about to receive clarified local planning authority with the Federal Construction Law of 1960. The need for a unified vision and coordinated action was pressing, for "the problems of orienting the residential areas towards those of employment and production as well as towards recreational areas were becoming more and more urgent … while the areas of population concentration were getting to be overburdened with people and functions," according to the Housing Minister.[11] The Housing Ministry, in fact, was now renamed Federal Ministry of Housing, Urban Affairs, and *Raumordnung*, even though some of the *Raumordnung* concerns were still with the Ministry of the Interior and other appropriate ministries, such as traffic, finance, or agriculture.[12] In 1961, Chancellor Konrad Adenauer himself approved a policy of *Raumordnung* aiming at "unburdening" the areas of population concentration, where nearly half of the West German population was said to be living at the time, by means of housing and job creation programs for the structurally weaker areas. One study in particular was commissioned to examine the need for renewing and replacing buildings in seventy representative villages, especially in their core areas. The impending census of 1961 was expected to include information about the state of buildings throughout the Federal Republic that would permit estimates of the cost of what the 1963 report called "the great task of the future—renewing our cities and villages."[13]

Ordo-Liberal Raumordnung

In the meantime, the government had passed from the hands of the aged Adenauer to a new chancellor, Ludwig Erhard, who was known not only as the architect of the West German "economic miracle," but also for his ordo-liberalism, the economic philosophy of state intervention not into the processes of a market economy, but in the creation of a basic economic and social order in which the market forces of free enterprise would work to everyone's advantage. The housing minister, Lücke, reflected this ordo-liberalism in his report when he equated *Raumordnung* with "basic economic structural and social policy" and stated that[14]

> the federal government is concerned about the spatial development of the Federal Republic and fears that, failing state intervention, this development is bound to undermine and reduce to empty formulas the basic values of the constitution, and to endanger the [ordo-liberal] "social market economy". ... The federation would like to see to it that the *Länder* and communes coordinate their respective planning and responses to structural changes so that they may be in harmony with the interests of the whole. Moreover, it would like to make sure that common principles of *Raumordnung* and "rules of the game" will be established and guaranteed which harmonize the interest of the individuals and the whole just as did the Anti-Cartel Law in the economy.

This law, also known as the Law for the Regulation of Competition in the Economy, was the cornerstone of Erhard's concept of a "socially-concerned market economy (*soziale Marktwirtschaft*)."

The four main tasks of *Raumordnung* policy, consequently, were to be:

(1) The creation of a comprehensive overview over present and future trends, as well as the elaboration of goals and recommendations to guide the communes and other parties interested in spatial utilization and order in recognizing their tasks and opportunities;

(2) The drafting and execution of a federal framework[15] law on *Raumordnung* that would secure the optimal development of the economic, social, and welfare conditions of the whole republic and adjust it to the structural changes going on in every part of the federation;

(3) The creation of the prerequisites for individual *Land* or communal action that would enable them to do the right thing in the public interest without adverse effects to their own planning, administration, and finances;

(4) The elimination of obstacles that hitherto stood in the way of optimal development in each particular sector.

The minister for housing, Urban Affairs, and *Raumordnung* then spelt out the guidelines[16] of federal *Raumordnung* policy[17]:

(1) Full opportunity for the individual citizens and families to develop their potential within the wider community;

(2) Elimination of all obstacles to the optimal utilization and development of the territory and its productive forces;

(3) Careful cultivation and maintenance of the natural sources of soil, water, climate, etc.;

(4) The most effective utilization of existing services such as roads, schools, health care facilities, etc., and the in the long run most cost-effective renewal or building of new facilities;

(5) The promotion and elaboration of our settlement patterns in harmony with their natural basis and in such a way as to develop the most rational and functional settlement units.

By the end of 1963, the lower house of parliament, the *Bundestag*, had a federal *Raumordnung* bill before it for which the government had provided ample material in a first *Raumordnung* report.[18] But the upper house, the Federal Council (*Bundesrat*)—which represents the *Länder* governments—objected to the bill on constitutional grounds, arguing that existing administrative compacts were quite adequate for the coordination of reasonably uniform principles of *Raumordnung* under the authority of each *Land*. It took until 1965 for the Federal *Raumordnung* Act to be accepted by the Federal Council that had meanwhile inserted the requirement to consult the *Länder* governments on all basic questions of *Raumordnung* and regional planning.

The new law proposed to (a) secure and further develop the healthy areas while improving the structure of those less healthy; (b) accept population concentrations as long as they made for "spatially sound and well-balanced conditions," and to counteract concentration if the opposite was true; (c) maintain, in rural areas, "adequate population density," appropriate economic capacity, and sufficient non-agricultural job opportunities; (d) help the borderlands with Iron Curtain countries; and (e) promote communes of "centrality."[19] There was also mention of "the formation of larger communes," a first hint of the merger movement that lay ahead for West Germany's micro-communes. Furthermore, the *Raumordnung* Act proposed a federal-state ministerial conference on *Raumordnung* and prescribed that the federal minister of the interior was to issue a widely circulated *Raumordnung* Report every two years, beginning in 1966. A cabinet committee of the relevant ministries, moreover, was now established on the subject of *Raumordnung* and the Ministry of the Interior had a special experts council (*Beirat*) working on the same subject.[20]

Armed with these legal and organizational supports, the work of guiding future policies proceeded apace. Even the Council of Europe in Strasbourg picked up the topic in broad, international perspective. The *Raumordnung* Report of 1966 presented the present state of development in the Federal Republic[21] in numerous maps, graphic charts, and tables and reported on what was about to become a veritable flood of research by various institutes. Interestingly, the report revealed that the glaring increase of discrepancies between rural areas and the burgeoning conurbations of the 1950s had noticeably slowed down—as compared to the *Raumordnung* Report of 1963—because the people leaving farming now could find industrial jobs in the new industries of "lower central places" of the rural areas, rather than migrating to the old areas of urban concentration. The promotion of economic and cultural activities in these smaller centers in rural areas thus appeared as a natural pivot for improving the regional structures. The emigration from the smallest rural communes, especially from those oriented toward agriculture, was as large as ever, if compensated somewhat by the rural birth rate of the early sixties; and the educational differential between rural and urban areas appeared to play a major role in motivating people to migrate. Still, the partial reversal of the earlier migration patterns was not enough to outweigh the pressing need for imposing a better spatial order on the overcrowded conurbations nor for developing the areas left behind in the helter-skelter rush.[22]

New Demographic Trends Emerge

The basic research for *Raumordnung* quickly accumulated as the federal-state ministerial conferences and the various institutes[23] concentrated on mapping out central places of higher and medium significance—in a big atlas work entitled *Die Bundesrepublik Deutschland*—delineating the areas of population concentration and relating road planning and the railroad net to the task ahead. Terms and definitions were worked out to facilitate processing the information for a future data bank for regional planning. Aerial photography was explored as an aid to making the maps and a prognosis was prepared of the internal migration patterns expected between 1975 and 1995. Once more, the preparatory work had to await the census of 1970 just as a decade earlier that of 1961 had promised to be the definitive key to prognostication.[24] Finally, at the insistence of the *Bundestag*, the new government of Willy Brandt began work on a Federal *Raumordnung* Program that was not completed until 1975. In the meantime, parts of it were released in the form of a first "program concept" (1971) and a "goal system for spatial development" generated by the council of experts on *Raumordnung*, which showed the axes and nodes of both the concentration areas and of future development.[25]

The research uncovered new demographic trends. As early as 1970, the Ministry of the Interior had already noted that, with the exception of the Munich area, the cores of the great conurbations had begun to lose population to smaller and medium-sized towns at their periphery and that the towns outside the areas of population concentration were growing the fastest. Now, it discovered the dramatic impact of the *Pillenknick*, the bend in the population curve caused by the birth control pill, which threatened to undercut many prognostications as it drove inexorably toward a negative balance of population growth. The rural areas, which until recently had made up for the urban shortfall by producing far more than their share of births, now dropped to the urban level that greatly reduced one of the motives for rural-urban migration. At the same time, some of the rural areas of Bavaria, Hesse, and Lower Saxony were gaining in industry and employment at a rate well in excess of the healthy average growth in jobs of the end of the 1960s.[26] For a state like Bavaria, all these trends were a compelling argument to begin its own *Raumordnung*, the sooner the better, to channel development at all levels.

At the federal level, the activities of the seventies with respect to *Raumordnung* seem almost anticlimactic, at least with the benefit of hindsight. Although further *Raumordnung* Reports continued to appear, in 1972, 1974, and 1978, supplemented by structural economic, agricultural, and transportation reports, they amounted to a continuation and execution of the insights and decisions made earlier rather than presenting new departures. To be sure, the subject of *Raumordnung* now even rated passing mention in the government declaration of Willy Brandt of 18 January 1973, who had just been reelected after a landslide election[27]: "For all the citizens in our federal state, equal opportunities must be created and secured. To this end we are working out a concept for the spatial development of West German territory and aiming at a better regional balance of federal measures. Urban concentrations and rural areas must complement each other. … It stands to reason that we must supply our cities and communes with the institutions and services they have been denied in the past. …" It had become clear by that time that urban lifestyles were spreading throughout the last remote villages of rural areas.

At the same time, the need for recreational use of the rural and remaining natural areas had mushroomed, posing further problems of regional planning. Recreational needs frequently motivated the decisions of city families and individuals to relocate outside or at the edge of the conurbations, and so did the cultural and infrastructural services of cities and towns, according to surveys commissioned by federal agencies. People in industrial and metropolitan areas also became more conscious of the environmental pollution and degradation that had increased in geometric proportion with the industrial growth of the fifties and sixties.[28] In the countryside, on the other hand, one out of five residents—in 1972 about as many as in 1984—expressed a desire to leave their small town or village in quest of qualified employment and better cultural, social, and shopping opportunities. The other 80 percent, by way of contrast, cited home ownership, a farm or garden by the house, or a sense of belonging with family, friends, or the place of their birth as their reasons for staying.[29]

Federal *Raumordnung* activity for the rest of the seventies visibly wound down with less frequent *Raumordnung* reports and an amended prognosis of population and economic development up to 1990. With the impact of two oil crises and changed fertility behavior, the curves in the Federal *Raumordnung* Program of 1975 had to be adjusted for population shrinkage and economic stagnation almost as soon as the ink was dry on it. Since the changes were common to most of Western Europe, moreover, a Europe-wide prognosis really would have made more sense in any case. Bilateral *Raumordnung* commissions with France, the Benelux countries, Switzerland, and Austria, were set up to discuss common border problems. Essentially, the initiative had long passed to the planners at the *Länder* level.[30]

Bavaria Tackles Territorial Reorganization

"If you ask me," said the middle-aged mayor of a fair-sized small town south of Nuremberg to me, "this local territorial reform is ridiculous for Bavaria. It makes sense in heavily urbanized North Rhine Westphalia but not here among our old towns and scattered villages." He pointed with the stem of his staghorn pipe at the rolling countryside, with its distant clusters of farm houses and woods, and nervously tugged at one end of his bushy moustache. His own community had grown under the reorganization and he had gained status as a mayor with civil service qualifications.[31] He tilted the pipe stem in the direction of Munich, the state capital, and added with a derisive edge in his voice: "Just because the *Nordlichter* (North Germans) did it, they are making us go through the same agony." Or, as my Hessian grandmother used to say, "die wolle ja nur mit die grosse Hund' sache gehe" (they only want to go and piss with the big dogs).

Precedents for Bavaria

It is doubtful that the state planners of the Bavarian ministries of the interior and of planning and the environment saw the enterprise in these terms. Many of the other West German *Länder*, beginning with North Rhine Westphalia, had indeed begun to reorganize long before Bavaria tackled the job, and so, for that matter, had many of the neighboring countries in Europe.[32] The first *Land* to reorganize its local government,

Rhineland Palatinate, in fact began as early as 1965. North Rhine West-phalia, the richest and most populous state of the Federal Republic, passed the legislation for the first phase of its reform between 1967 and 1970 and completed the undertaking in 1975.[33]

Baden-Württemberg also started reorganizing in 1967–1968, when the state government committed itself to the course of reform and voluntary mergers were encouraged among the smallest communes. In 1970, a "to-tal territorial reform conception" was before the *Landtag*, which in 1974 passed the last of the relevant legislation.[34] This reform involved a situa-tion that was more comparable to that of Bavaria than, say, North Rhine Westphalia. In 1968, Baden-Württemberg still had 3,378 communes, of which 1,827 were below one thousand inhabitants. By 1978, their number had shrunk to 1,001, including 371 administrative unions of smaller units (of no fewer than two thousand each) in sparsely populated areas. There was also a need for redrawing county (*Kreis*) boundaries. The county reform came early (1969–1971) in the process, creating particularly in rural areas counties of comparable population size and usually following the boundaries of several hinterland areas of cities of medium centrality. Furthermore, eleven groups of counties were joined together in regional planning areas that took over the task of regional planning for smaller planning units designated originally by the *Land* Planning Law.[35]

In Hesse, the reorganization reduced 2,216 (1969) communes below a population of two thousand to a mere 23 (1978), halved the number of counties, and generally aimed at a structure consisting solely of unitary communes.[36] Even the Saarland began its reorganization with a first pre-paratory law in 1970, while Schleswig-Holstein's reorganization legisla-tion started in 1966 and the implementation took place between 1969 and 1976, including not only voluntary mergers but also the creation of over one hundred "multiple communities." Lower Saxony, finally, had its reform between 1970 and 1974, preceded by a wave of voluntary mergers among the 4,138 smaller places below the county level and ultimately leaving 142 collective communes (*Samtgemeinden*). Here, the county re-form came last, after the lowest level of communes had all been taken care of.[37]

If Bavaria seemed late in completing its territorial reorganization, it was not for lack of homegrown precedent. In fact, there is the often-cited example of the sweeping reforms of Count Maximilian Joseph Montgelas (1759–1838) who at the beginning of the nineteenth century was the first minister of the newly created kingdom of Bavaria. The state had been enlarged by the addition of Suebia, Franconia, and smaller entities and was faced with a welter of diverse, secular and clerical, "sovereign" cities and territories, as well as with a wide range of self-governing town and market constitutions that were quite beyond the control of the old Bavarian state government.[38] Franconia, where all of our fifteen communes are, was particularly difficult to integrate, both because it was composed of heterogeneous, independent parts (including the Teutonic Order and the Margravedoms Ansbach and Bayreuth) and because at least some of the Franconian knights and cities bitterly resented in turn the Prussian, Imperial Austrian, and Bavarian claims on them and the French machinations behind them. The Bavarian takeover at Napoleon's behest involved considerable violence and rumors of Jacobin conspiracies.

Montgelas had been plotting the territorial and secularization changes since 1796 in a high game of diplomatic chess against his antagonist, Prussian Minister Karl August von Hardenberg who, against the background of the dissolution of the Holy Roman Empire and Napoleonic advances, strove unsuccessfully to expand Prussia into southern Germany. Montgelas, the winner, in the spirit of enlightened absolutism, unified the Bavarian state by dividing the new territory into four equal *Kreise*—the Rezatkreis and the Altmühlkreis included most of our communes. With the Organic Edict of 1808, the great reformer gave all Bavarian local government a uniform basis of French-style communes that, among other things, involved the reduction of the pre-existing number of some 40,000 small entities by means of territorial reorganization to about 7,300 (without the Palatinate).

As the Organic Edict put it,[39]

> the best guide for determining the communal boundaries is in the natural conditions; for the situation often has already united neighboring locations in common and frequent intercourse which this instrument ... ought to link even more closely ... if the natural situation gives no clues as to communal boundaries, other existing demarcations, such as administrative offices (*Schultheissämter, Obmannschaften*), church parishes, school districts, etc. can help to draw or connect boundaries of communities. ... The extent of the village communes, with some regard for area, should be measured so as to include no more than 200 families or 1,000 souls, and no less than 50 families or 250 souls.

This 1808 Edict and Bavarian organic law gave the present form to villages and small towns that since medieval times had been recognized only as settlements by their feudal/clerical masters and by their *Gmain*, a kind of commons or organization for the cooperative use of common lands and communal welfare. But it also aimed at dethroning, aside from feudal and clerical authorities, the free city elites and the trade guilds that had long taken over the governance of *Stadt* and *Markt* in a mixture of *Gmain* and economic management. After a mere decade as first minister, Montgelas[40] was overthrown and a measure of local self-government (which he had destroyed and expropriated) restored in 1818, along with a ballyhooed new Bavarian constitution, albeit essentially in the new territorial form, for the smallest unit of the Bavarian state. His extensive secularization and mediatization measures remained intact. The seven districts (*Regierungsbezirke*) of Bavaria also date back to Montgelas, while the 143 pre-reform counties originated from district administrative offices created in 1862 and received the name Landkreise (rural counties) only in 1939.

The Weakness of the Smaller Communes

The tasks assigned the communal level in 1818, of course, were far more modest than what they are today: The communal councils were in charge of conferring their own "citizenship" and licensing of trades, had authority over municipal building activity, fire protection, lighting, communal road building and maintenance, water supply, and care of the poor, of minors, and of churches and schools within certain limitations. They also had their own police as a matter of delegated authority. The ordinance of 1818 even commissioned the village teachers to take care of such writing and accounting chores as the elected communal officials might not be able to discharge. These minimal functions corresponded to the role assigned to public authority by nineteenth century liberalism, and even then, there was considerable doubt whether the smaller communes were able to take care of these functions adequately.

The dramatic growth of communal functions after the Second World War—in larger cities already since before the turn of the century[41]—had left the communes helplessly floundering in the wake of the modern state: Without the help and guidance of the county prefecture, the *Landratsamt* and their omnibus welfare and vastly increased infrastructural functions—nor the enormous public investments at the communal level, two-thirds of West German total public investment—were clearly beyond their capacity to control.

As long ago as 1932, an American political scientist wrote,[42] "It is undoubtedly a fact that many *Landgemeinden* [rural communes] are too small to be satisfactory local government units. Yet such places frequently have a very keen sense of their own individuality and a strong objection to losing their corporate existence by annexation or even to being formed into various types of unions of *Landgemeinden*." As the author of the 1978 reform, Interior Minister Bruno Merk, wrote to me twenty years after the reform: "[regarding] the territorial reform, one has to admit that territorial corporations (like local governments) are not a purpose in themselves but a means to an end. They must have the size and capacity to carry out the functions assigned to them. Even the communal top associations did not deny that the majority of Bavarian communes were no longer able to do that."

Immediately following the reform, some critics also fastened upon the size of many communes, frequently long overgrown by urban sprawl and inter-communal patterns of interdependence, but also on the lack of suitable administrative personnel, paid or honorary, and on local factionalism and lack of financial resources. The reform of the smaller communes, the authors of a definitive study (published by people close to the Bavarian Communal Association [*Gemeindetag*]) wrote, "is the core piece of the whole reform" because they have been "the weakest territorial structures" of Bavarian local government. They were to take care of the governmental tasks closest to the public and yet remain intimately linked to the state administration at all levels. As long as the smaller communes could not handle many of the new concerns, the tendency was to address them at a higher regional level, thereby leaving the old self-governing communes even farther behind the new technocratic state, and the rationale of democracy farther behind that of bureaucracy and neo-corporatist solutions.[43] When the local citizenry and its elected officials no longer seemed capable of making many vital decisions, well-organized interests and the bureaucracy were likely to make them at the higher level and far removed from democratic control.[44]

Regional Planning and Administrative Reform

Against the background of federal *Raumordnung* activities, the mapping of central places in particular, the Bavarian government moved at several levels of action at once. Beginning with a formal announcement in the government declaration of 25 January 1967 by Minister President Alfons Goppel, it initiated the administrative reform of communes, counties, and districts. A year later, the Bavarian minister of the interior, Bruno Merk, convened a Working Group "Communal Reform," which included representatives of the three communal associations,[45] along with ministry officials, and called upon local and county officials to participate in the shaping of the policies. By April of 1970 the state government had a draft before the legislature of a Law to Strengthen Local Self-government, including county and city levels.[46] At the beginning of 1971, Goppel launched the administrative reform itself, in his opening *Landtag* speech, beginning with the rural counties that were to be reorganized by the summer of 1972. He also called upon the communes to start merging voluntarily before the mergers, beginning in 1976, would be mandated.

Mapping Places of Centrality

At about the same time, the planning process was set in motion with the Programs for Bavaria I and II (1969–1970) and the Bavarian Land Planning Law of 1970, which embodied the *Raumordnung* principles to be applied. This law also requested the executive to come up with *Raumordnung* Reports at regular intervals, of which the first appeared in 1971. A Land Development Program gradually took shape as the state was divided into eighteen planning regions of which, for example, West Middle Franconia was one (No. 8), and the mapping of central places and their respective hinterlands began.[47] A first draft with maps was published in 1974 and circulated until the final version in several volumes appeared in 1976. It contains all the supporting material and spells out the development policies and their justification along with identifying the central places in the state.[48]

(a) Large Centers (*Oberzentren*) with a hinterland radius of twenty miles (thirty kilometers), such as Augsburg, Munich, Nuremberg/Fürth/Erlangen, Regensburg, Würzburg, and Ulm/Neu-Ulm.[49] The plans also identified sixteen "possible large centers" of the future that included some of the locations of new universities—the presence of university-level institutions is one of the criteria for the status of a large center—such as Bayreuth (population 70,600), Bamberg (72,000), and Passau (51,000), and also such cities as Ansbach (38,183) and Rosenheim (51,604), which are of particular interest to this book. These latter two, it should be emphasized, have no central place of competing importance within their respective counties or, for that matter, their respective planning regions.

(b) Middle Centers (*Mittelzentren*), of which there were seventy-five in Bavaria, including Wasserburg (10,614) in Rosenheim County, Rothenburg (11,882), Gunzenhausen (14,890), Weissenburg (17,469), and Neustadt on the Aisch (10,636), which are mentioned throughout this book. The middle centers were defined by a minimum of 7,500 in their urban core, and of 30,000 in their core and middle-range hinterland as well as by a minimal twenty million marks in retail turnover and 2,500 manufacturing employees, and a like number of in-commuters. The average values of existing middle centers were considerably higher. Another twenty-eight towns were considered "lower centers with partial middle center functions," really with an incomplete array of middle center functions.

(c) Lower Centers (*Unterzentren*) were defined as having a minimum of two thousand inhabitants in their core and ten thousand in their hinterland, as well as about nine hundred gainfully employed in manufacturing and eight hundred commuters. The annual turn-over in their retail stores was supposed to be at least 7.5 million marks. They included Feuchtwangen, Heilsbronn, and Uffenheim, which are mentioned in this book and are said to be important centers of services and industry in their respective areas.

(d) The Two hundred and seventy-two Small Centers (*Kleinzentren*) had to have at least one thousand in their core and five thousand in their hinterland, three million marks retail turnover, three hun-dred commuters, and 350 manufacturing jobs. They were generally expected to supply the basic needs of their hinterland. The regional planning associations of their respective regions designated them as small centers.

These classifications were supported with lists of indispensable and dis-pensable institutions and services that were said to typify each level of centrality: Small centers, for example, had to have a school center or *Hauptschule* (middle school), adult education courses, a public library, pub-lic kindergarten, various sports facilities, a youth center, a doctor, dentist, pharmacist, post office, a bank or savings institution, an inn, and a garage for repairing automobiles and agricultural machinery. In many cases they might typically have also a movie theater, a facility for public events with two thousand square feet, a nurses' station, taxi service, tourist office, and an annual fair and a small weekly one as well. Lower centers had to have a public health insurance office, and other health insurance offices, an elementary school and facilities for special students, a movie theater and an events facility as described above, at least five doctors and three den-tists, a veterinarian, optician, nurses station, youth center, taxi service, four or more bank branches, a cafe, dancing school, driving school, at least four car repair shops, and a tax accountant. They might also possess a vehicle inspection station, a *Gymnasium* (public secondary school) and vocational schools, a hospital, school counselors, sports facilities, county offices of the Bavarian Farmers Association (BBV) and of the Raiffeisen cooperative, a travel agency, a notary public, an attorney, architect, and a hall for industrial exhibitions.

Middle centers such as Wasserburg and Rothenburg had to have a *Gymnasium* (public preparatory school) and other schools, especially for differentiated vocational training, a large multipurpose events facility, a hospital with differentiated specialties, four to eight specialists, a senior home, educational counseling center, welfare services, an indoor pool and sports stadium, a travel agency, notary public, tax accountant, architect, and an engineer's office. They also might, but did not have to, possess a range of government agencies such as the county prefecture (*Landratsamt*) including construction and finance, road construction, water supply, land surveyors, agriculture and fire insurance, an employment office, and public health agency. They also might have state courts of the two lower levels (*Amtsgericht* and *Landgericht*), a labor court, a specialized hospital, county offices of industry and trade associations, a trade union (DGB) office, and the farmers association (BBV), a branch of the Land Central Bank, and an industrial exhibition hall. It should be noted that these specifications, except for the "might have" ones such as courts and government offices, differ little from places of lower centrality, although population size and economic capacity constitute a significant gain in critical mass. The science of centrality[50] and *Raumordnung*, it would appear, is not that exact although Bavarian towns and cities present such an obvious scale in size and importance that there is little doubt about the difference, say, between a middle and a lower center. In fact, the state planners never even bothered to specify all the criteria for the large centers.

The staff of the Ministry for *Land* Development and Environmental Problems collected relevant material on each of the eighteen planning regions and developed plans to reflect difficulties specific to that area. Task forces composed of members of the Bavarian diet and state-level administrators worked with the counties, cities, and communes, and with representatives of public and private interest groups to establish guidelines for the subsequent reforms.

Administrative Simplification

In addition to the area reforms, other administrative reforms were planned, including some timed to occur in conjunction with the area reforms. The planning and design of the area reforms took seven years and about 850 suggestions were made in that period to simplify and/or improve state administration. The reforms can be subdivided into three major types: Simplification of administration, functional reforms (which have not all been completed), and other administrative reforms. The first type of reforms relates to the various branch offices of state agencies located throughout Bavaria. The second type of reforms involves a redistribution of public services among the levels of the reorganized governmental system. The rest refers to the centralized organization of state agencies, most of which are located at the state capital of Munich. Here is a brief summary of the type and extent of these reforms.[51]

The branch offices of the small district courts, the tax offices, the agricultural bureaus, the forestry, health, and water agencies, and the departments of roads were all reduced in number, in many cases so that only one agency existed for each newly organized county after the county reform.

In addition, police reorganization was continued. Local police forces were gradually disbanded, as the state gradually took over all police duties. These reforms were completed in 1975.

The beginnings of the functional reorganization also addressed questions of personnel, including which agencies had the right to hire and promote personnel and regulations concerning working a second job and flexible working hours. A number of taxes were increased, including the motor vehicle tax, taxes involving permits, and taxes on telephones, and the assessment of property was re-evaluated. Improvements were made in the administration of rent and heating oil subsidies, and emergency aid. The construction of buildings and roads was also simplified, and public roads were standardized and color-coordinated uniformly throughout the state. The public registries were reorganized and would henceforth be subject to regular inspection. Public health offices were to concern themselves more with industrial pollution while many of their former activities were relegated to other agencies. Some of the functions of the public schools were standardized and simplified while recognizing the educational problems engendered by an increasingly mobile society. The reformers also standardized agricultural regulations for milk, viniculture, and rabbit raising, and for hunting and fishing. Finally, the government developed new regulations regarding the sale and transfer of property, and passed a stronger, more comprehensive law of historical preservation.

The *Kreisreform*

The first phase of the territorial reforms rearranged the administrative seats and boundaries of the *Landkreise* (rural counties), halving their numbers and doubling their average size. At the same time, the ranks of the independent (*Kreisfreie*) cities were reordered and redistributed, which reduced their numbers as well.[52] Before the county reform the 143 rural counties ranged from about 17,000 residents in 71 square miles (County Beilngries, Upper Palatinate) to 155,000 people in 135 square miles (rural Munich County). From 1 July 1972, there were only 71 rural counties averaging slightly over 100,000 residents in 374 square miles each and ranging in population from 68,000 (Lindau on Lake Constance, soon 73,151 [1990]) to 227,000 (rural Munich County, soon 266,629).[53]

The county reform was intended to strengthen the capacity of county governments to plan and develop their respective territories, maintain there a general hospital, take over the maintenance and construction of the entire public school system, including the secondary *Gymnasium* and vocational and special education. Also to maintain and supervise the supra-local water supply, sanitation, and waste-removal systems, supra-local fire protection equipment, sports facilities, and to operate social services ranging from youth centers to senior homes. Many an old Landratsamt (county prefecture) had been too small and understaffed to be able to do justice to these challenges of modern government. Enlarging their population and tax base, it was hoped, would give each of them a capacity that would allow the provincial, or district (*Regierungsbezirk*) offices between them and the state government to devolve additional functions upon the counties in the future.[54]

But the county territorial reforms were also enjoined to "maintain the unity of the living, administrative, and investment territory with respect to historic and tribal-traditional (*stammesmässige*) ties" and to assure, aside from economic and administrative rationality, their "closeness to the citizenry and the simplicity of the arrangement."[55] The redrawing of county boundaries and, most of all, the abolition of about half the counties and the demotion of many former county seats naturally brought a storm of protests: There were 161 petitions to the state diet, one abortive attempt to launch an initiative, and unsuccessful suits by the old county of Wolfratshausen before the Bavarian Administrative Court, and of the counties of Ingolstadt and Coburg before the constitutional courts of Bavaria and of the Federal Republic, respectively.

In the areas we discussed in the previous chapters, to give examples, the new county of Ansbach (population 155,165) was created from the old Ansbach county (population 54,000) plus the old counties of Rothenburg, Dinkelsbühl, and Feuchtwangen, with some territorial changes and the subordination of the once independent town of Rothenburg to the new county administration. The county seats of the three abolished counties, furthermore, lost that status. The new county Neustadt on the Aisch/Bad Windsheim (population 85,000), where our communes of Ippesheim and Weigenheim are located, likewise included not only the old county Neustadt (population 42,000) but county Uffenheim and about two-thirds of the county of Scheinfeld. The new county Weissenburg-Gunzenhausen (population 86,000) was formed more or less from the old counties of Weissenburg (39,000) and Gunzenhausen (40,000) and the demoted city of Weissenburg, where parts of the northern wall of the Roman empire (*Limes*) have been excavated. Since this whole area has a history of extreme territorial fragmentation, it was not difficult to construe ample lines of historical tradition for almost any set of redrawn boundaries.[56]

It was a rather contrasting story in the county of Rosenheim, southeast of Munich, which shares neither the population decline nor the economic stagnation of West Middle Franconia. The new county of Rosenheim (population 186,000) included the old county (90,000) as well as most of the old counties of Bad Aibling (48,000) and Wasserburg (53,000). Here there were few historic boundaries except for the Salzburg enclaves in the midst of the Old Bavarian duchy, which were promptly ignored when the new boundaries were drawn. The demotion of the ancient, proud city of Wasserburg from the status of a county seat at the hands of a Christian Democratic (CSU) state government provoked an angry rally of its small citizenry. Not only was the old county Wasserburg destroyed, but a part of its old hinterland was now in the next county, Mühldorf. Six of seven CSU city council members resigned from the party and, with other independent elements, formed a nonpartisan *Wasserburger Block* for the next local elections. Three local notables, a hotelier, a transport business owner, and the scion of another old Wasserburg family—one can see the gilded, wrought-iron trade signs with two of their names on entering the town square—were instrumental in forming the new local party that promptly sent a large delegation in a motorcade to complain to the Bavarian minister president in Munich. "Some hard words were said," as an informant told us who was present at the confrontation. The *Block* then put up an independent mayoral candidate and a full slate of twenty councilor candidates for the city elections. Their choice, a well-educated but little-known former county administrator and not even a native of Bavaria, won handily and proceeded to govern the city with a coalition of small parties including the *Block*. The small-town citizenry had given a patently political response to what they perceived as a largely political decision.

The Independent City and Hinterland Reforms

An Independent City Reform was implemented in two parts. The first phase occurred in 1972, in conjunction with the county reform, when twenty-three smaller independent cities lost this status and were subordinated to the newly formed counties. The original forty-eight cities ranged from a population of 10,400 (Eichstätt) to the metropolis of Munich with 1.3 million inhabitants, which again raised the question of the capacity of the smaller ones—in particular those under thirty thousand—to handle functions on a level equivalent to the county governments. The "guiding figure" for the new independent cities was a minimal population of fifty thousand but the planners did not have the courage of their convictions, or they would have ended up with only seventeen independent cities. Aside from population size,[57] the new independent city also was supposed to have substantially more per capita tax revenue (in 1971, an average DM 281 as compared to DM 132 for the counties) than the rural counties, but with this surplus it also had to supply the basic needs of its hinterland. The losers in the selection of county seats were re-designated "Large County Towns" (*Große Kreisstädte*, abbr. GKSt.) and retained part of their original privileges, and the title *Oberbürgermeister* for their mayor instead of First *Bürgermeister*. Their subordination to the county also increased the base of the latter, as in the case of the GKSt. Rothenburg.[58]

The second phase occurred in 1978, in conjunction with the communal reform, when in the course of the City Hinterland Reform a number of suburban communes were consolidated into the remaining twenty-five independent cities. In contrast to the other two reforms, in this one some large, economically strong units lost their independence on the grounds that these suburbs had long enjoyed the services and employment opportunities provided by their larger neighbors without having to pay for them. In other cases, predominantly agricultural areas were nevertheless incorporated into urban areas, in order to provide much-needed land for economic expansion.

The City Hinterland Reform followed generally different rules from the communal reform in rural counties. On the one hand, there was no reason to take away the autonomy of viable, fair-sized communes in the hinterland of a city even if they were, so to speak, within the magnetic power of their large neighboring star. Even multi-community administrative unions—not including the central city itself—might be a better solution to give smaller communes in the sparsely settled hinterland the required administrative capacity to take care of their local government functions. Where the city was clearly about to grow along its development axes and where the proximity of built-up areas and their interrelations had grown to the point of denying the smaller entity a life of its own, on the other hand, it might be better to annex it to the city. Annexation also made sense if it would help a given center to attain the degree of centrality desirable for its role in the development of the region.[59]

The Communal Territorial Reform

The local territorial reform got underway in March 1969 with an amendment of the Financial Equalization Act to provide for financial rewards for voluntary mergers among communes. These special inducements and low-cost credits produced 265 mergers the first two years and another wave in connection with the communal elections of 1972, which reduced the total number of communes from over 7,000 to 4,406 by July of 1972 and frequently merged micro-communes to achieve at least the size of 1,000 residents. Meanwhile, the government had submitted its first bill for the "strengthening of communal self-government"[60] (1971), which introduced the term *Verwaltungsgemeinschaft* (administrative union) or VG. A further financial amendment promised rewards for forming a VG as well. At the same time, the Bavarian Communal Statute (*Gemeindeordnung*) was amended to replace the usual requirement of referenda for territorial changes with a wholesale legislative mandate to change the entire system at one stroke.

The *Verwaltungsgemeinschaft* as an Alternative

The administrative union, or VG (of several communes of about one thousand residents each), was to be the means whereby even sparsely settled rural areas with under-sized communes could achieve a form of local administration comparable to the unitary communes (*Einheitsgemeinden*, or EGs) of the more populous areas. It had been tried before with considerable success, most recently in Baden-Württemberg. According to the 1971 Law on Strengthening Local Self-government, Art. 2, a VG had to be large enough to take on the new administrative functions, with a combined population at least approaching the "guiding figure" of five thousand that an EG also had to possess (Art. 11). Furthermore, the formation of a VG had to take into account all the concerns of *Raumordnung*, traffic patterns, school districts,[61] economic geography, and cultural and historical patterns. If necessary to form a viable VG, according to Art. 4(2), even communes that were quite capable of discharging their own and delegated government functions in an orderly fashion could be ordered to join a VG to give it critical mass. The law was equally explicit in spelling out under what conditions the provincial governments could draconically order territorial changes or annexation to unitary communes against the will of the commune involved: If (a) a commune was too small to be a viable administrative unit, or (b) if the administrative unity and rationality of governing an area suggested it, and (c) if the degree of centrality required to serve the needs of the hinterland suggested increasing the core area of a center.[62]

The Bavarian government was at pains to counteract the rumor that the VG was only a temporary, transitional institution that in time would lead to the creation by annexation of a unitary EG, thus reducing the last shreds of the identity and autonomy of the VG member communes to a mere shadow, an *Ortsteil* (part of a commune) name under the name of the more encompassing community. The VG is a corporate entity[63] with the right to employ civil servants and other public employees in full-time positions at its seat, which, along with the name of the VG, was picked after some consultation by the provinvial government.[64] Its member communes each retained their name and territory—often after mandated mergers that gave them the minimum size of 1,000 residents and a new name—as well as their honorary *Bürgermeister* and communal council. The VG administers

(a) tasks delegated by the state, such as the civil registry, passports, conscription, elections at all levels, census operations, and welfare and public health functions;
(b) the execution of decisions made by its member communes, such as those regarding budgets, taxation, and tasks delegated to it by the member communes, or such as maintaining or improving the common water supply, sanitation, and road systems. This makes the VG the successor of many special districts and shared functions of the past, although some special districts and multi-communal cooperative groups have continued to flourish[65];
(c) the school district functions, where the VG coincides, as it often does, with the elementary and middle school (*Grund* and *Hauptschule*) boundaries, likewise in delegation by the member communes.

What then, we must ask, is left to the member communes to decide? The remaining functions are comparable, perhaps, to the broadly defined police powers of Anglo-American local government by which a community can take charge of its own zoning, plan its roads and recreational facilities, fire protection, school maintenance (if the commune still has one), cemeteries, tax assessment, social services, and local water supply and sanitation to the extent that these functions have not been turned over voluntarily to the VG. But a member commune no longer has administrative personnel, except perhaps attendants of municipal pre-schools, cemeteries, or tourist offices, or a part-time secretary for the mayor. The preparation and execution of its decisions is left to the VG office. The mayor of a member commune still wears the traditional mayor's chain across the chest and can perform marriages, preside over elections, or arbitrate disputes, but there is no more pretense of administrative functions.

The mayors and one to five of the council members in each of the member communes form the assembly of the VG,[66] which is also supposed to represent partisan and other factions of the members' communal councils. The VG assembly decides about the staff and budget of the VG, selects one of the mayors as the VG president, and designates several vice presidents from among its own membership. The VG president represents the VG toward the outside, presides over assembly meetings, and oversees the preparation and execution of its decisions. The VG staff must include civil servants,[67] or similarly trained full-time administrators, and varies in size according to the size of the VG. On the average, Bavarian VGs have about three member communes each and a population size between four and six thousand residents. But VGs with eight—like the VG Rothenburg of chapter 1—or more member communes are not unusual in sparsely settled regions, and some VGs exceed a population of ten thousand. Since 1979, the VG staff on the average has been about nine civil servants and employees per VG, while 1,083 member communes had only 3,964 employees between them,[68] evidently including a number of social and health service personnel, construction and traffic specialists, managers of municipal enterprises and institutions, and very few mayors' secretaries.

During the formation of VGs, the elected executive (*Landratsamt*) of each county usually needed to guide also the mergers of the smallest communes to attain the required size of a VG member commune or, in the more densely settled areas,[69] into larger unitary communes (EGs). In so doing, the counties themselves needed the guidance of the state via the provincial governments to maintain uniform standards and procedures in the process. A typical EG, at least after the "reform of the reform," was likely to have between two and ten thousand inhabitants, rather than something nearer the original "guiding figure" of five thousand.[70] It usually occupied an area with a radius that would require citizens to travel no more than five miles to reach their local administrative center, with the possible exception of outlying areas connected to it by a freeway.

An EG was supposed to permit the optimal concentration of local administrative capacity on a basis of adequate economic resources, social and geographical unity, including the elementary and middle school (*Grund-* and *Hauptschule*) districts and most other special district functions. Hence it is quite capable of handling all of its own local government functions as well as what may have been delegated or may in future be delegated to it from the county level. EGs were also meant to be so uncomplicated in their arrangement of offices and functions that the citizenry could easily maintain a clear picture and a sense of democratic controllability.

Notes

1. See also Merkl, *Germany: Yesterday and Tomorrow* (New York, 1965), 187–189, where the apex of West German economic recovery in the late fifties is linked to a wave of self-critical reappraisal of the Third Reich. From there, the self-critical reform spirit went on to other targets, including "democratization" of Bonn's democratic struc-

tures, an extremely controversial goal that the founders' generation of the Federal Republic took as an insult to its achievements.

2. See, for example, Helge Pross, *Über die Bildungschancen der Mädchen in der Bundesrepublik* (Frankfurt, 1969), whose author demonstrated that rural-born women, especially Catholics, were rather unlikely to enter, much less graduate from a West German university.

3. This percentage refers to member communes of administrative unions as well as independent unitary communes under two thousand. In 2008, the percentage had shrunk to 7.9 percent in Bavaria and 6.0 in Middle Franconia. *Jahrbuch Bayern 2009*.

4. See *Jahrbuch Bayern 1981*, 12 and 18. In 1961, 37.3 percent of the population lived in communities below two thousand, while 18.6 percent were in those between ten and one hundred thousand.

5. *Raumordnungsbericht der Bundesregierung 1971*, 56–61 (hereafter, *Federal Report* with the year).

6. Release of Bavarian Ministry of Development and the Environment, 18 August 1980. There were two thousand respondents in the *Landkreise* Cham, Kronach, Hof, Miesbach, and Passau, and four hundred in the three metropolitan areas.

7. See, for example, *Regional Development in Western Europe*, Hugh D. Clout, ed. (London, 1975), and *Public Policy and Regional Economic Development: The Experience of Nine Western Countries*, Niles M. Hansen, ed. (Cambridge, MD, 1974).

8. See the ministerial activity reports in *Deutschland im Wiederaufbau* (hereafter referred to as *DIW* with the reporting year). A first draft based on the Prussian laws of 1926, a *Reichstag* bill of 1931, and a 1942 ministerial draft had been circulating as early as 1950. In 1951, the *Bundestag* called on the cabinet to submit a bill, but then constitutional issues were raised and it took until 1954 before the bill passed. In the meantime, appropriate materials and maps of economic geography were being prepared, among other agencies, by the *Institut für Raumforschung* in Bad Godesberg. See *DIW 1952*, 192; *DIW 1954*, 78; *DIW 1955*, 107; and *DIW 1959*, 199.

9. There had been important precedents in the form of plans to reorganize the *Länder* boundaries, beginning with Hugo Preuss's 1919 proposal to dismember Prussia, the 1928 plans of the *Länderkonferenz*, and post-1945 attempts to create meaningful *Länder* units and, in 1951, the creation of Baden-Württemberg. See esp. *Die Bundesländer*, ed. by Institut zur Förderung Öffentlicher Angelegenheiten (Frankfurt, 1950); and Federal Ministry of the Interior, *Die Neugliederung des Bundesgebietes* (Bonn, 1955), where a possible territorial reorganization under Article 29 of the Basic Law is discussed.

10. See *DIW 1956*, 112, and *DIW 1958*, 463 and 287. The quotation is from *DIW 1957*, 378.

11. See *DIW 1949–1959*, 231. Beginning in 1960 the ministerial activity reports appeared under the title *Deutsche Politik 1960* (hereafter, *DP* with the reporting year). See *DP 1960*, 395–396 where the quotation appears.

12. Agricultural policies had been linked with it as early as 1957. The Federal Ministry of Transport had an obvious concern with the impact of road construction on *Raumordnung* and, in 1961, established a commission of experts to study this subject. See *DP 1961*, 342–343.

13. See *DP 1961*, 393, and *DP 1963*, 363. A law for the Promotion of Urban Construction followed in 1963.

14. *DP 1963*, 359 and 362. The report also contains maps of the Federal Republic showing the per capita gross domestic product in 1957 and the population decline of

1950–1961 county by county. Ordo-liberalism particularly aims at restraining monopoly positions and creating level playing fields so that market competition can work its magic.

15. Under the constitutional division of legislative powers, the federation was permitted only to legislate a "framework" on this subject within which each individual *Land* government could fashion its own *Raumordnung*.

16. A first set of principles of *Raumordnung* agreed upon by the federal and *Länder* representatives was published in *Bundesanzeiger*, 4 August 1962.

17. See *DP 1963*, 362.

18. See Deutscher Bundestag, *Drucksache IV/473* and *Drucksache IV/1492*, for the report itself. The bill is *Drucksache IV/1204*.

19. The reference is to the categories of centrality set forth below. By 1965, the subject of *Raumordnung* had been transferred from the Ministry of Housing and Urban Affairs to that of the Interior and, in 1966, the Housing Minister of many years, Paul Lücke, became minister of the interior of the new grand coalition. *DP 1965*, 57–58 and 292.

20. This council of experts formed eight working committees on such subjects as federal construction funds and *Raumordnung*, central places and the communes in their hinterlands, nature preserves, administrative structure, mono-industrial areas, industry in rural areas, long-distance roads, and the financial aspects of *Raumordnung*.

21. The international aspects and the possibility of all-German *Raumordnung* in case of German reunification were by no means neglected in the report.

22. See *Federal Report 1966*, and *DP 1966*, 26–29.

23. The most important public institutes were the *Bundesforschungsanstalt für Landeskunde und Raumordnung* and the *Institut für Raumordnung*.

24. See the ministerial activity reports in *Jahresbericht der Bundesregierung 1968*, 112–115 (hereafter referred to as *JB* with the reporting year.

25. See *Federal Report 1972*, 154–172.

26. *JB 1970*, 128–133. See also *JB 1969*, 138–139, and *JB 1971*, 213–221.

27. Quoted in *JB 1972*, 54.

28. See *Federal Report 1972*, 12–14, 30, 44, 82–89.

29. The 1972 survey of public opinion regarding location is described in ibid., 56–61: 25 percent of the West German adult population at the time expressed a preference for living in conurbations and another 48 percent for living within twelve miles (twenty kilometers) of their urban cores. Forty-five percent of the population actually lives within the hinterland of one of twenty-four such conurbations, although many of them seem unaware of the fact.

30. See *JB 1977*, 445–449 and 473, and *JB 1978*, 425–433. A revision of the Federal Construction Law of 1960 perhaps deserves mention as do the stepped up federal expenditures for improvement and maintenance of the historic city cores.

31. The Bavarian territorial reform enabled a number of younger, ambitious "honorary" mayors to qualify by taking a retraining course with examination as "professional (*berufsmässige*) mayors" with civil service privileges.

32. See esp. the accounts of Danish, Dutch, Belgian, Swedish, British, French, and Italian local reforms in *Local Government Reform and Reorganization: An International Perspective*, Arthur Gunlicks, ed. (Port Washington, NY, and London, 1981); and, for the same countries as well as Norway, Finland, Ireland, and Eastern Europe, in *International Handbook on Local Government Reorganization: Contemporary Developments*, Donald C. Rowat, ed. (Westport, CT, 1980). See also the contributions to Merkl, *New Local Centers*.

33. The reform reduced some 2,300 local authorities, including federated communes, to 373 unitary communities (EGs).

34. See esp. Baden-Württemberg Kommission für die kommunale Verwaltungsreform, *Teilgutachten A, B, and C* and Landtag 5. Wahlperiode, *Drucksache V/3300*, 15 October 15 1970.

35. The four districts (*Bezirke*) stemming from the pre-1952 predecessors of Baden-Württemberg were retained for a transitional period. The county administrations also were enlarged by the inclusion of public health, agriculture, and educational administration under the same roof.

36. See Hesse Ministry of the Interior, *Hessen, Gemeinden und Landkreise nach der Gebietsreform, eine Dokumentation 1977* (Melsing, 1979).

37. See Georg-Christoph von Unruh, *Gebiets- und Verwaltungsreform in Niedersachsen, 1965–1978* (Hannover, 1978), 71–81; as well as *Federal Report 1972*, 20–21; and Frido Wagener "West Germany: A Survey," in *International Handbook on Local Government Reorganization*, 332–340, esp. 336–337. See also Arthur Gunlicks, "Restructuring Service Delivery Systems in West Germany," in *Comparing Urban Service Delivery Systems*, Vincent Ostrom and Frances P. Bish, eds. (Beverly Hills, CA, 1977).

38. In 1748, as Mack Walker relates, 176 communities of the Electorate of Bavaria alone were legally defined as "bearers of sovereign rights and special judicial authority," not derived from the Elector. The constitutional powers and immunities of these and other territorial towns and markets fill fifty volumes of the archives of the state. Walker, *German Home Towns: Community, State, and General Estate* (Ithaca, NY, 1971), 21, and also chapters 2 and 8.

39. Quoted in Otto Reigl, Josef Schober, and Gerhard Skoruppa, *Kommunale Gliederung in Bayern nach der Gebietsreform* (Munich, 1978), 1–2. Also *König Max I Joseph*, II, 153–154 and 163–165, where the resistance and legal obstacles are also discussed. Montgelas also commissioned a twenty-five–volume population and economic survey of Bavaria that served both his policies and those of the future.

40. On Montgelas, who had already a long and distinguished career before becoming prime minister, see esp. his biographer, Eberhard Weis, "Die Begründung des bayerischen Staates unter König Max I: (1799–1825)," in Spindler, *Bavarian History*, I, 3–15, 38–60.

41. See also Merkl, "The Urban Challenge Under the Empire," in *Another Germany: A Reconsideration of the Imperial Era*, Jack R. Dukes and Joachim Remak, eds. (Boulder, 1988), 61–72.

42. Roger H. Wells, *German Cities. A Study of Contemporary Municipal Policy and Administration* (Princeton, NJ, 1932), 29.

43. Reigl et al., *Kommunale Gliederung*, 11–15, 18–19.

44. See also Lothar Albertin, "Local Territorial Reform in the Context of West German Social Development," in Merkl, *New Local Centers*, 123–139.

45. The three associations are the Bavarian *Gemeindetag* (communal association), *Städtebund* (small town federation), and *Städtetag* (urban federation). There are also associations of communal enterprises and of other corporate local entities.

46. See Bayern, Landtag, *LT Drucksache 6/3207*.

47. Bayerische Staatsregierung, *Raumordnungsbericht 1971*, 9–20 (hereafter, *Bavarian Report* with the year).

48. See the draft *Landesentwicklungsprogramm Bayern*, A and B (Entwurf). In his introduction to the final *Land* Development Program, Goppel also mentions a 1962 statement of Principles and Goals of *Raumordnung* in Bavaria. See also Bayerisches Staatsministerium für Landesentwicklung und Umweltfragen, *Landesentwicklung*

Bayern. *Zentrale Orte und Nahbereiche in Bayern, 1972* (hereafter, *Zentrale Orte*) and *Landesentwicklungsprogramm A, 2.*

49. The last-mentioned center straddles the state border with Baden-Württemberg, in which Ulm is located. Only Neu-Ulm and some smaller suburbs are in Bavaria.

50. See also Leslie J. King, *Central Place Theory* (Beverly Hills, CA, 1984), a critical appraisal of the theory and practice of mapping central places and their hinterland, and Gerhard Isbary, *Zentrale Orte und Versorgungsnahbereiche* (Bad Godesberg, 1965).

51. For details, see Bayerische Staatskanzlei, *Verwaltungsreform III* (Munich, 1973), 14–82.

52. See Landtag, *LT Drucksache 7/1445*, 27 December 1971, esp. 34 ff. A chronology of the several waves of committee proposals and hearings can be found in Reigl et al., *Kommunale Gliederung*, 35–37.

53. The "guiding figure" (*Richtzahl*) for the new counties was only 80,000, which should be contrasted to the post-reform averages of more densely-populated *Länder* such as Rhineland Palatinate 102,000, Schleswig-Holstein 156,000, Hesse 165,000, Baden-Württemberg (with twice the population density of Bavaria) 200,000, and North Rhine Westphalia 300,000–365,000. See Reigl et al., *Kommunale Gliederung*, 33–34 and the tables on 44–46. Lower Saxony favored an average size of 155,000.

54. Ibid., 30–32.

55. Ibid., 32. See also the principles for county reform spelled out in Baden-Württemberg, Innenministerium, *Denkmodell der Landesregierung zur Kreisreform in Baden-Württemberg,* (Stuttgart, 1969), 7–8; and "Gutachten zur Kreisreform," *Staatsanzeiger für Baden-Württemberg,* July 1970, 67, Supplement, 10–15, where communal and state administrators aired their somewhat differing views.

56. See the descriptions in Landkreisverband Bayern, *Die bayerischen Landkreise und ihr Verband* (Munich, 1978), 206–207, 212–213, and 218–219. Weissenburg remained county seat but lost its independence from the county administration.

57. Population was a necessary but not a sufficient criterion of the surviving independent cities, and this is even more true of the *Große Kreisstädte* that are frequently outranked in population by ordinary towns.

58. Here again, the territorial reform of Baden-Württemberg permits comparisons: Its sixty-three rural and nine urban counties were reduced to twenty-five new counties of at least 130,000 population, including four of the nine cities that were henceforth known as Large County Towns, as in the case of Esslingen, once a county seat of its own county. The government also offered to help the demoted cities by locating certain state agencies there. Only five independent cities remained, namely Stuttgart, Karlsruhe, Mannheim, Freiburg, and Heidelberg.

59. See Bayerisches Staatsministerium des Innern, *Gutachten zum Stadt-Umland-Problem in Bayern*, December 1974; and *Gebietsreform*, 11.

60. See Bayern, Landtag, *LT Drucksache 7/330*; and the final version GV Bl., 27 July 1971, 247.

61. Regarding the intimate connection between the drawing of new VG or EG boundaries and the new school reform districts, see also *Bavarian Report 1971*, 184.

62. See Reigl et al., *Kommunale Gliederung*, 20–22, 26.

63. German law distinguishes between a corporation of public law, which can be a legal subject, concluding contracts like any EG or county, and a territorial corporation that a VG is not. It rather resembles a cooperative special district, which has to rely on the approval of its member communes for any action.

64. Presumably, the largest or most centrally located commune becomes the seat and gives its name to the VG, but it could also be the name of a shared geographic feature.

65. Special districts and cooperative arrangements beyond the extent of the VG have continued in effect. On the foregoing, see Bayerisches Innenenministerium, *Verwaltungsgemeinschaft in Bayern*, December 1973, 8–14.

66. Member communes below 1,000 inhabitants are represented by their mayor and one council member, those between 1,000 and 1,999 by the mayor and two councilors, and those over 2,000 by the mayor and three council persons, and so on.

67. The classification commonly expected is the *gehobener Beamtendienst* (elevated civil service) rather than the lower service or the highest classification.

68. See *Jahrbuch Bayern 81*, 287; and Reigl et al., *Kommunale Gliederung*, appendix. Since the "reform of the reform" of 1979 freed about two hundred member communes and dissolved forty-eight VGs, the 1978 statistics differ considerably.

69. An EG is also desirable in less densely settled areas that have a clear central community.

70. The 1979 "reform of the reform" of Minister President Strauss was a major factor in granting EG stature to nearly two hundred VG member communes ranging from under two thousand inhabitants to over five thousand. The twenty-five independent and larger cities are also EGs.

Chapter 4

THE IMPLEMENTATION OF THE REFORM

They came at three in the morning in two trucks full of uniformed men with side arms at the ready. Several county (*Kreis*) officials stood by in the dull light of the early hours as the doors of the old village Rathaus of Wolpertingen (not its real name) were broken and forced open. They rifled desks and jimmied the locks on the doors of a bookcase. Finally they removed all the records and accounts of the small rural commune, loaded them into their vehicles, and left before the dawn was breaking upon a handful of stunned villagers awakened by the noise and standing around at a safe distance. A prosperous farm village of less than a thousand souls, Wolpertingen was supposed to be annexed by the nearby town of Retschhausen, a rapidly growing community of mostly working-class families that had always been viewed with distaste and distrust by every self-respecting Wolpertinger. "We are not going to let them steal our rich village and give it to the spendthrifts of Retschhausen," one prominent Wolpertinger was quoted in the papers. Wolpertingen was far from rich, but it had husbanded its resources with care and foresight while everyone "knew" of the poor management of the neighboring town.

The proud Wolpertingers tried to fight annexation every way they could. Finally, when they had exhausted all other avenues of redress, they organized teams of stouthearted men armed with pitchforks and other farm implements to guard their Rathaus against attempts to seize the most visible symbol of their autonomy. County and state officials were turned back with hints of force and barnyard language that, in another age, would alone have brought serious charges of rebellion and *Beamten-*

beleidigung (insulting a civil servant) from a list of justiciable offenses. Officialdom decided to avoid a direct confrontation even though it had the law on its side. Instead, they decided to ignore the rebellion, outwait the Wolpertinger vigilantes, and then, suddenly, to carry out their successful *coup de main*, leaving the Wolpertingers to fume in impotent rage.

The threat of violent confrontation between the good citizens of Wolpertingen and the armed might of the state of Bavaria was fortunately avoided here and elsewhere as the state forced small communes to merge into more viable units. In most other cases, in fact, potential conflicts never escalated to the point of vigilante guards bearing pitchforks even though the wrath of the Wolpertingers was not unique. It is true that Bavarian officialdom had conspired to deprive disgruntled communities of most normal opportunities of legal and political recourse against the forced mergers, beginning with the removal of the requirement of a referendum for all territorial changes from the 1952 Local Government Statute (*Gemeindeordnung*). On the other hand, we must not overlook the fact that the mergers of micro-communes were supposed to be in their own best interest. Still, such a massive intervention in the basic democratic right of people to maintain their own local government is a serious breach of democratic faith and of the right to self-determination spelled out in the West German Basic Law (constitution) of 1949.[1] We need to weigh carefully the long-range goals of this local territorial reform against the patent short-term injustices of such coercion.

Implementation of the Local Reform

The actual implementation, following the early, voluntary mergers, took place in three different stages, not counting the discussion in the news media. These stages also became the battleground for challenges to the reorganization plans. The voluntary merger phase was to end 1975[2] and, by 1 May 1978, the whole reform would be completed by government fiat and sealed with local elections in the merged or federated new constituencies. The elections actually took place in March, *before* the reform, so that newly elected officials could be on hand by 1 May. Part of the ensuing struggle continued through administrative channels down through the districts and county governments to the local mayors and councils. Another part took place in the *Landtag* (state diet), even though an additional law (1975) had made sure that the mandated mergers below the county level could be effected by executive ordinance.[3] Nevertheless, in early 1976, the Landtag Committee on Constitutional Questions and Local Government had received some 282 petitions regarding the communal reform and, in thirty-six cases, decided to amend the plans. In March of the same year, the Ministry of the Interior also passed an ordinance decreeing minor changes in the boundaries among Bavaria's seven districts, which affected some communal and county boundaries. The district governments then each passed their ordinances for county-by-county communal reform. The *Landtag* received copies of these ordinances as well as two further bills to facilitate the territorial reform and the future redistribution of functions upon the newly created local entities.[4] Finally, the *Landtag* passed the law to hold local elections in the new units on 5 March 1978 and on 1 May of the same year the communal reform went into effect.

There was yet a third stage of conflict on which complaints about the communal reform were brought and resolved, namely the courts—despite all barriers to judicial challenges. The Bavarian Administrative Court handed down its decision confirming the legality of the concept of this reform. Already in late 1976, following 122 lawsuits by communes dissatisfied with the reform in their particular cases, the court granted fifteen complaints (one for lack of a hearing) and induced six plaintiffs to withdraw their suits. All of these trials involved on-site visits by the court, and the appearance before it of both sides. The court evidently accepted the reform in principle and appeared to find for the plaintiff only if it could be demonstrated that the planners had ignored their own guidelines. Among other things, the court held that VG member communes had no right to appeal the choice of the VG seat. Seven of the communes filed a second suit after the first suit was denied and fourteen went on to the Bavarian Constitutional Court when the Administrative Court turned them down. Early in 1978, the Administrative Court struck down a request by four communes to postpone the 1978 elections, seconded a few days later by the Bavarian Constitutional Court, which rejected a part of a class action suit (*Sammelpopularklage*) with the same objective.[5]

The class action had been submitted by a group of several hundred mayors, including the mayor of Türkenfeld, scheduled to be part of a VG Grafrath (near Fürstenfeldbruck). The group was known as the *Aktionsgemeinschaft Demokratische Gemeindegebietsreform Bayern* (ADGGB), or the Türkenfeld Circle. By November 1977, the ADGGB had collected nearly forty thousand signatures to put an initiative on the ballot to change the Bavarian Constitution (Art. 11) and force the government to submit the communal reform to the people. Two months later, 211 ADGGB communes submitted their class action suit to have the reform declared an unconstitutional violation of democratic procedure. But the court declared the reform act and, in particular, the new institution of the administrative union (VG) unobjectionable and, in the end, threw out the entire class action. Some of the unhappy plaintiffs of the Türkenfeld Circle ominously pointed to the date of the decision, 20 April 1978—Hitler's birth-day—and proclaimed it the death knell of communal liberty. As we shall see below, this was not yet the end of legal actions to reverse or alter the outcome of the reform,[6] nor was it the end of political challenges.

In 1979, in fact, the incoming new administration of Minister President Franz Josef Strauss decided to yield to the multiple pressures and carry out a "reform of the reform," or "*Korrektur*" involving 53 of the 392 VGs. There had been much criticism of the many exceptions to the five thousand minimum population stipulated for both the EGs and the VGs. There were even some EGs with less than two thousand inhabitants. Now Strauss promised to consider well-reasoned—some critics said "well-lobbied" or "of the right political party membership," that is of Strauss's party, the Christian Social Union (CSU)—challenges. The challengers could claim such attributes as a sufficient tax base, potential for growth, and available administrative staff for their community's independence. After acrimonious debate in committee, the *Landtag* voted along partisan lines, ninety-seven to fifty-seven, in favor of the "reform of the reform." One hundred and ninety-eight communes thus regained their independence, although the protests over allegedly one-sided decisions never stopped. The opposition wanted the same criteria to apply to all communes but the government was in no mood to open the floodgates again. Minister President Strauss also favored a number of small Alpine resorts with tiny year-round populations but large numbers of seasonal tourists who were allowed to ignore the stringent rules.

The Reform in Middle Franconia

It may be appropriate at this point to show the impact of the communal reform on the fifteen Franconian communes we described in chapters 1 and 2. Table A12 in the Appendix shows:

(a) the number of separate communes that still existed in 1966;
(b) the considerable reduction of these numbers occurring at the time of the county reform 1971–1972, or earlier;
(c) the VGs formed and their seats;
(d) the number of member communes in each; and
(e) the changes, if any, brought by the "reform of the reform" in 1980.

The table speaks for itself: these seven areas went from 131 separate communes, many of them micro-communes indeed, to seven VGs with a total of 40 member communes in 1978. The *Korrektur* then increased the number of VGs to eight and gave three member communes, Merkendorf St., Arberg M., and Langfurth EG status. These three new EGs had the following populations: Langfurth 1,885, Merkendorf St. 2,100, and Arberg M. 2,005—the first two also grew about 5 percent in the following decade. They were hardly of the size demanded by the functional requirements envisioned by the reform. *Stadt* Merkendorf, in fact, had already been turned down once by the Constitutional Court.

Looking at the observable impact of the communal reform in the early 1980s, it appeared that the internal integration of the member communes, in other words the very first step of the reform, was often still far from complete in 2000, less so than the institutionalization of the new counties and VGs. Most of the citizenry of the consolidated member communes still identified somewhat with their original place name and partial community, sometimes to the point of insisting that the old place name rather than that of the larger member commune be on the personal identification card carried by each adult. As one of the mayors put it, "each partial commune (*Ortsteil*) has a mentality of its own. The reform cannot influence this." Another mayor opined that it wasn't that partial communes thought of each other as rivals, yet they were "of course" on the lookout so their old community received its share. Many of the old Bavarian communes joined by the reform were known to have ancient conflicts or grudges that then became the main reason for the communes to bring lawsuits or turn to the incoming state administration for relief against the unloved merger. There is, for instance, such an ancient conflict between old Steinsfeld and the communes (now *Ortsteile*) Gattenhofen and Bettwar, the causes of which have long been forgotten. In the 1978 elections, the mayoral candidate for greater Steinsfeld—who had been the long-time mayor of Gattenhofen—received only 12 of 360 votes from old Steinsfeld. However, he was confident of doing much better next time by force of his personality and the benefits of the merger for both old communities. The mayor of another hamlet happily reported that a new church choir had now been formed from all parts of his enlarged member commune, which he interpreted as a first sign that the merger had "taken."

The Formation of VGs

The formation of a VG in West Middle Franconia was a complex multilateral process involving far more than the suggestions of the *Landrat* and the fulfillment of the legal requirements. Many small communities began to negotiate early for mergers just to reach the one thousand–person minimum for members of a VG. Their willingness to merge was sometimes facilitated by the approaching retirement age of their mayors, or their willingness to retire prematurely, as with Oberscheckenbach and Habel-see, which agreed readily to join Ohrenbach once the fate of their old mayors was no longer an obstacle. It is worth noting that their communal councils evidently did not receive the same degree of consideration as the old mayors. The patterns of long tenure and near-unanimity in mayoral voting further underline the traditionally patriarchal nature (*père de famille*) of this office. Frequently, mergers were favored also by the certainty of the reform and the thought that during the voluntary phase it might still be possible to get one's way rather than having to accept the plans of outsiders. Bruckberg nearly missed the opportunity for early negotiations and was faced with possible annexation to Weihenzell when, in 1976, VG memberships were worked out for both.

The complex and often impenetrable negotiations that led up to the formation of a VG were easiest among hamlets faced with only the choice between annexation into an EG and membership in a VG. In that case, of course, a VG was preferred—witness the case of Bruckberg. In 1977, Mitteleschenbach was the object of unsuccessful annexation schemes by both Wolframs-Eschenbach and Windsbach, a nearby dwarf *Stadt* of 769 residents in 1972. Then came the oversized VG Triesdorf I of 1978, which was dissolved again a year later and replaced by the VG of Wolframs-Eschenbach and Mitteleschenbach, and a VG Triesdorf II of Ornbau and Weidenbach. In the vicinity of Rothenburg, greater Adelshofen strove to avoid incorporation into Rothenburg, which would have destroyed its overwhelmingly agricultural character and swamped it with tourists. A VG with enlarged Steinsfeld and stagnant Ohrenbach as well as five other enlarged member communes—Gebsattel, Geslau, Insingen, Neusitz, and Windelsbach, all ranging from eight hundred to fourteen hundred inhabitants each—was more attractive. In view of the likely rivalries among otherwise similar communes, the formation of a VG was facilitated also by naming it Rothenburg and placing its administrative seat in that town even though Rothenburg itself is, of course, not a member.

Joining a VG was a much harder choice for communes that hoped to be allowed to continue as a unitary commune (EG). Thus *Stadt* Ornbau sued unsuccessfully against inclusion in the VG Triesdorf I but was denied because it had neither the population (1,246 in 1972, and 1,484 in 1989) nor the tax capacity of an EG. When this VG was dissolved, Ornbau once more tried to attain independence, but was instead put into the new VG Triesdorf II together with the market town Weidenbach, which obtained the administrative seat.[7] Wolframs-Eschenbach was foiled in its attempt to absorb Mitteleschenbach and, alternatively, to become an EG. In the end, it had to settle for the name and seat of a new VG Wolframs-Eschenbach, with Mitteleschenbach as a member commune. Sometimes the formation of a VG was made to depend mostly on reaching agreement about the location of the administrative seat. Markt Berolzheim, for example, agreed to join the VG Altmühltal only on condition that it would become the VG seat. But Meinheim won because of its central location between the two even though it was much smaller (825 residents, and 833 in 1989) than Markt Berolzheim (1,157, and 1,250 in 1989). There may also have been political considerations: Two decades before 1978, Markt Berolzheim had an SPD mayor,[8] a rarity among small communes in a CSU-dominated state.

The status of Röckingen was put in limbo since, in 1975, the community voted for incorporation into Wassertrüdingen (*Stadt*) but then changed its mind a year later, opting for membership in the VG Hesselberg instead. The state authorities agreed to the second choice, but there was a lawsuit by Wassertrüdingen that insisted that Röckingen abide by its earlier decision.[9] Langfurth had also been a member of the same VG, in fact its seat, but regained independence as an EG because of its size (1,981 in 1989 and 2,148 in 2008), although its tax revenues were only 71 percent of comparable EG communes.

What benefits did the communes receive for being willing to merge or join a VG during the voluntary phase, aside from the incentive grants? Most of the communes received no additional buildings or personnel positions. Weihenzell got a new administrative building to house the VG seat. There was also a new kindergarten and the bus connections were improved. In Meinheim, another VG seat, the old city hall was enlarged for this purpose. Some mayors who became VG presidents received additional personnel. In greater Adelshofen, the old commune of Grossharbach was hooked up to the Franconia Water Supply (FWF) and Tauberzell and Tauberscheckenbach were given a sewer system. Real estate and business taxes were usually made uniform at the time of incorporation, either by adjusting them to the level of the receiving commune or at a compromise level. In VGs where there had been some rivalry for the VG seat, the mutual envy and suspicion was not completely laid to rest but sometimes it was attenuated by such devices as for instance giving Wolframs-Eschenbach the VG seat but the mayor of Mitteleschenbach the presiding role. Having the seat was considered quite a boon because it came with at least one middle-level (*gehobener*) civil servant and better facilities at no extra cost.

Examining how a new—or old and moribund—center came to reemerge from the territorial reform also tells us how the many micro-communes of Bavaria lost their autonomy and were swallowed up like inferior stars by the black holes in their galaxies. Among our fifteen Franconian communities, many a once-independent micro-commune survived only as a partial commune (*Ortsteil*) of a larger neighbor. The number of *Ortsteile* per larger commune bears witness to the extent of the earlier dispersion of population and the intensity of the integration process at work, whether it was voluntary or mandated by the state or the county prefect. Weihenzell, east of Ansbach, for example, acquired no fewer than twenty-two *Ortsteile*, each with its name and that of Weihenzell on its local signs. It nearly doubled its population to 2,846 (2007). Stadt Merkendorf of the original VG Triesdorf I, but not one of our fifteen, has thirteen *Ortsteile* and has become an EG. Steinsfeld near Rothenburg o. T. and Wolframs-Eschenbach have ten each and Langfurth nine. But there are also some like Ohrenbach (pop. 645) and Ornbau St. with only six each, or Mitteleschenbach with two. Even tiny Röckingen (pop. 756) has five *Ortsteile*. The sheer number of these *Ortsteile*, of course, goes far to explain how Bavaria's well over 7,000 communes with a population of less than three thousand shrank down to 1,279 (1978) and ultimately 1,226 (1987).

Ortsteile of Wolframs-Eschenbach

Let us focus on the case of Wolframs-Eschenbach that grew from its marginal population size before the reform (1,774 residents) to the respectable size of 2,911 and the status of the seat of an eponymous VG. We

Illustration 4.1. Wolframs-Eschenbach in 1919: Old town walls, upper gate (on the left); Ortsteile beyond picture.
Source: J. B. Kurz, *Wolframs-Eschenbach: Kulturbilder aus einer deutschen Kleinstadt* (1919).

have an aerial picture of the post-reform town, in the middle its walled
old town visible from its Lower Gate to the turreted Upper Gate. The
aerial view shows that much of the area annexed to the original town
consists of rural hamlets miles away with but few houses. The population
of Wolframs-Eschenbach St. consequently rose to 2,525, i.e., 87 percent
of the total, a hegemonic position by any measure.

The next largest *Ortsteil* is named Biederbach with 111 residents on
twenty-five lots, including nine cattle farms, seven full-time. There is a
small 100-year-old chapel and, until a few years ago, Biederbach had its
own grocery store, the only one among the smaller *Ortsteile*. A village
inn, Schuster, also went out of business and community events are now
held at a Reiterhof (horse ranch) Geidner. The *Ortsteil* still has its own
voluntary fire brigade, but it gave up its old firehouse along with three
other communal buildings in exchange for a new firehouse, a children's
playground and a soccer *Bolzplatz*. Biederbach has its own hunting association, but its Protestants have to go to church in neighboring Merkendorf
St., as do many in Catholic Wolframs-Eschenbach.

Adelmannsdorf, the next largest *Ortsteil* (sixty-nine residents) used to
be joined to what is now another *Ortsteil*, Selgenstadt (fifty-one) with
which its still shares the hunting association and a voluntary fire brigade.
The Village Renewal Program (*Dorferneuerung*) of Bavaria financed the
building of a new communal *Gemeindehaus* (with a children's playground)
that houses Adelmannsdorf's fire equipment, agricultural scales, and refrigeration storage. There is a village inn, Wagner's, and every May a May
Pole is erected. There are eight cattle farms, five full-time, but twenty
years ago, Selgenstadt alone had fourteen cattle farms. The latter *Ortsteil*
also has an inn, owned by the Keims family, which serves as a location for
public meetings.

Another rural *Ortsteil*, Waizendorf (sixty-two residents) in 1972 split
by mutual consent along religious lines from neighboring Gerbersdorf.
Waizendorf shares fire protection with Wolframs-Eschenbach, but retains
its own hunting club. Since the village inn, Teubner, closed, the Village
Renewal Program helped the village build a communal room into the
existing *Gemeindehaus* (city hall), which otherwise stores machinery and
refrigeration facilities. There are seven cattle farms, all of them full-time.
In 2007, Waizendorf reported proudly that at long last a bicycle path had
been completed to Wolframs-Eschenbach. Previously, it seems, the necessary rights of way had not been available.

Finally, there is the *Ortsteil* Wöltendorf (thirty-six residents), which
used to be together with the *Ortsteile* Reutern (forty-five residents), as well
as the Sallmannshof and the Bölleins- and Utzenmühle (altogether another fourteen residents), for a total of ninety-five residents and five cattle

farms, four full-time. Their earlier rural micro-communes apparently gave up their lives in 1972 and, one by one, joined Wolframs-Eschenbach during the voluntary phase of the territorial reform. Wöltendorf still shares its voluntary fire brigade and a hunting association with Reutern. A *Gemeindehaus* was renovated. The two mills and the Sallmannshof hamlet are at some distance from the rest. All these cattle farms, of course, have added a considerable agricultural element to Wolframs-Eschenbach, even though they may not figure highly in its population. In any case this allowed the town to apply for funds to the Village Renewal Program, which has long assisted with ameliorating rural neglect and poverty conditions. All the rebuilt *Gemeindehaus* structures probably needed it badly. Joining an urban community both highlighted rural neglect and helped villages to partake of such urban resources as roads, water supply, and orderly planning. Wolframs-Eschenbach also benefited greatly from the state's Urban Renewal Program (*Stadterneuerungsprogramm*), which funded not only repairs to the infrastructure but also historic preservation projects. Its present glory reflects this aid in splendid facades, especially along its Main Street. It is also worth mentioning the prevalence of the word *Dorf* (village) in so many of the *Ortsteil* names. The recurrence of earlier patterns and coexistence in these *Ortsteil* descriptions should also remind us that the great reform of 1978–1980 was just a phase in a long history of local territorial changes.

The incorporation of additional areas and population, of course, added to the workload of the new *Bürgermeisters* of each VG member who had to take over some of the functions of their several predecessors in each formerly autonomous part. The work also became more complicated as the newly incorporated parts often had different kinds of problems, including in some cases high indebtedness and neglected conditions. The presiding mayor of greater Steinsfeld began to make two visits a week to all the incorporated areas of his commune. As he made his rounds, he now covered a distance of about seventeen miles roundtrip each time, hardly the cozy little village of old. On the other hand, the pooling of administrative functions considerably lightened the workload of the honorary *Bürgermeisters* of the member communes. Some mayors were glad because over the years their administrative duties had required more and more record-keeping and legal expertise. Others began to miss their functions, although they now had the new go-between role described above. The constituents usually came to the mayor they knew for advice before approaching the strangers at the administrative seat of the VG. The city of Ornbau began to maintain a part-time secretary to take care of minor business on the spot and the mayor of Wolframs-Eschenbach even used to keep open the old city hall[10] and to pay for such a secretary out of his own pocket during the time the first VG Triesdorf had its seat in distant Weidenbach.

In wine-growing Weigenheim and Ippesheim, which had joined the VG Uffenheim already in 1974, special arrangements prevailed. For example, the mail from the state authorities now went directly to the member commune Weigenheim where most business was taken care of before it went to the VG administration in Uffenheim, rather than vice versa. Ippesheim still issued its own identity passes, a function normally handled by the VG. Some mayors also still performed weddings although the change in status had to be recorded by the civil registry of the VG administration. The work of the community councils, incidentally, did not change noticeably in quantity although they, too, tended to be thrust more into the role of mediators between constituent interests and the VG administration. Their sessions became more formal over the years and minutes were kept regularly since the reform.

The presiding mayor of a VG, of course, now had a greatly increased workload, which required some knowledge of conditions in the entire VG and a detailed knowledge of relevant law. This latter requirement had at first motivated some communities before the reform to opt for a "professional mayor"—one with civil service qualifications—in the hope that this might qualify them to become the seat of their VG. However, of the eleven VGs in Landkreis Ansbach, for example, only four had professional presiding mayors and one was a civil servant to begin with.[11] The presiding mayor has knowledgeable civil servants at his elbow but may not wish to appear dependent on their legal advice alone. After all, he already faces an uphill struggle every day against the alleged "Sachzwang," the standard bureaucratic argument that the "objective conditions of each decision" prejudice the choice and greatly restrict the political options open to the politicians.

After the Reforms

So far, the common fear among the member communes that the VG seat would become the new center of social, political, and cultural life also seemed not to have been borne out although there was at least a likelihood of long-term developments in this direction. No obvious shifts of infrastructure and no particular increases of cultural activities at the VG seat seem to have occurred as yet. In the VG Uffenheim, for example, it was still only the clubs of the member communes who fielded concerts in *Schloss* Uffenheim or entertained at the hospital and senior home. There was, perhaps, more of a willingness to share facilities now, as with the community of Weihenzell, which permitted the Table Tennis Club of

Bruckberg to use its indoor hall since Bruckberg lacked one. Even after decades, it may be still too early to assess the lasting social patterns that have been evolving under the new system.

Whether the fifteen mayors of our communes regarded the reform as a whole as appropriate or not depended largely on their concrete chances of independent survival as a commune. Those whose communes could be spared the fate of absorption into a nearby EG by joining a VG now put their trust in the continuation of the VG system. Those who strongly believed they could have survived by themselves as an EG were more skeptical and expected the VGs not to last. On the whole, the centralization of administrative services was viewed in a positive light provided the personnel were truly competent. On the other hand, mayors and citizenry expressed regrets at the degree of bureaucratization and the greater distance, both spatial and psychological, to get to the seat of administration. Some mayors of member communes tried to make up for this in small ways: in Burk, the citizens could pick up their new passports at the mayor's office and, in Röckingen, he/she had the local registration forms for them, all this in order to maintain the highly prized closeness (*Bürgernähe*) of local government to the citizenry.

The appreciation for the VG system also involved other aspects that cannot be ignored: the 1971–1972 formation of much larger counties in place of the small ones of the 1960s[12] had often placed the county offices much farther away. The VG administration now helped citizens to prepare all kinds of administrative applications and requests to the counties and state agencies, which the communes of old could not do. Considering how social change has broadened the circles in which most people move, even the size of a VG seemed proportionally not much larger than a scattered old rural commune in the horse-and-buggy days, at least in terms of getting around. As long as the mayors of member communes cooperated among themselves and with their VG, there was no reason to mourn the loss of personal contact with the citizenry, which continues to be maintained faithfully by mayors and community councils of the member communes. And there is, of course, the superior financial and planning capacity of the VG office, which has all the expertise and resources required for the solution of most of its own local problems.

Given the enlarged communes, the VGs, and the likewise enlarged EGs, there appeared to be but one thing left to do to complete this process: the state government must return some of the communal functions that have migrated over the years to counties, special districts, and higher levels of local government—for example, garbage removal and preservation of historic monuments—and include the EGs and VGs in other functions that the state had long delegated to local levels above the communes, such as zoning and licensing. This *functional reform* was the logi-cal complement of the chief aim of the *territorial reform*, namely of the creation of local units more capable of performing important local gov-ernment services, and an appropriate governmental response to the three decades of social change we have described in previous chapters. There is also a parallel of sorts here to the most glaring defect of Montgelas's centralization of functions in 1808, and their return to the communes in 1818 and since.

Summing up the Reform

The author of the 1978 reform, former Minister Bruno Merk probably was not too far off the mark when, in his letter to me in 1998, he claimed that "developmental realities had meanwhile relativized the original ob-jections to the territorial reform. The changing opinions are reflected in the rising number of twenty- and twenty-five year jubilees of the newly formed communes and the reports accompanying them." By 2008, less than 1 percent of Bavarians lived in independent communes below one thousand residents, 7 percent in those between one and two thousand, and about one-fifth in communes between two and five thousand, for a total of 27.7 percent under five thousand. Occasional changes were still going on then as court decisions or political bargaining amended even the supposedly ultimate[13] form of the local territorial reform. Nevertheless, we need to come to a point of at least assessing the broad outlines of what has been done and compare it to the reforms of the other large West Ger-man *Länder*, say, as of the 1990s. For this purpose we have prepared sev-eral tables summarizing the territorial, population, and political changes and putting them side-by-side with those of the other seven extensive Länder[14] of the West German Federal Republic (tables A13–A15).

Our table A13 shows at first the gradual patterns of migration and urbanization over the century prior to 1970, a period notable not only for metropolitan growth, but also for the conspicuous increase of places between two and fifty thousand inhabitants. It was this development in Bavaria that, aside from the twenty-two major and potential major cen-ters designated by the regional planners, gave the seventy-five middle centers—and the twenty-eight lower centers with some middle center functions—the critical population mass. Setting these centers in declin-ing order side-by-side with the communes of 1970, we can account for al-most all the ones above ten thousand in population, and a few below that line. Add the lower centers and they correspond roughly to the remain-ing 1970 communes above five thousand. Add the small centers and you have most 1970 communes above a population size of three thousand.

This three thousand mark, then, could be considered the critical lower limit for a rational territorial reform in Bavaria. Setting a population size of five thousand as the "guiding figure" for both the EGs and VGs, in a manner of speaking, might have given all local administrative units a threshold from which to aim at lower center functions.

The 1978 reform instead aimed considerably lower than the targeted levels: Even though the EGs between 3,000 and 4,999 are not broken down further by size in the table, it is easy to see what has happened. A quick check of the district Upper Bavaria alone shows that about 43 percent (44.9 percent in1989) of the communes given EG status there in 1978 were below 4,000—including eleven (5 percent) below 2,000 (1,700 in 1989 [5.9 percent]),[15] twenty-four (10 percent) between 2,000 and 2,500 (thirty-one or 10.5 percent in 1989), and twenty-eight (11.5 percent) between 2,500 and 3,000 (thirty-four or 11.6 percent in 1989) in population size. The willingness of the state to go below one thousand for the member communes of a VG in a mere 20 percent of the total seems far less consequential since they had no more administrative functions that might be jeopardized by a lack of capacity. The overwhelming majority of VG member communes, in any case, was near or above one thousand.

The VGs formed as of May 1978, with only 16 percent below a total population of four thousand (22 percent in 1989)—given a "guiding figure" of five thousand with allowances made for sparsely settled rural areas—also seem within tolerable margins considering the alternative, that is the status quo ante. After all, the differentials in Bavarian settlement patterns were extreme, which may explain the glaring county-by-county differences in the ratios of EGs to VGs: Generally speaking, alpine counties with a lot of tourism—counties Berchtesgadener Land, Bad Tölz-Wolfratshausen, Miesbach, or Starnberg—and densely settled metropolitan hinterland counties such as Landkreis Munich, have a preponderance of or nothing but EGs, including some rather isolated resorts of under-sized, year-round populations.

On the other hand, there are counties with as many or more VGs than EGs, such as counties Erding, Landsberg on the Lech, Weilheim-Schongau, and Rottal on the Inn in Old Bavaria, Cham and Neustadt on the Waldnab in Upper Palatinate. Similarly the Franconian counties of Bamberg, Forchheim, Kulmbach, Neustadt on the Aisch/Bad Windsheim, Kitzingen, Rhön-Grabfeld, and Würzburg, and the Suebian counties of Dillingen on the Danube and Donau-Ries, or of Lindau, East Allgäu and Lower Allgäu in the southwest. These counties are typically agricultural and sparsely settled.[16] Counties such as Ansbach and Weissenburg-Gunzenhausen of the preceding chapters are not even on this list, despite their fitting the stereotype, perhaps because of the presence of many old historic towns that (barely) qualified as EGs. These are also the areas where many of the old pre-1971 counties were far below population averages and capacity—if not area—and had to be merged with others, which may account for the fact that the reduction of the number of counties to conform to a more or less standard population size was much greater in the districts of Upper Palatinate, Lower Bavaria, and Lower and Middle Franconia, than in Upper Bavaria.

The 1979 *Korrektur* (table A14), not to mention the piecemeal changes since then, further lowered the territorial thresholds for EGs and weakened some VGs. Many of the new EGs, especially in Alpine areas (but not only there) were below two thousand or between two and three thousand—sixty new EGs between one and two thousand, and eighty-four between two and three thousand—so that now well over half (58.4 percent) of the total EGs were below the "guiding figure" of five thousand, as compared to 50.5 percent in 1978. The formula for the *Korrektur*, among other things, allowed for a minimal size of two thousand and permitted a shortfall up to 10 percent on even this limit, provided there were such other attributes present as a certain tax capacity or tourist volume measured in overnight stays. In some instances, a quick splicing job—for example, of the member communes Babensham (pop. 1,358) and Kling (821) of the VG Eiselfing in Rosenheim County—produced a semblance of conformity to the rules for an EG. In many cases, it was simply a matter of overruling earlier, carefully documented decisions, as with Merkendorf St. and Arberg M. in Ansbach county, where the change left in place of a large VG Triesdorf I (10,855) created two VGs of about thirty-three hundred population each. The number of VGs over five thousand statewide, in fact, dropped by seventy-two and those under three thousand tripled (table A14). The question remains in the cases of both undersized EGs and VGs whether it was true, indeed, that a "guiding figure" of five thousand was necessary to achieve the desired capacity and, if so, why the reformers seem to have lacked the courage of their convictions.

It may be helpful at this point to compare the Bavarian reform to those in the other West German *Länder*, bearing in mind the differences in population density and reform design. As will be observed (table A15), some *Länder* abolished, or did not preserve their VG-type arrangements although they may still have some major communal or metropolitan co-operative organizations not listed in our table. All of them reduced their number of rural counties, some more than others, and strove for a uniform county size. But average Bavarian counties are clearly smaller than most, with over half below a size of one hundred thousand inhabitants in contrast to, say, twice that size in North Rhine Westphalia.[17] The sizes of the remaining twenty-five independent cities in Bavaria also are notably smaller than those of the independent cities left in the wake of the reforms elsewhere: eight of the Bavarian cities are below fifty thousand; only six above one hundred thousand (eight in 1990). By comparison, all twenty-three North Rhine Westphalian cities are above one hundred thousand inhabitants. Even the most comparable *Länder*, Lower Saxony and Rhineland Palatinate, gave their 164 VG-like municipal federations a size of ten thousand or more, while choosing to leave many micro-communes intact, including some of only a few hundred residents.[18]

East German Community Sizes

How do the communes of the five new East German *Länder* compare with Bavaria and West Germany? The German Democratic Republic under-went an Administrative Reform in 1952, which abolished the *Länder* level in favor of fifteen districts, including East Berlin, and turned the country into a unitary state. After German unification in 1990, these five *Länder*, more or less, were restored prior to admission to the West German federation, and East Berlin was merged with West Berlin. At that time there were 8,505 West German communes—after two decades of territorial consolidation in the West—and 7,621 in the East, with a total population of only one-fourth of that of West Germany. In the West, only 6 percent of the people were still living in communities of two thousand or less, but in the East 24 percent. On the average, eastern *Länder* had about five urban and thirty-seven rural *Kreise* and over 1,500 communes each. There had been some consolidation since 1972 when there were still 8,777 communes, including 7,689 rural communes with less than two thousand residents each—in fact 4,289 of these were no larger than five hundred and another 2,260 between five hundred and one thousand[19]—a distribution rather similar to Bavaria before the communal reforms. From 1973, there were also communal associations and federations. Bavaria's low population density (in relation to the rest of West Germany) also resembles that of the former GDR, which ranges from a very low level in Mecklenburg-Vorpommern and Brandenburg to nearly twice the Bavarian level in Saxony.

But here the similarity of the communes ends because the pre-unifica-tion system of the GDR was so very different. The economic basis of local autonomy was gradually taken away and, from 1961 and 1965, integrated into the total planning apparatus and command economy of the cen-tralized communist state. The representative assembly of deputies of the cities (*Stadtverordnetenversammlung*) and rural communal assembly (*Ge-meindeversammlung*) and the councils based on them were "elected" with a unitary (communist) list without competition and with no independent representatives. Under "democratic centralism," they were bound by central directives and elected a *Bürgermeister* from their midst. Their basic function was to carry out the decisions made at the center. It was at best a system of administrative decentralization under the tight reins of the communist Socialist Unity (SED) party and the Stasi secret service.[20]

Will the East German *Länder* also take the plunge, sooner or later, and undergo territorial reorganization? Some already have. Thuringia, for example, concluded a territorial reform in conjunction with local elections, sharply reducing the number of counties, enlarging EGs and creating VGs. Most likely others would follow, considering the relative weakness of East German counties and towns as compared to the West and their diminished ability to generate resources. But at first there was formidable opposition from office-holders who sought to retain their positions at any price and feared consolidation of *Kreise* and communes. Many activities that their Western equivalents considered the core of their functions, such as social services, transport, energy, and waste abatement, had long been turned over to the central government. As Wolfgang Seibel has pointed out, moreover, the East German administrative service was very inadequate and required extensive retraining and replacement before it could take on a position equivalent to that of Western civil servants in state and local government.[21]

The purpose of this comparison was to bring out the distinctive character of Bavaria and of its reforms. Regional differences require accommodation and the Bavarian approach was obviously inspired by the sparse settlement patterns of the state. Since the choices involved, moreover, were inherently political, we should also take a closer look at the incidence of protest or resistance to the communal reforms.

Patterns of Reaction to Bavaria's Reform

A reform of this magnitude was bound to provoke resistance even though little of it at first seemed to meet the eye aside from the abortive citizens initiative mentioned above.[22] There was a lot of old-fashioned state paternalism in the sweeping manner in which the Bavarian state decreed and carried out the reform. And some of the reactions rather resembled the ineffectual grumbling of old-time lower officials and subjects citing reasons against the reforms—"*raisonnant*" as it was called in the absolutist age—right in the middle of the torrential wave of environmental protests and citizens initiatives convulsing West Germany in the 1970s.[23] There were, of course, a number of incidents such as the one we described at the outset of this chapter and other protests involving communities at the edge of large cities such as Nuremberg, Ingolstadt, and Augsburg. But on the whole, the citizenry seemed far less upset than were local mayors and communal council members whose positions were in danger of being downgraded or eliminated by the reform and who were interested, for that reason, in exaggerating the adverse popular response to the reform. This may have been true in some cases, but hardly explains away the considerable evidence of popular resonance to the pleas of these officials.

I decided to probe the dimensions of the reactions of officialdom by post-reform interviews with a number of *Landräte* and mayors, and to send out a questionnaire to mayors of a sample of 121 of the original Bavarian communes that had *not* become the seat of a new EG or VG. Using 1975 reorganization maps (which turned out to contain a few errors), I selected communities throughout Bavaria that

(a) had a population over twelve hundred, in fact as large as could be found, and had been above one thousand since 1840 (some only since 1950);

(b) had been given the title of a *Stadt* or *Markt*, or were an important historical site, all likely indicators of a strong sense of identity;

(c) were not at the edge of metropolitan areas;

(d) were nearly as large as, or larger than, the new VG or EG seat;

(e) were rather distant from the new VG or EG seat.

I expected both (d) and (e) to serve as indicators of rivalry and separateness, although the places closest to each other often turned out to be worse rivals than those far apart.

I attempted to select no more than three from any county, but took care also not to miss some of the obvious clusters of likely choices. The selection turned out to include many of the communes that filed lawsuits against the territorial reform which was as strong an indication as I could hope for, of hard feelings about losing out.[24] Questionnaires were mailed to the mayors of record of these communes, with a self-addressed, stamped envelope, in the expectation that this might be the surest way to gather a representative expression of dissatisfaction with the reform. To be sure, a strong sense of local identity, civic independence, or local rivalry might just as well have been found in smaller units. But it seemed to me that, all other circumstances being equal, a certain size might make a commune feel that it deserved better, that it had the capacity to act independently, while smaller units would have less self-confidence.

In the questionnaire I asked the mayors whether they expected, at least, to be reelected to the new communal council and found that a surprisingly large number indeed did. Those who did not often cited advanced age or retirement. One was about to become a *Landrat* (prefect) and two said they chose not to because they had fought the reform. Some may have anticipated finding a niche in the new administration after the reform.[25] Being reelected to the council of the new VG or enlarged EG, of course, could just as well signify a determination to continue the battle against the "winners" of the reform,[26] or at least to defend the best interests of one's original constituents against the encroachments by a majority of outsiders. The mayors were also asked whether anyone in their commune objected to the loss. Close to nine out of ten said so, but for lack of polls[27] or referenda I have no way of gauging how strong this sentiment may really have been.

Table 4.1. Mayoral responses to the question: Do you believe you will be elected to the next communal council?

District	Yes	No	DK/NA
Upper Bavaria	7	4	2
Lower Bavaria	3	–	5
Upper Palatinate	6	–	1
Upper Franconia	3	1	1
Middle Franconia	4	3	1
Lower Franconia	5	3	5
Suebia	2	2	1

Table 4.2. Mayoral responses to the question: Did some of the citizens of your commune object to the reorganization?

District	Yes	No	DK/NA
Upper Bavaria	9	1	1
Lower Bavaria	8	–	–
Upper Palatinate	7	1	–
Upper Franconia	5	–	–
Middle Franconia	9	–	–
Lower Franconia	5	–	–
Suebia	5	–	–

How did the "losers" among the communes—fifty-one of our sample became member communes of VGs and eleven were annexed to unitary communes (EGs)—compare to a random sample of the "winners," that is communes that either remained independent EGs or became the seat of a new VG? The losers were generally more anemic in their population indices, more agricultural, and less characterized by rapid industrialization.[28] They also exhibited inferior per capita tax revenues, which presumably signified their diminished capacity for local functions.

The Mayors' Responses to the Goals

I also presented the mayors of the sample of losing communities with a list of goals that the communal reform was supposed to achieve:

(1) Equal opportunity for all citizens in economic, educational, and cultural pursuits.
(2) Creating a foundation for optimal economic development.
(3) Administrative rationalization by employment of trained professional administrators in place of the untrained honorary personnel of old.
(4) Equal delivery of public services.
(5) Others to be named by the respondents.

Our respondents made hardly any use of the opportunity to name other goals except for the repeated, possibly ironic mention of "bringing government closer to the people." One said "to stop emigration to the big cities." They could also have mentioned the stated goals of preserving open, natural spaces for recreation, preventing "leapfrog" development and despoliation of the countryside, and others.

These goals were presented to our group of mayors for ordinal ranking, which many of them did somewhat unevenly.[29] Quite a few, in fact, wrote into the space provided for the ranking phrases like "We are supposed to become a member of the VG T. and I can see no advantages to that" or "The commune of O. does not expect any improvement in its situation from this." One wrote "local government will be not cheaper but a lot more expensive because there will be fewer honorary functions." Another said, "the reorganization means greater distance to the citizens and more expense."

Table 4.3. Ranking of reform goals by mayors

	1st	2nd	3rd	4th	5th	Index (n)
Equal opportunity	27	12	3	5	1	4.2 (48)
Economic development	9	16	15	3	—	3.7 (43)
Administrative rationalization	9	7	9	12	—	3.4 (37)
Equalize public services	2	5	13	12	1	2.8 (33)
Others	3	2	1	0	3	3.2 (9)

Our question, "Do you think the reform will be able to achieve the goals you consider most important?" received the following responses: fourteen "Yes"; seventeen "Partly, yes"; and twenty-nine "No." One respondent explained his balanced view with the words: "Local administration will become more rational and effective (*schlagkräftiger*), but the often-praised 'closeness to the citizens' will be lost." Another was more hostile: "No, there will be no administrative simplification. On the contrary, the whole state and administrative apparatus will be *even more inflated; administration close to the citizen now pure utopia!* [underlined in red] ... The consequence of reducing citizens' participation will be the development of citizen initiatives." One response took specific issue with each of the suggested goals and argued rather colorfully that the reorganization in the case of his particular VG would have the opposite effect. "Instead of 13 local salaried employees, there would now be 22, etc. There should have been two VGs instead of one."

The skeptical attitudes of the mayors of "losing" communes—many of the mayors themselves expected to continue a career in local government, it will be recalled—also extended to lists of "lost values" we suggested at the end of the questionnaire. The questions were:

(a) Do you suppose the merger of naturally grown communities might lead to the loss of important values, such as historical tradition, communal pride or freedom, self-government, small-town character, or access to local government?
(b) Do you think the reorganization might also have the additional side-effect of changing typical features of local politics (for instance, by bureaucratization, or by the creation of a monopoly of the parties in local politics,[30] or alienation of the citizens from local authority)?

Altogether, four out of five mayors perceived losses and undesirable side effects as described. The write-in responses were sporadic and tended to limit themselves to picking up some of the themes suggested. Some mayors sent me leaflets and even small illustrated books about the ancient history of their towns or villages, many of which date back to the Middle Ages. Of specific mentions, historical unity and tradition, as well as the citizens' alienation from their local government, drew the most. A loss of self-government was next. Bureaucratization and politicization drew only passing attention. One mayor felt that, for his community, membership in a VG rather than absorption into an EG was crucial to saving community values. One respondent opined: "In my experience, the citizen now tends to seek refuge more in associations (*Vereine*) which he sees as a substitute for the loss of political community. ..." Another wrote "I know a large share of the opinions of communes all over Bavaria and, in many cases, the effects of the reform. On the whole, I must conclude that this was not the great work of the century, but rather the screw-up of the century (*Jahrhundertpfusch*)."

Even if we ignore the emotional nature of the responses, which may in part reflect community sentiments, it is obvious that the mayors of these "losing" communes saw far more losses than gains in the reorganization. They rarely distinguished explicitly between the goals of the reform for the whole state (the winners as well as the losers) and the advantages for their particular commune. But there was no mistaking the bottom line of their judgments: The reform goals seemed to them elusive, perhaps not even worthwhile, whereas the values about to be lost were concrete and their loss inevitable.

Criticisms of the Procedures

An obvious target for criticism were the procedures followed in the reform and especially of the limited opportunities of citizens and local officials to participate in the decisions made. I asked this group of mayors:

(a) Do you consider the procedures used in the reorganization to be on the whole appropriate?

(b) Do you feel that the reorganization should have given the citizens of the communes involved more of an opportunity to have their say, for example, through local referenda?

(c) Did some of the citizens of your commune resist the reorganization? If so, for what reasons? (The first half of this question was already mentioned above, linking protests to the mayor's career expectations.)

The responses tended to be negative on the appropriateness of the procedure in general, and positive on the need for more citizen input and on citizen resistance to the reform. This, at least, was the nature of the responses in Old Bavaria (Upper and Lower Bavaria and Upper Palatinate) and Middle Franconia. In Lower and Upper Franconia and Suebia, for some reason, the critics and the supporters of the procedures were more in balance. The comments from these districts, however, were no less stringent: Regarding (a) one Lower Franconian mayor wrote, "the VG was the stupidest solution they could come up with," and another, "they pretended that it was voluntary, when in fact we were being forced." Suebian mayors complained that the will of the citizens was not respected, their solidarity destroyed, and "their right to govern themselves trampled underfoot." The Old Bavarians, who are said to have a comparatively quick temper, had responses such as

"The decisions were made over the heads of the citizenry by the politicians";

"It was not a democratic procedure; the people's will was often ignored";

"The proposals of the *Landrat* offices dominated the proceedings. Those affected by the decisions hardly were given a hearing";

"In the last analysis, the government does as it pleases. The advisory polls were mostly eyewash";

"The will of the inhabitants of our market town was ignored";

"This was not a reform with objective guidelines, but directed by the ... will of a domineering ministerial bureaucracy ... doing favors whenever influential personages were cooking up their own stew";

"These were decisions made at the 'green table.' The ministerial bureaucracy has too much power."

The idea of real referenda was picked up with enthusiasm and especially where there had been an advisory poll on the reform. "Indeed," one mayor wrote, "our poll should have been taken into account in the decision." Another said, "The people should have decided the issue wherever several reasonable possibilities presented themselves. Whatever happened to the idea of a democratic territorial reform?" Democracy was mentioned by many of the critics. Several mayors also wrote something like, "the reform was necessary, but this procedure made for more damage than benefit." Finally, the desideratum of "closeness of local government to the citizen" was said to have been disregarded and the citizens "steamrolled" in many of the write-in comments. Some tied in these complaints with the reasons given for citizen resistance to the reform. Several mayors claimed that overwhelming majorities in the advisory polls had opposed the government solutions and had been simply overruled.

There is one theme in the responses of our group of mayors, finally, that deserves our attention even if it is a swan song for a communal life that is dying out. These are some of the reasons attributed to citizens objecting to the reform:

"as a result of the incorporation in T., a community that grew over many years is disappearing";

"the shattering of communities that have grown over 150 years of tradition";

"in our area, the VG is a step backward because our present government has enough qualified personnel ... and is able to take care of all the needed functions";

"because our commune O. wanted to retain its independence under any circumstances. We could have done it without further ado";

"ninety-eight percent of the citizens felt that our present administration works effectively and cheaply enough";

"W. was financially well off, but now we must share with communes that did not provide so well for themselves";

"because we want to keep our independence";

"because the formation of an EG, given our number of inhabitants, was certainly feasible and would have been the best solution";

"because this old town with so much tradition is to die while they are forming a VG in a place smaller than ourselves, a place without a past and without an old city hall. This green meadow has only 1,200 inhabitants in its core ... and an inn to feed the hungry. ..."

Responses of County and State Officials

Perhaps it would have been worth collecting answers systematically from mayors who presided over the winners as well and, then again, perhaps not. Sour grapes aside, the mayors of losing communes at least had a clear vision of what it was they were losing. The winners more often than not were likely to see the great change from the angle of bigger things to come, perhaps obliterating thereby in their minds a whole world they once knew just as well as their melancholy colleagues. In fact, I did interview some mayors of "successful" communes but not on as broad a scale because their responses were more likely to address different points of emphasis such as the practical problems following the reform. The survey of the mayors of "losing" communes obviously measures only one dimension of a complex, ongoing process.

The state officials I talked to in the Ministry of the Interior staunchly insisted that the adverse reaction was limited to disgruntled office-holders who would not accept the opportunities for career retraining or the "honorary pensions"[31] offered them. They also complained that some of the *Landräte* who, after all, were supposed to be the major conduits for "selling" the advantages of the reform to the mayors and communal councils in their respective counties were dragging their feet. They were supposed to acquaint their charges with the available options and talk them into voluntary mergers. Naturally, I made a special effort to talk to these "lazy" *Landräte* as well as to those eager to push the reform. Being an executive that is both elected by the people of the county and the quasi-prefectural representative of the Bavarian state in the countryside, a *Landrat* has to be at once a dutiful official and a skillful politician who knows how to get along with the mayors, councils, and voters of the particular county.

The *Landräte* I interviewed were mostly favorable to the reform, but with some important qualifications. One of them objected to the long duration of the voluntary phase. "If an operation is necessary," he said with a

Machiavellian glint in his eye, "It must be done faster." Another *Landrat*, a member of the opposition SPD, called the voluntary phase a hoax since the state had financial rewards for communes that agreed to merge and, in the end, the intended mergers would be imposed anyway. Still another Landrat, of the ruling CSU, felt that a minimal size of two to three thousand inhabitants would have been more appropriate.[32] As we have seen, the actual results were often closer to his suggestion than to the mandated size of five thousand.

Another common theme among *Landräte* and new mayors of enlarged units were the regrets expressed about the discarding of the honorary local officials of old. This was true especially in mergers of many units of member communes, which made it unlikely that many mayors and local councillors of the original communes would be employed again in the new context. Even though the old honorary mayors had received appreciable expense allowances, it was the pride that these volunteer officials took in their functions, and the voluntary services of all these thousands that were perceived as a great loss. Still another *Landrat*, however, expressed skepticism of this honorary status and pointed to the fact that not only had the current expense allowances been rather high and tax-free, but most of the honorary mayor's work was done by a salaried communal secretary, in any case. As one new mayor, who had been nimble enough to acquire civil service qualifications after eleven years as a mayor in a smaller town, of a Middle Franconian VG put it:[33] "When I first became [honorary] mayor of G., a mayor got 30 marks and no allowance for coming in to do his job. People took pride in coming in and doing whatever they could." Now the honorary mayor and council members received a per diem just for showing up at the Rathaus.

Landräte who were reputed to have encouraged, or at least failed to discourage, protests and lawsuits against the reform, on the other hand, conceded the necessity of the reform and, in one case, even wished it had happened prior to the school district reform, which often anticipated the mergers of small communes. One saw it as a long chain of events of decline for local government: the successive loss of a commune's own elementary school, the replacement of its local gendarme with an occasional motorized patrol, and the loss of autonomous post office, telephone, and railroad connections: "For decades, I have witnessed the hollowing out of local autonomy. What is really left of local self-government? What do they really have to decide these days? They just spend state and federal funds." He also said that he saw the politicization of local politics at this level coming. His only regret was about the loss of a local sense of identity among the citizenry. Some were cynical about the assignment of centrality to a place: "They didn't just pick the centers, but whenever they decided on a place, they called it a center." Another *Landrat* suggested that the local citizenry had long changed its image of local government from the "keeper of public order" of old to that of a "dispenser of services." He felt that the citizenry really cared about improved services, such as road repair, snow removal, water, and sanitation. And there would be better services under the new system. If the reform had occurred sooner, he believed there would not have been all this build-up of separate, inefficient communal facilities—such as sports and tourist centers—in competition with neighboring small towns.

Toward a Modern, Functional Society?

All the planning and the measures of administrative and territorial reform aim at the goal of adjusting the territorial-administrative structures which grew from the agrarian, pre-industrial social order to the requirements of the evolving [modern] functional society.[34]

This formulation by the federal government against the background of the complaints by the mayors of "losing" communities challenges the observer to come to a final judgment about this territorial reform. First, there are value questions—especially in an era of acknowledged limits—that are so basic as to be unanswerable without bias. To quote the state government[35] "The time of the 'growth euphoria' is past and, with the recognition of the changeability and imperfections of the newly-created values, there has been a rising recognition of the value of a natural environment for human existence and, parallel to this, there have been nostalgic images and a thinking back to a proven past."

But who is to say that this modern functional society is intrinsically better, more desirable, or that it will make people happier than the patriarchal, "agrarian pre-industrial social order" in Bavaria that it has replaced? Both Bavarian conservatives and the post-materialist Greens party may voice legitimate doubts and, perhaps, express nostalgia for the "good old days" of a nearly closed village community and the nearly self-sufficient small hometown. These conditions, however, if they ever existed in this idealized form, may have passed irretrievably into history. The only question that remains for the policy-makers, then, is whether to speed up the transformation, or at least not to let the laggards among the regions and communes suffer too long from the incongruities of the transition, or whether to let social change take its slow and unequal course. The fundamental value questions, from this perspective, pale beside the more practical questions of whether the particular mode chosen for the transition could have been better, and whether the particular shape of the post-reform local government setting is really to be preferred over its antecedents.

In particular, we need to examine the criticisms posed by those who are questioning whether the post-reform order of things was less democratic than the old one. Does it provide less of a sense of community, and more distance between local authorities and the citizen? Just what are the merits or demerits of the undeniable bureaucratization of local government as a result of the reform? What is the value of civic enthusiasm? Does halving the number of the 69,000 mayors, communal council members, and representatives of the county councils (*Kreistage*) and district assemblies (*Bezirkstage*) of 1966 to a total of 36,700 in 1978 automatically mean less democracy? A handbook on the reforms whose authors and publisher are close to the Bavarian Communal Association (*Gemeindetag*) argued that "the representative mandates in the small and smallest communes hardly had any communal policy-making substance left," because smallness and social change "hollowed out the democratic participation" of both citizens and representatives. This is an echo of Bruno Merk's argument that local government is not a purpose in itself but a means to an end, namely "to carry out its functions effectively. The majority of the [pre-reform] communes were no longer able to do this, as even the communal associations had to admit. So the reform was necessary, even overdue. ... I am convinced that, in spite of the political disputes and ensuing difficulties, we achieved a result worth showing off."

A representative of a community of five thousand at least has a meaningful role, they suggested and pointed out, besides, that recent laws had increased the communal and county councils. They also introduced the neighborhood spokesperson (*Ortssprecher*) to represent the remaining communes of old, the *Ortsteile*, and enlarged the rights of the town meeting (*Bürgerversammlung*).[36] The effort of the authors, alone, to point out the small augmentations of the number of representatives to balance the loss of some thirty thousand honorary mayors and council members suggests that they were well aware of the democratic significance of the loss of all these local volunteers and citizens who had staked their personal pride and talents on these positions.[37]

There is a great loss involved also when representatives, by dint of their numbers, are less considered ordinary people, "neighbors," and more likely a technocratic or social elite. On the other hand, we should remember that the old representative system was largely of a patriarchal, not exactly democratic nature in which the typical village, or small-town mayor was a rich farmer or upper crust notable whose social authority was merely underlined by the public office. Even a benevolent *père de famille* type of mayor is really a village patriarch, and hardly a democratic image.

What about the declining sense of community, and of communal identity? We have seen, in the preceding chapter, how social change has been eroding both the sense of community and of local identity, and we may return to this theme below.[38] The local government reform, in this context merely reacted to or, at worst, completed a process long underway. Still, there is no denying the sense of loss expressed especially by an older generation that clearly recalls the days when the farmers of small rural communes engaged in prodigious feats of cooperative construction and services with their teams of horses or oxen, and their volunteer manual labor—the German equivalent of barn-raising in the American Midwest. However, these volunteer community efforts, too, began to atrophy some time ago, when rural communities acquired non-agricultural populations who had neither the draft animals nor the skills or free time to perform such work during the slack winter season. When the farmers saw that their non-farming fellow-citizens were neither able nor willing to join in the efforts anymore, they understandably stopped performing these cooperative services, and the custom fell into disuse.

On the other hand, the active local associational and club life, albeit on the basis of the original communes, has not diminished very much. Where local taverns or inns have had to close, moreover, the new, enlarged communes have been able to supply community centers for club events, and even for youth activities and sports.[39] Finally, there is the perhaps more symbolic loss of all those beautiful old place names of dissolved communes, some 4,500 of them,[40] except for those retained on the signs for the time being as *Ortsteil* names under the name of the new commune. The reformers were very emphatic in discouraging hyphenated place names. What's in a local name, aside from the nostalgic memories of old-timers? Does the modern functional society only need zip codes and identification numbers?

The often-cited closeness of government to the citizenry (*Bürgernähe*) is not only meant to denote actual physical distance, but even this has become controversial. The omnipotent *Landrat* offices used to be an average of only six miles away from all the communes of a county before the county reform of 1972. Now the average distance to the county offices is 8.5 miles, but—or so the argument goes—now there are twelve to fifteen very capable EG or VG administrations nearby in a county where there used to be only two or three.[41] And these new local government administrators can handle most citizens' applications for residence matters, social security, welfare, health insurance, and tax matters for which they used to have to go to the *Landrat*. Furthermore, the *Landtag* has delegated passport, civil-registry, and road-building authority to the EGs and VGs,[42] Car registration was next, thanks to their new capability of processing electronic data. But did all this really make up for the loss of the old micro-commune mayor and council members who used to be friends—sometimes enemies—omnibus personal advisers, and symbolic representatives, though anything but competent administrators? The answer really hinges on how true it is that the public above all wants the services that the new government personnel can deliver rather than the "closeness" of the old village—or small town oligarchs who are now being idealized along with forms of a primary, neighborly community. The old German village or small town, moreover, was at times as oppressive and stultifying as at other times it may have been comforting.

Somewhat the same doubts can be raised about the slogan of the "bureaucratization" of small towns and village life that accompanies the communal reform outside of larger towns and cities. There can be no mistaking the spread of trained full-time administrators and their professional functions throughout a countryside hitherto quite devoid of real administration, nor of the considerable increase of cost resulting from these many new salaried positions. If it is true that there are now twelve to fifteen capable EG or VG administrations where there used to be only two or three—and there is an average of nine employees in some two thousand such units—it stands to reason that this was hardly a reform motivated by economy. On the other hand, how else were the desired services to be delivered throughout the countryside, if not by a better distribution of competent personnel and equipment? It was precisely the need for the honorary mayors to depend on the *Landrat* offices for these services that constituted their great weakness.

Critics may still mourn the passage of the central role of the old "communal parliaments," meaning the councils—or remember how even the remaining local politicians often find themselves out of their depth in the face of the new professional administrative processes in their own bailiwicks.[43] Experts on German constitutional law flatly deny that communal councils were ever meant to be "parliaments" in the sense in which *Landtage* and the *Bundestag* are. Instead they call the council an administrative organ. "The risk that the bureaucratic communal administration would sideline the elected officials," as a commentary close to the communal association put it,[44] "is far smaller than the danger that local governments continue to be under the tutelage of the state [county] agencies."

This formulation, indeed, describes the trade-off that has occurred, and it may also describe the bureaucratic direction in which the "modern functional society" is evolving for better or worse: As the entire state, from top to bottom, is becoming less and less of a vessel of sovereign authority, less of an instrument to maintain a workable civic order, this change also affects the lowliest of the old authority figures, the patriarchal mayor and communal councilor, robbing them of some of their authoritarian dignity just as it despoiled the authority of village priests and teachers. In its place, the rising "service state" requires of modern local government first and foremost the delivery of specific services—and this in as egalitarian and efficient a way as possible.

This change in function, by necessity, shifts the center of gravity toward those who are able to deliver the desired services, and the services themselves, but it does not necessarily take away the representative and steering function of the elective politicians. Instead, it might be taken by them as an incentive to prepare themselves better to oversee and control the EG and VG administrators who are supposed to take orders from them. There is no intrinsic reason why small-town and village politicians, given the greater selectivity implied in the reduction of the numbers of local units, should not be able to rise to the challenge that their colleagues among the mayors and city councils of medium and larger towns began to master long ago.

Notes

1. Art. 28 guarantees local communities "the right to regulate, under their own responsibility and within the limits of the laws, all the affairs of the local community."
2. September 1975 was the deadline for dissenting opinions by the communes. The financial rewards offered by the state for voluntary action could be claimed only until 1 January 1976, when all communes involved had to give their consent.
3. See GV Bl, 23 December 1975, 413. The changes in the boundaries of districts, counties, and independent cities were also proposed in the form of an ordinance. See Bavarian Landtag, *Drucksache 8/2083*, 27 January 1976, and GV Bl, 12 March 1976, 37.
4. For the district reorganization, see GV Bl, 25 March 1976, 111. For the two bills before the diet, see Landtag, *Drucksache 9/7158 and Drucksache 8/7433, and GV Bl*, 28 March 1978, 56.
5. See Reigl et al., *Kommunale Gliederung*, 53–55.
6. The experience with lawsuits to challenge the communal reform in Baden-Württemberg had been similarly discouraging: The courts rejected all individual or generalized attacks upon the reform with the sole exception of actions that could demonstrate that the government had ignored or violated its own planning and legislative guidelines in a particular case.
7. Merkendorf (*Stadt*) had also sued unsuccessfully, but eventually received EG status, as did Arberg (*Markt*), as a result of the "reform of the reform." They were larger and growing (2,106 and 1,986 inhabitants, respectively), but had a tax revenue level far

below (58 percent and 74 percent, respectively) their reference communes in the state.

8. The 1966 ticket identified the endorsement as Non-Party Voters Association and that of 1972 as Workers association. The new mayor was a carpenter who was elected in 1978 upon endorsement by a joint ticket of CSU and Free Voters.

9. As of 2000, Röckingen still was in VG Hesselberg.

10. This symbolic keeping open of the city hall had dramatic parallels in some small communities in Bavaria that resisted annexation to neighboring places by force, defending their city hall and records with road barriers, sirens, church bells, and men armed with farm tools until a superior police force might have seized them.

11. Most of the professional and civil servant mayors seem to be concentrated in larger towns that are EGs.

12. Middle Franconia had seventeen *Landkreise* before the *Landkreisreform* of 1971, and emerged with only seven, three in West Middle Franconia.

13. For Middle Franconia, the corresponding figures were only 11.9 percent between two and five thousand and a total of 17.9 percent in communes below five thousand. At the time of the *Korrektur,* Merk's successor, Minister of the Interior Georg Tandler, had solemnly announced that this was to be absolutely the last territorial change connected with the communal reform, but there have been a number of additional court decisions and other changes since then. Another striking difference is that in communes under five thousand, the average household has 2.34 persons whereas in cities over one hundred thousand, the average household has only 1.8 members. One half of the latter, in fact, are one-person households, which is true of only one-third in communes below five thousand, where social life apparently is less anomic. *Bayern Jahrbuch 2009.*

14. Hamburg and Bremen were city-states, and so was West Berlin, which technically was not a part of the old Federal Republic, but still an occupied territory until 1990. All the others, and the five new *Länder* of East Germany, were regarded as "extensive" states (*Flächenstaaten*).

15. The EG below one thousand is Jachenau (845), a mountain community in the county of Bad Tölz-Wolfratshausen. Since 1979, there is also Wallgau (1,190) in the county of Garmisch-Partenkirchen.

16. The average area of a Bavarian VG was about 27 square miles in 1980, as compared to an average of 16.4 square miles for an EG (other than the independent cities). The EGs and VG member communes were encouraged to annex what little county land did not already belong to a commune. Unlike most American incorporated communities, German communes typically include all surrounding county land so that the counties rarely have any unincorporated areas.

17. Rhineland Palatinate's average county size, perhaps, most resembles that of Bavaria while all the others favored a much larger unit.

18. See also Frido Wagener, "West Germany: A Survey," in *International Handbook on Local Government Reorganization*, 332–340. The Lower Saxonian VGs (*Samtgemeinden*) and those of Schleswig-Holstein (*Amtsgemeinden*) also appear to be larger than those of Bavaria.

19. See Statistisches Bundesamt, *Datenreport 1992* (Bonn, 1992), 42–43; and *Statistical Pocket Book of the GDR, 1973* (Berlin, 1973), 11–12. "Urban communes," that is those over two thousand, numbered 565 between two and three thousand. Only 29 of the urban communes were over fifty thousand in population, which exceeds the size of the cities that will be discussed below. See also *DDR Handbuch* (Cologne, 1975), passim.

20. See also *SBZ von A bis Z* (Bonn, 1966), 84, 160, 261–262, and 424–425; and *DDR Handbuch*, 160–161, 350–351, 477–478, and 769–770. The party (SED) had its strongest leverage through the first secretary of the district.

21. See his "Necessary Illusions: The Transformation of Governance Structures in the New Germany," in *The Domestic Politics of German Unification*, Christopher Anderson, et al., eds. (Boulder, 1993), 124–126.

22. A similar policy of mandated mergers, say in Switzerland or California, would very likely have triggered major civil unrest.

23. See Jutta Helm, "Citizen Initiatives in West Germany," in *Western European Party Systems: Trends and Prospects*, Merkl, ed. (New York, 1980), 576–596. The epithet *raisonner*, or its German equivalent *räsonieren*, was broadly applied to all criticisms of the old, absolutist practices as late as the turn of the century (1900). The clash between the "reasoning" of the Enlightenment and the traditional authority exercised by the nobility and its minions is implicit in the word even though it was used for all kinds of resistance, "reasonable" or violent.

24. In most cases, the plaintiff communes were not trying to defend their local autonomy as much as they aimed at preventing a rival town from enjoying the fruits of a merger.

25. Under certain circumstances, the honorary *Bürgermeisters* that were losing out could be given an honorary pension (*Ehrensold*) and even a transitional stipend. They and other honorary communal officials also were offered special eight-week retraining courses by the Bavarian School of Administration to facilitate their acquisition of the administrative skills required for the new local administrations. See Bayerisches Innenministerium, *Gebietsreform Bayern. Gemeinden in der Reform*, 1975, 19–20.

26. As was the case in Edling, near Wasserburg.

27. In some cases, advisory straw votes were actually held on particulars of the reform, but the unsystematic nature of this procedure and the tendency to simplify the options undermined their validity.

28. The average industrial employment of the new EGs corresponded to the average posited for small centers.

29. We compiled an index from these by multiplying the first ranking times five, the second ranking times four, the third times three, etc., added up each row, and divided the totals by the number of entries in each row. Thus, the score should have run from a high of five to a low of one.

30. In the past, West German small towns under five thousand, and especially below three thousand inhabitants, tended to have a personalistic, non-partisan style of politics. See Merkl, "Factionalism: The Limits of the West German Party State" in *Faction Politics*, Frank Belloni and Dennis Beller, eds. (Santa Barbara, 1978), 254–260.

31. These "honorary pensions" were of a magnitude to pacify many a disgruntled office-holder.

32. He suggested that the state government had picked the minimum of five thousand only in order to avoid North German ridicule of "small-thinking" (*kleinkariert*) Bavaria.

33. His town, south of Nuremberg, had already absorbed two other communes and parts of four more in 1971–1972. The reform boosted its population by another 50 percent and made it the seat of a VG with two other member communes.

34. *Federal Report 1972*, 18. The preface to the *Fourth Bavarian (Raumordnung) Report* (1978), 3, furthermore, speaks of and distances itself from "voices that propose totally abandoning the goal of equal opportunity in all parts of the *Land*, and instead want us to proceed toward the concept of a purely functional *Raumordnung*." The Bavarian government expressed healthy skepticism toward such an excess of functionality.

35. See its *Third Bavarian Report* (1976), 9–10, where the state government also cites the Club of Rome's report and the energy crisis.

36. Reigl et al. eds., *Kommunale Gliederung,* 47–48. The references are to Bavarian Administrative Court decisions of 10 February 1977 (*no. 17 V 76,* 24 f.) and 27 May 1977 (*no. 35 V 76,* 20 f.) and the 1971 laws for the local elections of 1972 and for Strengthening Local Government, as well as a 1974 statute. The neighborhood spokesperson is now incorporated in Art. 78 and the new rights of the town meeting in Art. 18 of the Communal Statute.

37. This is an argument somewhat similar to the one that considers federal or regional devolution inherently more democratic than centralized government. The sheer numbers represent quality as well, namely the quality of democratic, grassroots self-government.

38. See the account of education and religion above, chapter 2.

39. Some observers, however, have pointed out that the newly merged EGs and the VGs often favor the development of their central cores at the expense of outlying areas. See Albertin in Merkl, *New Local Centers,* 128–131.

40. See the lists in *Die Gemeinden Bayerns,* 169–190, and Reigl et al., *Kommunale Gliederung,* 529–685.

41. See Reigl et al., *Kommunale Gliederung,* 49–50. These figures are presumably based on the new counties.

42. See *LT Drucksache 8/7433* for the draft bill to this effect.

43. Albertin, in Merkl, *New Local Centers,* 130–134.

44. Reigl et al., *Kommunale Gliederung,* 51.

Chapter 5

No Town is an Island

In historical perspective, the great Bavarian local government reform represents a final step in the centuries-long process of territorial integration of the Bavarian state, not counting its earlier history. The process began in the eighteenth century when Bavaria was still an Electoral Princedom (*Kurfürstentum*) of the Holy Roman Empire and consisted merely of Old Bavaria, roughly the areas of Upper and Lower Bavaria and the Palatinate, which it had acquired a century earlier. Small towns and villages such as our fifteen West Middle Franconian communities still were independent or belonged to other German states, such as the Kingdom of Prussia. Even in Old Bavaria, many an isolated small township or village may have felt as far from the capital, Munich, as an island in the South Pacific. This insular consciousness, of course, was never immune to the impact of wars, pestilence, and major economic crises such as years of bad harvests. But even peasant rebellions touched only a few areas. The great political upheaval of the French Revolution probably left hardly a mark until the great innovator, Napoleon Bonaparte, purchased the support of the Great Elector (*Kurfürst*) of Bavaria by making him a king and enlarging his territories with Suebia and Franconia, including the area of my research. Napoleon thus was the first territorial reformer here and the profound influence of the modernizing, revolutionary reforms in France also paved the way for Count Maximilian von Montgelas's local reorganization of the new kingdom early in the nineteenth century. Of course, we should not imagine that these Montgelas reforms—his tenure as State minister was of short duration—penetrated very deeply into the most remote reaches of the new Kingdom of Bavaria, into all of the insular and largely agrarian small communities he sought to reorganize. Only the Catholic church, the well-established rival and enemy of the spirit of the Enlightenment, of the French Revolution and Montgelas, had an effective presence everywhere, except perhaps in Protestant Bavaria.

Despite the spread of literacy and of the print media, the insularity of provincial Bavarian small towns and villages probably did not completely break down until after World War I, when the monarchy fell and—after considerable political turbulence—a Social Democratic government launched a timid effort to reform elementary education. After World War II, again, it was educational reform and the social changes we examined in chapters 1 and 2, above, that put an end to the geographic isolation of the smallest communities. In a manner of speaking, the war had centralized, even nationalized popular sentiment but the immediate postwar years of occupation had then produced considerable decentralization at the local, state, and federal levels. As the pendulum swung back, the school reforms of the late 1960s in any case were preceded by the universal spread of television, that great educator of the masses in everybody's living room. And it was no accident that the replacement of one- or two-room village and small-town schools with trans-local school centers and districts in many instances set the patterns for the local territorial reform we have examined in this book.

It was the governmental reaction, if rather out of synchronization with the popular sentiment, which swung from one extreme to another: Popular opinion leaders and their following in the 1940s and fifties first tended to favor the larger population centers and their opportunities, even migrating there, over living the life of the periphery. This popular inclination led political elites in the 1960s into the years of planning euphoria and administrative reform from the center, orientation toward large spatial relationships and the merging of territorial units for greater efficiency. But by that time popular sentiment was changing again: "now again small-scale relationships, and administration close to the citizenry, communal problem-solving, and regionalization are in demand."[1]

Policy-makers and politicians then tried to combine both approaches, from the top down and the bottom up by building structures of vertical integration, by "interweaving intergovernmental levels" (*Politikverflechtung*).[2] People however had rediscovered the attractions of living in rural settings or, at least, at the edge of urban centers rather than in their midst.

Either way the small places are now quite connected to the larger world around them in contrast to earlier centuries. Today no town is an island that could be examined entirely by itself as if it was not part of the larger system of German government. And whether the trend for a while seems to favor centralization or a return to the grassroots, to the lower levels of government—as in the citizen initiative movement of the 1970s or the Greens' slogan "think globally but act locally"—local government and politics remain tied and bound to the larger system of government. Until about thirty years ago, two thirds of West Germans supported centralization over decentralization, which has been favored by similar majorities since the end of the seventies.

In the reform era, the central government seemed a natural choice for tackling the many problems of social and economic reform with spatial planning, increased financial leverage, and powers to reach into the traditional preserve of states' (*Länder*) rights by the creation of new constitutional "common tasks" (*Gemeinschaftsaufgaben*) of federation and *Länder*. Within less than a decade, however, the federal government had, by common consensus, failed to demonstrate sufficient capacity to solve the problems at hand.[3] Some observers, in fact, felt that this failure was perhaps inherent in the increasing inability of most advanced industrial societies to govern themselves and to "steer" their own further social and economic development democratically and without recourse to neo-corporatist or bureaucratic solutions. "Ungovernability" and inadequate "steering capacity" were the buzzwords of the late seventies and early eighties.[4]

Local Government in the West German System

Before we can raise questions about where small towns such as Wolframs-Eschenbach or smaller communities like Adelshofen fit into the larger picture of German society and government, we need to clarify their changing position amidst these conflicting trends. Let us set these lowest-level communities and their officials and citizens into the wider setting of government in Germany: Above the member communes of a VG and the smallest unified (EG) town communities in Bavaria, there is the county (*Kreis*), represented by an elected county executive officer or prefect (*Landrat*) who is also appointed by the state government and, both, represents the *Kreis* toward the state and the state toward the *Kreis*. It was this key official, for example, who was entrusted with talking the small communes into a VG and negotiating the mergers and annexations necessary for optimal reform. Above the *Kreis*, Bavaria also has planning regions and the seven provinces or districts (*Regierungsbezirke*). There are elected assemblies at all levels. Above the provincial level, then, there is the state

(*Land*) with its parliamentary system: a bicameral parliament (*Landtag*) formed the executive cabinet with ministers and a minister president.

Above the states, there is the federal government, another parliamentary system whose legislature represents both the individual citizens via political parties in an elected federal parliament (*Bundestag*) and each state in the non-elective upper house, the Federal Council (*Bundesrat*). The state delegations in the *Bundesrat* consist of varying numbers of state officials specifically instructed by their respective state governments and they have to vote en bloc. This system has not changed, only expanded with German unification. And even this government, the Federal Republic of Germany, is only partly sovereign because it belongs to the European Union, yet another level. Its citizens are represented in a weak European Parliament, which imposes laws and advisories on them. Their member government, Germany, has a voice in the executive councils of the union. Is it any wonder if the people and officials in the smallest Bavarian communes feel a bit helpless in this multi-tiered setting, nearly powerless to shape their own lives and ward off bad developments?

The constitutions of Bavaria and the Federal Republic, themselves products of a half century's development, assigned the Bavarian commune a modest place among the levels of government. The federal Basic Law guarantees the existence of local self-government but only in the vaguest of terms. Under the traditional federal arrangement, local government is supposed to be a creation of the constituent state governments who each have their own local government code, determine local boundaries and structures, and have discretion over most matters of local jurisdiction, including the financial resources of the local authorities. In modern industrial societies, moreover, cooperative linkages between local and federal governments have developed that complicate the original blueprints. Most recently, the transfer of some *Land* powers to the European Union has further added to the complexity.

German local government, however, has long-standing regional traditions that make for different forms of local institutions and processes in different parts of the Federal Republic.[5] In six decades of governmental practice since 1949, the position of the local authorities has changed very considerably from the original specification in the West German Basic Law. Not only has the subordinate role of local units of the *Länder* governments taken on a quasi-constitutional position in the federal hierarchy: at penalty of losing political support, *Land* governments cannot ride roughshod over the express will of especially the larger local units. The federal system itself has been in continual flux toward complex forms of cooperative federalism that tend to undermine the original model of German federalism. Thus the local governments, depending on their size, have been drawn increasingly into participatory roles in an evolving system that is also characterized by both centralizing and decentralizing trends, by mushrooming growth of governmental functions and intervention into economy and society, and by an ever more confusing intermingling of finances and administration of all levels. The new buzzword of the seventies and eighties was "vertical interweaving," *Politikverflechtung*, the integration of decision-making authorities from all levels. Since then, some observers have become quite critical of it, if from varying points of view.

To locate the place of the local governments under discussion in the larger system and to penetrate the various conflicting long- and short-range trends, this chapter will address a number of topics one at a time. To begin it will try to bring out the character of the original model of West German federalism of the 1949 Basic Law both in the context of German federal traditions and in contrast to the better-known Anglo-American models of federalism. Secondly, it will sketch a picture of the actual evolution of intergovernmental relations in Germany in the light of group and representative processes, of social and economic history, and of the history of financial arrangements among the levels that, of course, also mirror the growth and changing distribution of governmental functions over the long run. The third vantage point will be the development and transformation of West German cooperative federalism and *Politikverflechtung* through the financial reforms of 1969 and the development of intergovernmental "common tasks." There will also be a critical discussion of *Politikverflechtung* and of the situation in which it has left the communes. We will conclude with an account of the impact of German unification and European integration on the role of *Länder* and communes.

Federalism in the Basic Law

In 1948–1949, when the Parliamentary Council in Bonn was busy drawing up a provisional constitution for the three Western zones of occupation, it chose to revive German federalism but not, as is sometimes claimed in ignorance of the circumstances, because the Western Allies, notably the Americans, wanted it to.[6] The framers of the Basic Law chose federalism because they equated it, rightly or wrongly, with grass roots and "organic democracy," with hundreds of years of an older, pre-Nazi German governmental tradition—they even credited federalism as a bulwark against totalitarian centralization—with principles of Catholic social philosophy (subsidiarity), and with a commitment to European integration.[7] At the time, they also found themselves in a de facto decentralized country that

consisted of ruined cities but intact *Länder* and occupation zones that restricted transport and communications among one another. There was no
national or federal government. There was however a sense of the complete collapse of the German nation-state, disgraced by two world wars
and made lasting by devastation and defeat, by division into West and East
Germany, by the abolition of Prussia, and the separation of West Berlin
from the rest of West Germany. After such a "zero hour" of political, social,
economic, and last but not least *moral* eclipse, it made sense to think of
rebuilding what was left from the bottom up, as a child might pile up building blocks, using the largely occupation-made *Länder* as the blocks supporting a "provisional" central government in a Western location, Bonn.

The acceptance of the occupation mandate to draw up a constitution
did not induce the framers of the Basic Law to adopt the model of the
United States constitution nor of other Anglo-American models of federalism such as Canada or Australia. Instead, they insisted on recreating the
distinctive pattern of Bismarckian and Weimar federalism and were quite
ready to face down repeated interventions by the Allied military authorities to change some aspects of this federal design.[8] German federalism
has always differed substantially from the American or Anglo-American
models in that, since 1871, there was no attempt to set up two separate
levels of government that are each nearly complete in their respective
executive, legislative, judicial, and financial functions.[9] There are several
distinctive features that set off German federalism from our own.

German federalism has always favored a federal council (*Bundesrat*)
as the upper house representative of the *Länder*, a chamber that is composed of non-elective delegations of varying size from each *Land* who can
vote only en bloc and as instructed by their respective state executives.
Through the legislative and administrative powers of the *Bundesrat*, the
Länder governments participate in federal decision-making to an extent
unparalleled in Anglo-American federalism. The imperial *Bundesrat* was
originally designed as a gathering of the princes of the realm under Prussian tutelage and each state delegation had its own embassy with extra-
territorial privileges in Berlin, which had to be accredited to the Kaiser
with full diplomatic pomp and circumstances. The old imperial *Bundesrat*
enjoyed equality in legislation with the lower house, the *Reichstag*, and
substantial additional authority over administrative ordinances and regulations passed by the federal government. Nevertheless, it seems to have
played a relatively minor role in actual decision-making until after the
fall of the empire when a committee of emissaries from the states—their
statehood and claims to sovereignty were buried when the Weimar constitution renamed them *Länder*—insisted on imposing a revival of the institution now called *Reichsrat* upon a reluctant Weimar Constituent Assembly.

The *Reichsrat* was only accorded a suspensive veto on federal legislation, but turned out to be a stronger institution than the *Reichstag* because, with the demise of the Kaiser, institutionalized Prussian hegemony,
and state princes, the representatives of the states—now demoted to regional public corporations, or *"Länder"*—lobbied with unrestrained determination for the interests of their respective *Land* governments. The
weakness and political fragmentation of the lower house, the *Reichstag*,
moreover, made the *Reichsrat's* suspensive legislative veto in most cases as
strong as complete equality with the *Reichstag* would have made it. The
Great Depression, in which many *Länder* went bankrupt, Chancellor von
Papen's coup over Prussia, by far the largest *Land*, and the final takeover
of the Weimar Republic by the Nazi dictatorship also meant the collapse
of German federalism.

The Basic Law of the West German Federal Republic of 1949, nevertheless, revived the old *Bundesrat* (without state embassies and princes)
with only minor modifications: The *Bundesrat* still has only a suspensive
veto on most federal legislative subjects, except for bills that involve administration by the *Länder*. This latter category, however, has turned out
to be the more important of the two, accounting for a majority of the bills
before parliament and including the most important legislative matters.
The *Länder* were fewer (ten at first) and more equal in size than before
1933. Their *Bundesrat* delegations now varied between three and five
votes, depending on the state populations. Unlike its secretive imperial
predecessor, the West German *Bundesrat* also admitted the press and public, but it was still an unimpressive spectacle to witness its proceedings,
mostly rapid-fire voting on several bills with rarely a word of debate. Its
politicking, if any, went on in topical committees and in direct contacts
among *Länder* governments and between them and their delegations.[10]

German unification introduced a further modification in the structure
and role of the *Bundesrat* in that the Unification Treaty of 1990 changed
the mode of representation. Since most of the newly created five East
German *Länder* were rather small in population (up to three million inhabitants each) in comparison with their West German equivalents, the
method of allocating seats in the *Bundesrat* was changed. For example,
each of the four largest West German *Länder*, including Bavaria, was given
six seats, followed by three West German and four East German *Länder*
with four seats each, unified Berlin also with four, and the remaining four
smallest *Länder* with three each, for a total of sixty-eight seats/votes of
sixteen *Länder*.[11]

To change the constitution or select judges for the Federal Constitutional Court now requires forty-six votes (two-thirds). The nineteen
votes of the five East German *Länder* cannot block an amendment of the

Basic Law if it is supported by all the West German delegations. Bavaria's vote of six of sixty-eight now gives the *Land* noticeably less clout than it had before 1990—with five out of forty-one (West Berlin only had an advisory role then)—but twice as much now as each of the four smallest *Länder* enjoys. Since a large part of the legislative activity of *Bundesrat* and *Bundestag* since 1990 has been directed at East Germany and the financial burden has been largely on West German shoulders, these proportions are significant.

The Division of Powers

A second German federal oddity then and now is the uneven distribution and, in fact, interlacing of legislative and administrative functions.[12] Most of the legislative activity and powers in the Federal Republic are concentrated at the federal level. After a hundred years of using the federal exclusive and concurrent legislative powers, almost all valid law is now indeed federal in origin or noticeably affected by federal regulation. Even the few areas once reserved to the *Land* legislatures (*Landtage*), such as local government, police powers, and education, are by now at least partially federalized. The typical workload of a *Landtag* is about one-tenth the number of bills that are pending every session before the *Bundestag*. On the other hand, the administration and adjudication of federal law takes place almost exclusively at the *Länder* level where the overwhelming majority of civil servants and judges are permanently employed—and according to uniform, federally mandated requirements. The only exceptions to this rule, other than the foreign service, border police, postal and railroad employees (these last two categories have now been privatized), are the small numbers of federal civil servants who operate the federal ministries, collecting information and preparing government bills.

Among the judges, too, the only exception to the rule of decentralization are the judges of the federal courts (*Bundesgerichte*) of civil and criminal law, administrative, social security, fiscal, and labor law, as well as the Federal Constitutional Court. The Federal Constitutional Court is sui generis in that its judges are political appointees outside of an otherwise Roman Law system who have the chief function of interpreting the Basic Law and serving as arbiters among the *Länder* and between them and the federation. The other federal courts exclusively handle the rare appeals in which the uniform interpretation of federal law by the courts of different *Länder* is at issue. All the other judges and courts are *Länder* judges and courts that handle all cases, including those involving federal law. In fact, the asymmetrical distribution of legislative and administrative powers between the levels means in practice that federal laws are almost invariably administered and adjudicated by *Länder* judges and administrators.[13] The growth of Big Government in Germany, unlike the hydrocephalic development of the American federal government in Washington, DC consequently was scattered over the ten (now sixteen) *Länder* governments.

The third difference between the basic designs of German and American federalism lies in the area of financial federalism. Not only does the same asymmetric arrangement of federal fiscal legislative and *Land* administrative powers apply—the *Länder* also collect some federal taxes by means of delegated administration—but there is the financial equalization procedure (*Finanzausgleich*) mentioned above. Equalizing tax revenues of different areas within a certain margin is a familiar technique to American practice but used only among local government units within the same state. To use it among the states of the union would be considered a violation of the federal principle. This is not to say that enhancement of the governmental resources of a particular, financially weak American state might not be attempted with the help of federal grants-in-aid, or by locating military bases and other beneficial federal programs there. In Germany, on the other hand, outright federal grants or subsidies were long considered a dubious method of promoting public programs, almost a bribe that deprived the recipients of the privilege of developing their own initiatives or, at least, to determine their content. By the process of "horizontal financial equalization" (*Finanzausgleich*) among the *Länder*, the Federal Republic distributed the proceeds from such major taxes as the income and corporation taxes, taking from the rich and giving to the poor. Vertically, it divides the revenues between the two levels according to a ratio—such as 35 percent for the *Länder* and 65 percent for the federation—over which the *Bundesrat* Finance Committee, composed of the *Land* finance ministers, haggles every year with the federal finance minister. As with the legislative functions, these divisions leave very little wherewithal in the hands of the *Landtage*. The *Länder* and communes could hardly function without their fixed share of the "common" major taxes, a condition that would alarm American practitioners accustomed to securing the survival of a level of government with at least a semblance of its own taxing powers.[14]

Here too the necessities of German unification cut an incisive swath beginning with the requirements of the Monetary, Economic, and Social Union Treaty of 1990, the first effort to infuse the bankrupt East German (GDR) economy with the currency and welfare transfers needed for the transition. Revised repeatedly and with the addition of a *Länder*-financed German Unity Fund of DM 115 billion and recurrent annual infrastructural subsidies by the federal government, this was the beginning of what was bound to be a relationship of financial dependency of the East upon the West. Concomitant with this flow of funds, the relevant constitutional provisions about the intergovernmental financial relations were suspended and, for a time, replaced with special fiscal arrangements. In particular, East German communes were thereby—in addition to receiving their real estate and business taxes as in the West—freed of the West German mandate of receiving a share of the common income and corporation taxes according to their own modest per capita tax revenue. Instead, their share was fixed according to their population figures.

It is important to recall that under communism, there were no income and corporation taxes and consequently no records of previous tax payments that could have been used for assessment in the West German mode. A special arrangement now assured all East German communes of a share of 15 percent of the proportion of income taxes collected within their *Land*, and this without the usual regional disparities. The most controversial part of the fiscal accommodation of East Germany, however, involved the respective shares of the sales taxes (*Umsatzsteuer*), which at first were separated into a West and East German fund until the enormous East German deficits forced the West German *Länder* to be more generous. Before 1995, the East German *Länder* and unified Berlin, moreover, were not to participate in the old process of financial equalization and instead to receive the subsidies mentioned earlier. This brief account of the basic institutional features of the federal system laid down in the Basic Law in 1949, of course, has to be seen in the light of the modifications of a transition that affected the communes in the system quite differently than similar transformations did in the US federal context.

The bare bones of the institutional structure also need to be related to the connective tissue of informal intergovernmental relations and to the physiology of the representative process. The latter, in particular, makes for close interaction along partisan lines as local constituency associations of the major parties select and promote candidates for municipal councils, mayor, county council (*Kreistag*) and *Landrat*, the *Landtag*, and the *Bundestag* itself. Once elected, the deputies of the higher levels naturally become notable local figures and *Land* or federal patrons who are frequently asked to intervene on behalf of local interests. These partisan ties are much stronger than in the United States and link the different levels at the same time that they invigorate at least the politics of the larger local units with partisan competition.

Organized and singular interests also tie the levels together with varying intensity, with actions originating from individual large businesses to labor unions, farm lobbies, and business organizations that can wield considerable influence in the *Landtag*, the *Bundestag*, or with the executive branches of both levels. At the *Land* and federal level, moreover, the communal associations of large and small cities and counties are the acknowledged voice of the local government interests and they are routinely consulted. In rural Bavaria, furthermore, there is the curious hybrid of partisan elective politics and state administrative clout of the *Landräte* (prefects), key figures and likely patrons to all kinds of local clients, ranging from certain businesses to particular communities. Good *Landräte* can call upon powerful allies at the provincial level and in the *Land* administration, patrons who help them reward their clients with favors and punish their enemies with neglect.[15] Bavarian politics, furthermore, features occasional figures of far-ranging regional influence who make themselves so useful both to the state government and local communities and *Kreise* that they sooner or later end up as state secretaries in the government cabinet, perhaps even ministers of agriculture or of the interior of Bavaria.

Social and Economic Change

It is easier perhaps to understand the great transformation of German federalism when it is placed into the context of a rapidly changing society and economy. We can leave aside the historical controversies about the motives and goals of the early nineteenth-century administrative reforms except for saying that they were invariably intended more to strengthen the *monarchic* state than to encourage citizen participation for its own sake.[16] In Bavaria, in particular, the early reforms were mostly meant to integrate the newly won state territories gained as a result of Napoleon's drastic reorganization of the German political landscape. Germany never really had a liberal night-watchman state—least of all in Bavaria—which might have provided a more suitable basis for an Anglo-American style federal system. Instead, there was an uneasy co-dominium of the monarchic state with the land-owning nobility and, in the cities, the newly rising industrial bourgeoisie.

It was the industrial revolution that gave the semi-emancipated cities real weight and eventually changed the fabric of the entire system. The emerging public welfare and regulatory functions of industrialization were placed with the communes[17] and the Gneist reforms of the late nineteenth century in Prussia emphatically accorded them the function of stoking the economic fires. Rudolf von Gneist also freed rural communes from feudal overlords and thought he was combining British and French models when he coined the phrase "the state rules, the commune takes care of the economy (*der Staat herrscht, die Gemeinde wirtschaftet*)." By that time however, the state had indeed taken away all the police powers that once belonged to the cities. Industry, on the other hand, required a number of new communal functions such as transport connections, sanitation and water supply, education, and the promotion of business activity. The infrastructural buildup was further reinforced with the new health and social services demanded of the commune[18]—at the same time that the emotional ties of individuals to their local community were visibly weakened and major new social conflicts threatened to break out between capital and labor.

The resulting changes gave cities the character of self-governing bourgeois enclaves of cooperative economic activity set off from, and ultimately superior to the rule of the authoritarian state. The newly rising city took on typical service functions, developing its own personnel and a variety of municipally owned enterprises—the gas, water, sanitation, electric transport, and street lighting of "municipal socialism"—and created a modicum of consumer satisfaction. It even succeeded in reducing the level of the new social conflicts. In this fashion industrialization effectively smothered the old authoritarian law-and-order function long before World War I destroyed the feudal basis of the states of the federal system.[19] Even at that, the duopoly of state and commune still favored the authority of the state, which, according to Hugo Preuss, the father of the Weimar constitution, stood behind the quality of municipal self-government. It was not until the collapse of the old authoritarian, and pseudo-federal order[20] in 1918, that the neo-interventionist state arrived with a vengeance in Germany to minister to the many new social and economic needs created by war and defeat.

By that time, postwar economic dislocations, massive unemployment, and poverty made for an enormous burden for the local level. The situation was further aggravated by the dramatic social and political conflicts erupting in the cities of the Weimar Republic. The end of the empire also brought the introduction of universal adult suffrage to cities that had been governed under extremely restrictive franchises. In most cases, this involved the ouster of the old patriciate and the arrival of partisan competition that, at least in the larger cities, brought Social Democrats and Communists into a prominent role. Adelheid von Saldern called this democratization of electoral law of 1918–1919 "the most dramatic reform" in the history of German communal self-government up to that point, though liberal and conservative politicians saw in it "the end of real self-government." This "Bolshevik takeover" in turn legitimized rightwing street demonstrations and stormtrooper violence to "reclaim the control of the streets."[21] Eventually, the Nazi stormtroopers won out over Social Democrats, socialist trade unions, and Communists at the local level because, at the national level in early 1933, the old establishment had sold out to the Nazis. To the extent that they had not already succumbed to Nazi landslides by March 1933, cities and *Länder* were simply taken over, in a coup-like atmosphere—the *Gleichschaltung* (political coordination). Federalism was abolished in 1934, and local government turned over to Nazi-appointed officials.

The Changing Federal Financial Constitution

The changing "financial constitution" of German federalism shows the long-range trends better than the constitutional formulae both before and after Germany's lapse into totalitarian centralism. There had been a conspicuous lag of German political institutions in the last decades of the empire as feudal rule survived into an urban, industrial, and democratic age. In a manner of speaking, some of this lag still continued under Weimar. The framers of the Weimar constitution did acknowledge the rights of communal self-government in Articles 17 and 127 and thus restored a semblance of constitutional realism. But the great financial reforms of minister of finance Matthias Erzberger, at the outset of the republic and in the face of their greatly increased burdens, doomed the communes to a permanent fiscal crisis and made them directly dependent on federal funding—of course usually with strings attached.[22]

Back in the nineteenth century, the *Reich* still had spent less than ten percent of total public expenditures that altogether amounted to only 15 percent of the gross national product. After World War I, in the twenties, the federal share of public expenditures had tripled while the total public expenditures at all levels had grown to 25 percent of GDP. By the end of the twentieth century, the federal budget accounted for about 39 percent of the total public expenditures, which by that time stood at 48 percent of GDP.[23] The communal level that in the 1920s still shared 40 percent of the public expenditures (when the *Länder* were at 30 percent) had now dropped to just under 25 percent while the *Länder* actually spent a larger percentage (37 percent) than in the relatively less-centralized twenties. Clearly, the growing federal share and the general growth of governmental expenditures have created a very different context for federalism today as compared to the nineteenth century.

It is in this context that we have to place the impact of the major financial reforms on federalism and on the communal level in particular. To begin with, there has been a dramatic differential between the expenditures of urban and rural local governments—such as our smaller communes and rural *Kreise*—from the beginning of the nineteenth-century wave of urban growth, with cities outspending their rural cousins three to one per capita (two to one today). Thus local governments have not exactly been united in their interests in the distribution of the financial shares although the communal associations always would prefer to present them as if they were. The considerable disparities among the *Länder* and, even more strikingly, among individual communes, especially big cities and small places, make for dramatic differentials of capacity and financial resources, not to mention conflicts.

The diverging interests of the federation, of the political parties and other organized interests and, inevitably, of individual *Länder* governments, moreover, make this a game the communes can seldom win. In the early years of the Federal Republic, while some of the *Länder*, including Bavaria, and their communes were groaning under disproportionate burdens still left over by war and defeat, others were already booming with the "economic miracle." The federal government followed a policy of accumulating cash surpluses—often called the "Julius tower" of avarice—of startling size from the beginnings of this uneven economic prosperity in West Germany. When this foolish hoarding policy was finally abandoned in the mid-fifties, there would have been an opportunity to redistribute these resources by means of the equalization procedure (*Finanzausgleich*) among the *Länder* to those that were most deeply in debt by that time. But with the 1957 elections looming ahead, the Adenauer administration decided instead to shower this largesse via a constitutionally questionable program of federal grants-in-aid, many with matching grant requirements, over the cities, villages, and *Länder* of the country. The few critical voices were drowned out by the eager acclaim of greedy recipients, politicians anxious to be reelected and, most interesting of all, by teams of policy specialists from federal and *Land* ministries and city departments happy to push their pet projects. With the applause of this last-mentioned "functional accompliceship (*Ressortkumpanei*)," grant-in-aid financing for common tasks thus was born a dozen years before such intergovernmental financial cohabitation was legal in West Germany.

As John Shannon pointed out in his comparison of local finances in Great Britain, the United States, and West Germany, the latter comes in last in a comparison of revenues raised locally versus outside aid: for every local mark, West German communes received five in outside subsidies. This has a powerfully equalizing effect, to be sure, though it does so chiefly by denying individual cities the right to shape their own budgets and expenditures. To quote Shannon, local government in West Germany can be compared to the dowager's pet poodle—"a creature noted more for its cleanliness than for its independence of action. The dowager in this case is the German State (*Land*). She tries to keep her poodle on a short leash to prevent the dog from being lured away by certain poodle fanciers headquartered at the federal capital in Bonn."[24]

The Intergovernmental Finance Reforms of 1969

The federal government indeed continued to pour out large sums in grants-in-aid regardless of the seesawing annual negotiations over the respective shares of the income and corporation taxes between it and the *Länder*. The communes had benefited considerably, though not equally, from the rising revenues of the business tax in the years of the economic miracle. Eventually, in 1966, the first major recession in West Germany cut short the chancellorship of Ludwig Erhard and the dreams of never-ending prosperity. The downturn forced the Bonn government to take a long and hard look at the country's economic situation and its possible leverage against business cycles.

As the new chancellor, Kurt Georg Kiesinger, pointed out in an address before the *Deutscher Gemeindetag*, the association of smaller communes, the communes played a major role in anti-cyclical policy because about two-thirds of public investments were usually invested in them. Their share of the public indebtedness (36 percent in 1972) had also grown prodigiously over the years even though as a percentage of GDP, the public debt had hardly changed in twenty years. The Kiesinger administration, in fact, initiated some immediate transfers to the communes to boost public investment and promised major long-range changes to ameliorate their parlous financial situation. Indeed, a commission of experts had already prepared detailed proposals for a grand financial reform that would include a reorganization of federal-*Land* relations and a communal finance reform. The communal associations endorsed these proposals with minor modifications. Further negotiations among the levels explored the limits of consensus.

The commission had proposed to lower the communal business tax substantially and to compensate and strengthen communal finances with a personal income tax of their own or, more likely, a share of the income taxes of federation and *Länder*. For the first time since 1919, it appeared, the communes might have a big new tax source of their own again besides business and property taxes, administrative fees and "bagatelle levies," such as dog and hunting license fees, and the beverage and entertainment taxes. The rising economic difficulties—the commission report still predated the recession of 1966—led to hurried negotiations over how to generate enough federal surplus to facilitate the transition and other promises to transfer substantial amounts, for instance of the gasoline taxes, from the federal to the local level. The impact of that recession on the state of Bavaria, in particular, also cut the annual amount from what had been redistributed by in-state equalization among the communes up until 1966, while the *Land* government itself took on another billion marks of indebtedness on top of the 7.5 billion outstanding at the end of 1967.

The latent conflict between smaller communes and cities finally surfaced with a broadside attack on the federal proposal by the cities' *Bayerischer Städteverband*, which argued that it could see no improvement for the communal finances of central places in taking away a substantial part of the local business taxes in exchange for a mere share of the income tax. The association also protested the absence of concrete assurances of structural investment at the same time that the capacity of cities to invest in their own future was declining. The cities wanted a "real" income tax including the full progression of the rates and not just a share of it.

The association of smaller and rural Bavarian communes, the *Bayerischer Gemeindetag*, on the other hand, welcomed the federal plans including a slight increase in property taxes, but emphasized the need for both quantity and quality of the communal tax system, especially by reducing its heavy reliance on business taxes.[25] As then federal minister of finance Franz Josef Strauss pointed out eloquently, these taxes made up, on the average, 80 percent of the communes' own revenue. They varied greatly from one township to the other and according to the business cycle, and were generally paid by a tiny minority of the taxpayers, about 5 percent.[26] There was an apprehension among the propertied and business classes and in the CDU/CSU that communal councils elected overwhelmingly by non-propertied and non-business voters might not show the appropriate prudence when it came to spending what a small minority had produced. Since the vast majority of the smaller communes depended mostly on transfers from *Land* and federation, moreover, Strauss was also concerned that this might not encourage a sense of democratic, responsible self-government. "We should enable communes that do not happen to have productive industries within their walls to draw on tax resources of their own to a higher degree than they could up to now … so that a minimal base for establishing their fiscal responsibility may be present."[27] The envisaged local tax system would then rest on three sources, a share of the income tax and the business and property taxes, and might more easily accommodate the differences between residential communities and those where the places of work were.

Early in 1969, the final shape of the communal finance reform began to emerge when it became known that, in 1970, Bavarian communes were expected to transfer 785 million marks (40 percent) of business taxes to the federal government in exchange for a 1.06 billion share of the income taxes. Again there was no agreement among the communal associations: the *Deutscher Gemeindetag*, *Deutscher Landkreistag*, and the *Deutscher Städtebund* supported the original government bill while the *Deutscher*

Städtetag, the representation of the largest cities, held out for a share of the entire progression of the local income tax. The representatives of the smaller communes and rural counties preferred a proportionally lower range of income taxation because it would encompass 80 percent of all the taxpayers and hence provide a more evenly distributed tax base for all communes than the progressive levy on the top incomes. They were not at all happy with a bipartisan compromise that quintupled the income ceilings from DM 16,000 (for singles) and 32,000 (married couples) a year to 80,000/160,000, a cap that would leave out, approximately, only the top 5 percent, and in communes under five thousand inhabitants hardly anyone.[28] Preliminary estimates set the 1970 range in per capita income taxes among Bavarian communes as follows:

Average for all Bavarian Communes in 1969: DM 474

Independent cities: DM 726

Range among independent cities: DM 318–1,279

Munich Grünwald: DM 2,640 (incorporated upscale suburb of Munich)

Kreis-dependent towns: DM 339

Even after the communal finance reform was passed and slated to go into effect at the beginning of 1970, the *Bayerischer Gemeindetag* was far from jubilant: "Strengthening the financial base of the communes," the president of the organization wrote in his annual report, "'only reached a part of the level that the communal associations considered desirable and necessary … still, it is a step forward—at about 240 million marks improvement for Bavaria—and we can avoid the erosion of the communal tax system only in this fashion and … stop our further movement towards a mere grant and allocation system."[29] As he pointed out earlier, political compromises had watered down the expected gains: the hoped-for cut in the business taxes had become a transfer and communal hopes of inserting a future right to set local income tax rates into the federal constitution were disappointed.

There were other problems that only came to light after the reform had actually been carried out and some hitherto unavailable 1968 statistics became available. The dilemma of the progressive zone of income taxation was resolved simply by starting with the lowest ceiling of eight thousand to sixteen thousand marks in 1970 and hiking it tenfold two years later. A last-minute effort in the *Bundesrat* to regulate only the years 1970 and 1971 and to leave the rest to future negotiations failed to make it to the conference committee between the two houses. It was a typical result of the year-end legislative rush in Bonn and the president of the *Bayerischer*

Gemeindetag expressed the "urgent hope" that the entire reform might be amended before 1972.[30] It was not to be. As the reader will recall, 1972 to 1980 were the years of the local territorial reforms in Bavaria.

The Common Tasks of Federation and *Länder*

The finance reform of 1969 and the constitutional amendments legalizing the advanced stage of cooperative federalism in the Federal Republic became the basis of the intergovernmental system henceforth. Article 104 (1) of the Basic Law had assigned separate tasks and the expenditures connected with them to the federal and *Land* levels, respectively, to be carried out by each level on its own, according to Art. 104 (5).[31] Separate tax sources had been assigned the two levels from the beginning, except that the income, corporation and, from 1969 on, the "turnover/value-added" (VAT), that is, sales taxes, were to be shared as per Art. 104 (1–3), covering almost three fourths of all tax revenues on all levels, in the hope of insuring equal development at the federal and *Land* levels. In 1983, right after the reform, for example, the purely federal taxes amounted to 47 billion marks, the *Länder* taxes to 18.4 billion, and the exclusively local taxes to 33 billion; the shared taxes were 291.4 billion, of which the communes received 14 percent of the income taxes (about 10 billion).[32]

The most important innovation of the 1969 reforms were the constitutional amendments that made shared or "common tasks (*Gemeinschaftsaufgaben*)" of federation and *Länder* part of the constitution. Article 91a (1) of the Basic Law succinctly defined the "common tasks" as original *Länder* tasks (according to Art. 30), which are so significant for the whole nation that federal participation may be required to improve general living conditions. Three such common tasks were specified: (1) the expansion and new construction of universities, including university clinics; (2) the improvement of regional economic structures; and (3) the improvement of agriculture and of coastal protection. In addition to these three common tasks, Article 91b authorized federal-state agreements covering educational planning and research promotion, a hitherto reserved *Land* category that had earlier been regulated by cooperative, voluntary *Länder* action (and also penetrated by federal grants) by the Permanent Conference of (*Land*) Ministers of Culture and Education. Further additions to the list were headed off by the determined resistance of some *Länder* governments.[33] For each of the three specified tasks, implementing legislation was issued that had to define more precisely the common tasks involved, delimit them toward the remaining *Länder* jurisdiction, and provide for "framework planning" and other procedures to safeguard the undertaking. Each *Land*, moreover, had a veto over particular common task measures in its territory that assured it of some degree of participation and consultation. In fact, it could even pursue its own solutions of the problems involved provided it was willing to finance them itself. The planning committees for joint planning and financing for each common task were composed of the federal finance minister and the appropriate ministers of federation and all *Länder,* such as all the ministers of agriculture. Decisions required a three-fourths majority of the committees, and the federation was granted eleven votes that made it impossible to outvote the federation or the *Länder* as a group. Regarding its own territory any one *Land* could veto action.

The role of the communes in all that, both finances and common task planning, remained small and mostly indirect, that is via their *Land* minister. The reactions of the communal associations to the long-range effects of the communal finance reform, in fact, became no less dyspeptic with the passage of the years even though the *Bayerischer Gemeindetag* was deeply embroiled in the controversies of school and territorial reform in the seventies. The establishment of the "common tasks," for example, elicited at first only a sigh of relief that federal authorities were still barred from interference in the local details of planning that were of the greatest concern to local government: "It certainly matters to the communes, where they are going to build a new university, and where new industry, regional economic structures, agricultural produce markets, or coastal protection by dikes … are to be improved." The communes also evinced great interest in federal financial aid to the *Länder* for *Land* or communal investments in traffic or housing improvements, urban renewal, and hospital construction (Art. 104 [4]).[34]

The communes were understandably looking for more federal grants-in-aid because, even though their gains from the trade-off between business taxes and their share of the income tax continued to improve, rising costs soon left them and their public indebtedness not far from where they had been in 1969, before the reform. The *Bayerischer Gemeindetag* referred to this as "the great sell-out" of federalism and of communal self-government because the shrinking communal fiscal capacity progressively robbed the communes of their ability to be autonomous agents and responsible for their own management.[35] By the mid seventies, the financial misery of Bavarian local government was said to turn into a "financial catastrophe," as the height of public indebtedness (16 billion marks in 1975) and the consequences of the first oil crisis came home to roost, in particular in the *Kreis*-dependent communes that had emerged from territorial reorganization. Comprehensive tax cuts decreed by the federal government in 1975 hit the local level worst of all: even though local authorities only claimed 12 percent of the total revenues they had to accept 18 percent of the cuts.

Their own ability to invest had shrunk from an annual 12 billion marks in 1967 to 4.2 billion in 1975 and 2.4 billion in 1976.[36]

The urban growth rates of the heyday of the economic miracle had long slowed down and begun to reverse, especially in the rustbelt areas of the German northwest. But even though the south, including Bavaria, eventually benefited from the great regional shift, in the short run southern cities suffered from the same cutbacks. For decades Bavaria had been a beneficiary of the horizontal financial equalization in favor of poorer *Länder*. Starting in 1989, the state became a contributor to equalization.

Further tax cuts in 1978 once more generated a discussion of how the communal finance reform should be improved so as to give the communes more financial stability and to shield them from federal and *Land* anticyclical expedients that, more often than not, had placed the largest burden on the local level. Even though 1979 once again brought temporary relief, the financial situation of West German communes continued to present a depressing picture that certainly justified the Catonic *ceterum censeo* of the *Bayerischer Gemeindetag* that "the communal finance reform of the sixties simply must be continued … in order to secure to the communes the revenues needed to fulfill their tasks. Their ever-increasing dependence on grants-in-aid must be reduced!"[37] The national trend during the seventies, the decade of the local territorial reforms and of the oil crises, instead saw West German local government expenditures double, especially in the areas of salaries, social services, and the debt service.

How real this situation was to the communes under consideration in this book can be gathered from an eloquent plea of the mayor of Wasserburg, one of the Old Bavarian towns researched by my then collaborator, Patricia Gibson Heck. The mayor, Dr. Martin Geiger, was protesting plans to abolish the local "bagatelle taxes" (dog and hunting license fees and beverage and entertainment taxes). It is a swan song of the spirit of German local self-government[38]:

> These taxes stem essentially from the constitutionally guaranteed communal right to levy taxes. They are … taxes of which every taxpayer can see the immediate link between his obligation and what the commune's government does … with his money. To abolish them is just one more step in the destruction of the responsibility of directly elected communal officers. … Every reduction of the right of a commune to levy direct property taxes and responsibly determine their rate takes away something from our self-government, from the deliberate shaping of our communal budget on the basis of levies that we can realize from our own citizenry. … They can be taxed. … Substituting for these direct taxes means … to sunder the link of responsibility between communal government and the citizenry … which can now make demands without worrying about whether the community

can pay for them. In place of weighing priorities in the communal council and the necessary self-restraint then, there emerges a mechanism of demands which begins with individuals and organized interests, makes the elected officials act as claimants upon the financial mass of the state, and distributes the ... loot according to the whim or loudness of the various interest groups.

The state system of subsidies and grants has greatly increased in recent years ... and so have the possibilities of "program"-related aid, casting an evil spell upon how communes decide on investments in their walls. ... Notifications of particular grants are no longer first sent to the commune's government but to a particular councilor or deputy ... to give the impression that he "procured" these grants for his constituency. ... There is the deliberate and lasting image of communal dependency on the efforts of a representative ... with the larger government.

Cooperative Federalism or *Politikverflechtung?*

If small-town mayors at the low end of the totem pole felt they were suffocating for lack of financial autonomy, the word from the higher levels was by no means sanguine about the results of the financial reform. Somehow things had taken the wrong turn, or perhaps the elusive goals of the reforms were already beginning to change. After all, the original problem of the system was that West Germany's rather centralized society, as Peter T. Katzenstein has put it so succinctly,[39] was governed by an emphatically decentralized set of institutions. Therefore, when the age of social reforms (the sixties) suggested a need to increase the "self-steering capacity" for the entire society, the decentralized structure became a major barrier in the path of the reformers and planners.[40] The obvious remedy at first seemed greater centralization in spite of federalism, and there was a rash of publications on cooperative federalism, including discussion of the rise of cooperative federalism in the United States.[41]

But the German system from the beginning was much less capable of separation than American federalism and, for that reason, already open to an old-style version of cooperative federalism under its sweeping federal legislative and financial powers, as we have shown above. Unlike the Anglo-American fiction of statehood and territorial turf, the West German *Länder* were only meant to be huge, autonomous administrative corporations for the implementation of federal law whose most important function—at least in the practice of the Federal Republic—had been their direct participation, through the *Bundesrat*, in federal policy-making.[42] But if the central reformers could not convince some of the *Land* politicians (for instance, of the opposition parties) and administrators of the merits of their plans, they were even more likely to be stopped than, say, a reform administration in Washington that may establish a new independent regulatory agency or administration, or carry out its intention with massive federal grants. Even if the *Bundesrat* could be overruled on major legislation—political tradeoffs have sometimes undercut its veto on bills that involve administration by the states—it still has sweeping control over the implementation of federal law and could frustrate the intent of *Bundestag* and cabinet in one way or another.[43]

How then did this new version of cooperative federalism hope to succeed where old-style cooperative federalism had failed to satisfy the demand for central steering capacity? It hoped to institutionalize what an early comment had called the "increasing tendency towards the interweaving of the political processes and contents [of all three levels] to overcome the institutional separations."[44] This political interweaving (*Politikverflechtung*) theory, according to the experts, "at least got us out of the bind of federal constitutional theories and the economic theory of federalism." It also involved consultation of the communes in the planning process although they are not exactly favored by the existing politico-economic and constitutional leverage that determines especially the initial input of all participants into *Politikverflechtung*. A great deal, of course, depends on the nature of the problems to be solved, the heterogeneity of the interests involved, and the legitimation potential of a given policy.[45]

More often than not, the initiative toward tackling new tasks by means of *Politikverflechtung* may actually have come from the communes, as in the case of the promotional grants of the urban renewal program (*Städtebauförderung*) or at least from the poorer states. The richer *Länder*, by comparison, tended to either have it their own way with an intergovernmental program, or to go it alone. The participation of the communes in the common task areas is regulated by clauses in the relevant federal legislation and by the laws of their respective *Land*. The federal *Raumordnung* law, for example, specifies the communal rights to be informed, consulted, heard, and permitted to offer alternative plans, as guaranteed by Article 28 (2) of the Basic Law. In matters of the common tasks, communes are entitled to "parity in co-dominial participation" with the *Land* authorities, and any decision about a particular commune without its own participation—as distinct from "consent"—is null and void. They could, of course, seek judicial remedies, although as we have seen this has not helped most plaintiffs as often as, in Bavaria, did the recourse to direct political appeals to the new minister president, Strauss.[46]

The Bavarian Regional Planning Act (*Landesplanungsgesetz*) guaranteed communes, rural *Kreise*, provinces, and the communal associations a chance to "participate to the extent that they would have to conform to the plans" (Paragraph 14 [2]). But since regional planning bodies were formed in accordance with it, there was no more communal participation except for the hearings of the Regional Planning Council (Paragraph 11 [3]) of which at least the representatives of the communal associations were ex officio members. The communes on the other hand were obliged to supply all information desired for the planning process. In principle, all *Länder* grant their communes participation in the regional planning process. But Bavaria and a few other *Länder* restrict much of this participation to the communal associations. The planning regions in effect block the communes from direct access although they are obliged to report communal opinions, in particular those they have overruled. Their mission, however, has been not only to collect the opinions of their *Kreise* and communes, but to try to reconcile them with each other. In that process, the region often makes decisions prejudicial to a particular commune's interest. The planning regions, the selection of central places, and the criteria for the location of small centers were all decided without any communal input or participation. Communes were allowed their say at too late a stage and not in time to make meaningful alternative proposals.[47] No doubt, this procedure greatly simplified and facilitated the painful process of regional planning, but it also detracted from its consensual and democratic legitimacy.

Critics of *Politikverflechtung*

The communal finance reform and the legalization of the common tasks raised so much controversy that both administrators and academic specialists decided to examine more closely the course of the implementation of the three common tasks. A large research project carried on at universities in Berlin and Konstanz, in 1974, combined detailed case studies with critical comments from all sides. The project examined various approaches to the common tasks and surveyed earlier forms of intergovernmental cooperation—for instance agricultural subsidies and the Green plan since the 1950s.[48] It also searched the course of relevant intergovernmental disputes for clues. Some *Länder*, for example, had rejected the guideposts for the territorial reform.

Bavaria, in particular, insisted on federal subsidies for all central places whereas the federation was only willing to consider those with a hinterland of at least twenty thousand people. The clash produced a compromise that promised federal support to only 114 of the 332 centers selected by the state (see chapter 3). Bavaria's preference for creating widely scattered industrial opportunities for its part-time farmers rather than for the industrial concentrations of the federal plans created further friction, and so did the objections of Bavaria and Baden-Württemberg to the 1971–1973 project to improve agricultural structures. In all these conflicts, the *Länder* were clearly the "heavies," but could not always stop federal action completely. A lot of the details of the federal plans were changed during implementation: the planned aid for older farm workers, for example, became a social structural (welfare) measure; subsidies for farm machinery co-ops were dropped when it proved impossible to reach a consensus.[49] The *Länder* determined the distribution of program funds on their soil themselves, retained the right to aid supplementary policies—at their own expense—and continued to control their own aesthetic and cultural preservation of the landscape according to their own regional plans.[50]

Another common task considered by the group grew out of the rising burden of motorized traffic on communal roads from the 1950s to the finance reform of 1969. The federation had collected all the gasoline taxes and automobile license fees, sharing very little of the revenue with the other levels. In 1960 a "communal penny" was added to the gasoline tax, but only for local roads connecting to the long-distance road net and, starting in 1966, the communes also received a percentage of the *Länder* share of this tax. The Communal Traffic Financing Act (GVFG) of 1971 finally provided for complementary financing by all three levels, but with the *Länder* determining the distribution between themselves and their communes. Major road planning was mostly in the hands of state agencies, which often all but ignored the regional plans.[51]

The most intriguing area of intergovernmental cooperation was probably the evolution of urban renewal from its fifties' antecedents of rebuilding the devastated cities and providing much needed housing for the ethnic refugees and others desperate for shelter—after four decades of housing and rent controls in the cities. At first almost any addition to available housing was welcome. But by the early sixties, a variety of new concerns began to replace the mere desire to supply more housing. The need to renovate old housing, the role of old tenements on a housing market straining toward saturation, the crowding of the cities—overall urban and regional planning became more important than building apartments. The "functional weakness" of the urban core areas even suggested subsidizing them like central places. There seemed to be no market solutions or adequate local finances for these problems before the drawn-out debates of the 1960s over various versions of the Promotion of Urban Construction Act of 1971. The *Länder* and the communal associations resisted "mixed financing" by several levels prior to the communal finance reform. The addition of voluntary investment aid (Basic Law Art. 104 [a]) finally supplied the constitutional basis for it and the first funds began to flow in 1971–1973. The communes welcomed the investments in which the federal planners soon perceived their most "spatially related" development tool.

The *Länder* actually showed more reluctance than the communes to be drawn into the larger national planning process of the SPD-Free Democratic party (FDP) government in Bonn that manifested itself in statements such as "we cannot permit purely local development goals anymore without referring to the larger economic, interrelated whole."[52] Christian Democratic Bavaria protested the loudest, abstained in the *Bundesrat*, and (in 1972) sued to have the procedure declared unconstitutional by the Federal Constitutional Court. It felt that the federation had a habit of going beyond the *Länder* priorities. In practice, the communes initiating proposals had at first submitted many ill-chosen projects and, within a few years, by 1975, the number of new applications became negligible anyway. The funding came in thirds from each level, with private resources making up much of the communal share. Bavaria and several other *Länder* insisted on using urban renewal as a means to support the weaker areas of the state even though the latter had a much harder time to raise the private capital for their share. Needless to say, most applications came from conurbations and not from the weaker rural regions.[53] Neither the federal nor the *Länder* programs were really designed to ameliorate structural weaknesses and hence tended to aggravate the inequalities.

Politikverflechtung was not noticeably more successful with hospital construction where the government had inherited a fivefold cost inflation from 1950 to 1970 with only modest increases in the working load. The inevitable major deficits and cuts in further investment led to rival plans motivated by the unequal distribution of hospital beds and by fears of pushing the public health insurance beyond tolerable limits. Everyone seemed to accept the need for a federal subsidy combined with higher charges to the consumer. But the *Länder* rejected this as a "common task" and were then obliged to present annual hospital construction programs with lists of priorities.[54] Thus, the federal "steering role" had completely fallen to the *Länder* and the *Bundesrat* was able to veto any attempt to revive it on the grounds that this would represent an example of "unconstitutional mixed administration." The federation was not even in a position to determine the volume of its one third of the financing.

The researchers concluded that, on the whole, *Politikverflechtung* did not resolve the problems of level fixation, distribution, or interaction, and that the varying degrees of effectiveness had to do with the varying need to obtain a broad consensus for a policy. The difficulties of the process could be reduced by the simple expedient of reducing the number of participants. The finance reform of 1969 had put an end to bilateral decisions and the common task amendments (Articles 91a and 104a[4]) demanded that all the *Länder* and the federation be represented on the planning committees. Beyond this, programs such as low-income housing for large families, singles, the elderly, and the handicapped have always brought in representatives of districts and counties to determine the distribution of funding; this resulted in excessive complexity (*Überverflechtung*) and stalemate. Requiring unanimity on the joint committees was a poor formula for consensus, but majority coalitions were even worse. The functional ministries of federation and *Länder* preferred to handle intergovernmental cooperation along vertical, functional, or project lines rather than in the multilateral mode favored by cost-conscious finance ministries, although functional decision systems usually lacked alternative options. Segmenting the decisions into (a) *Land*-federal, (b) within *Land*, functional, (c) within *Land*, regional, and (d) bilateral *Land*-commune elements at least tended to reduce the need for consensus within each segment.[55]

In the process of technical evaluation of individual applications, such as for communal roads or low-income housing, the decisions are rarely made at a level higher than the *Länder*, or lower, as at the district or provincial level. Thus, there is more de facto coordination from the bottom than "steering" from above. Formulas such as "equal treatment," "maintaining the existing possessions" (*Besitzstandswahrung*), postponement of conflict, and foregoing conflicts greatly facilitated the negotiations. Federal grants without strings or a stronger process of vertical and horizontal financial equalization, the researchers believed, might have avoided *Überverflechtung* and the requirements of complex consensus structures. The Enquête Commission on Constitutional Reform, however, wanted to keep *Politikverflechtung*, and so did the communal associations and the *Land* and federal ministers even though many a member of parliament was dubious about it. Why this support? Because *Politikverflechtung* did reduce conflicts, or at least it made it easy to spread the blame when rejecting an applicant. They also credited it with the capacity to initiate and stabilize new programs.[56]

Retreat from Intergovernmental Interweaving?

If the "political interweaving" (*Politikverflechtung*) was viewed with misgivings by some of the planners and policy innovators, the communes felt even more at a disadvantage, considering their role in the political-economic system and their modest constitutional role. Their *Land* governments, some of the communal representatives felt, tended to "buy" their fiscal autonomy with subsidies that brought more strings than cash. Only the largest urban agglomerations had enough disruptive potential—often with the help of strong environmentalist or consumer groups—to counter this kind of "imperialistic *Politikverflechtung*" with insistent demands for participating in the decision-making process. Smaller communes, such as the ones considered here, lacked their capacity for information and conflict management and were unable to "undercut state *dirigisme*,"[57] as the big cities might.

However, the accusation of imperialistic manipulation was likely to surprise both the *Land* diets and their governments. The latter felt that the common tasks and their planning processes had greatly reduced their leeway for shaping policies that had long been exclusively or at least "concurrently" theirs. Even more emphatic was the complaint of the *Landtage*, whose shrinking sphere of action was small to begin with, that they were completely left out of representation on the planning committees—and so was the *Bundestag*. They had an ominous new slogan, the "emasculation of the parliaments" (*Entmachtung der Parlamente*), although the *Landtage* were not legally bound by the intergovernmental agreements concluded with respect to particular measures. But the critics in the *Landtage* were unlikely to stop the momentum of badly needed measures or to challenge, by means of parliamentary control over the executive, the discretion used by the planning committees, and the promised federal subsidies in practice.[58] The regional differences in the Federal Republic, moreover, tended to undercut the resistance of the *Länder* in the *Bundesrat*. Small wonder that minister presidents of *Länder* as different as Baden-Württemberg (Filbinger, CDU) and Hesse (Oswald, SPD) decided at an early point that they would prefer to see the "common tasks" abolished again. Some observers made a plea for "disentangling" (*Entflechtung*) the two levels, moving toward more "separative practices," and instead returning the authority to the *Länder*, and giving them a bigger percentage of the shared taxes to use as they may see fit.[59]

The well-known German political scientist Gerhard Lehmbruch had already in earlier writings on West German democracy raised the question whether *Politikverflechtung* was not undermining the competitive processes of democracy. Now he came back to this question, in response to the case studies in Konstanz and Berlin, and put the answer in the context of the economic crisis of the late 1970s, the second oil shock. The financial needs of the poorer *Länder* may have been the trigger for the establishment of *Politikverflechtung*, he agreed, but economic crisis management soon took over and introduced a kind of institutional conservatism born of the growing sense of crisis: Now everybody looked to the federation, under Helmut Schmidt's leadership, for all social welfare needs and it had to oblige for the sake of its own continuing legitimation.

The federal government, from its own point of view, was afraid to reduce the excessive "political interweaving" lest the *Länder* use their additional financial resources for purposes other than the urgent needs of the whole polity. Lehmbruch doubted that interweaving was working well and questioned whether the goals of the common tasks were really so clear that the federal government was in a better position to decide what to do than the decentralized levels of government. He concluded that there were still important policy areas that had better be kept out of the clutches of bureaucratic *Politikverflechtung* and saved for the play of competitive democratic forces.[60] He mentioned in particular the highly controversial subject of educational policy that had just been drawn into the common tasks under a federal-*Länder* commission on educational planning.[61] Furthermore, did the constitution really demand uniform living conditions throughout the country? He hoped that, following the recommendations of the Enquête Commission on Constitutional Reform, it might be possible to roll back the intergovernmental *Politikverflechtung* by turning the formerly concurrent and framework legislative jurisdiction of the federation into a mere power to determine policy guidelines (*Richtlinienkompetenz*).[62]

Critical voices from several *Länder* administrations joined the chorus of dissatisfaction with the constitutional changes and the planning and financing of the common tasks. They tended to agree on a number of points: (a) that the *Länder* would be much better off with funds obtained under an objective system of financial equalization and to be spent at their discretion; (b) that the southern *Länder* had different needs and should be allowed to go their own way in economic development; (c) that uniform solutions were no panacea; and (d) that the communes should not be allowed to establish an independent role for themselves in the constitutional system.[63] They also took a dim view of the "Marxist verbiage and critiques" of some reformers and flatly denied that the Federal Republic in the 1980s was somehow suffering from a greater degree of economic or social crisis than other industrialized democracies, as some of the reformers had alleged.

The Future Role of the Communes

Representatives of the communes, by comparison, were quite aware that there had been a politicization of local planning processes in the seventies that no one would have thought possible a mere ten years earlier. Young and radical activists found the big-city scene, in particular, irresistible as a theater for staging grassroots reforms.[64] A rising tide of citizen initiatives swept the calm lagoons of small-town and -county governments as well.

In the processes of macro-economic management through neo-corporatist mechanisms, such as Concerted Action, and Councils of Financial Planning, and of the Council for Cyclical Economic Policy (*Konjunkturrat*) in the seventies, the communes were granted a new standing in the constitutional system, but this also restricted their autonomy by assigning them a role in national anti-cyclical policy. The communal associations would really have preferred specific recognition of the local governments as the "third pillar" of the system—in an amended Article 28 (2[3]) of the Basic Law. They also wanted a requirement of consultation with them whenever appropriate in the rules of procedure of both houses of parliament and the executive departments.[65] There had even been proposals for establishing consultants of the communal associations in the *Bundesrat* and its committees, presumably selected and delegated by the *Landtage* to participate by constitutional right in the planning of the common tasks. An alternative proposal was for a federal *Kommunalrat*, as a third chamber of parliament, or a similar second or third chamber of the *Landtage*—most of the *Landtage* are unicameral; with the abolition of the Bavarian Senate all have become so—in order to maintain the autonomy of the communes in all measures affecting them.[66]

Though these proposals stood little chance of acceptance at this point, their proponents could point to significant precedents in German and Prussian constitutional debates of the last 130 years. Article 88 of the 1848–1849 Frankfurt constitutional draft proposed to give half of the seats of the larger states (which had a provincial level) in the House of States to representatives of their provincial estates. The Prussian constitution of 1848, also a product of the abortive 1848 uprisings, proposed that the First Chamber (House of Lords) be composed of representatives elected by the provincial, district, or *Kreis* deputies, including thirty deputies elected by the councils of the larger cities. This provision was removed entirely in 1853 when the monarchy made the House of Lords exclusively one of hereditary and lifetime peers, although the Prussian king by his grace granted some cities a "right of representations." The 1920 constitution of republican Prussia set up a Council of State for the representation of the Prussian provinces in legislation and administration. It was elected by the provincial *Landtage* and the Berlin city council. The original draft of the Weimar constitution had proposed dismembering the huge state of Prussia by more or less turning its provinces into *Länder* of the Weimar federation, thus "dissolving Prussia into the Reich." But this never came about even though it was still under discussion at the *Länder* Conference on Territorial Reorganization of ten years later. Instead, the successor of the old *Bundesrat*, then named *Reichsrat*, allocated half of the Prussian seats to the provinces and the city of Berlin (Art. 63 [1]).

None of this was really what the communal representatives were demanding now. There were also objections and not only to the direct representation of the communes, but even more to the representative rights of the communal associations as such.[67] Given the highly integrated nature of West German government and society, however, there is perhaps no use pretending that communal interests require a quasi-federal constitutional status within the *Länder*—in an age when the old-time image of federalism among quasi-sovereign states has become dubious and unrealistic anyway—to secure themselves against being strong-armed by the larger, organized forces of society and government. On the other hand, vertical *Politikverflechtung* involved forces of such difference of magnitude that perhaps only a constitutional basis can protect the lower and smaller local units from the larger and more aggressive ones. To be sure, the communes want to participate in decisions that affect them in crucial ways. Meaningful participation in such a highly integrated system, however, can be achieved quite effectively by being consulted, heard, informed, asked for one's opinion, and given a chance to make alternative proposals.[68] The desideratum is a kind of codetermination or a "paritatic codominial participation" (Henrich) in all decisions affecting a commune and its members. Party competition and democratic elections, moreover, are no less effective a device against being strong-armed than the constitutional devices of quasi-federalism.

Within a particular *Land* such as Bavaria, however, the participation of all but the largest of the communes indeed tends to be absorbed and mediatized by in-between layers of government and of planning: planning regions, *Kreise,* and districts all tend to keep the smaller commune from acting as independently as if they were located on the moon, or on an island many miles from the rest of German society. Regional associations do not just collect the opinions of the communes within their respective area but try to reconcile them with each other, which is bound to lead to planning decisions contrary to the will of at least some of them.[69] The smaller communes are even less able to resist the imperatives of the *Land* Development Plan even though the *Land* government is of course obliged to consult them and to permit them to participate, through their communal association, in the formulation of goals and determination of particulars. Again, the big cities of a *Land,* say Munich or Nuremberg, are likely to retain a great deal more self-determination in this process than little Wasserburg or the small communities discussed in our first chapters and the conclusion. Rosenheim has more clout than Wasserburg but not nearly as much as Munich. But as examples from New York to Rome and Frankfurt have shown, even big cities are not masters of their own fate and can go bankrupt like any small community in Middle Franconia.

What is true of the planning process of the *Länder* applies with redoubled force to the (not always successful) efforts at macroeconomic "steering" at the national level. Given the centralization of economic processes and organizations in the Federal Republic, it would be ludicrous for even a large city to pretend it was isolated from what affects everybody's livelihood and opportunities. This is not to exclude local initiatives or the right of each community to be heard and to participate in the complex process of national policy-making. A smaller commune also can take the initiative and demand to be consulted in decisions affecting it, although its leverage and options are likely to be more limited. Despite the presence of at least three good reasons that tilt the balance toward local initiative we must not overestimate its de facto capacity for local self-determination: (1) the often unsatisfactory results of the "steering" efforts of the seventies and eighties; (2) the built-in bias of the institutional fabric of federalism that has been amazingly effective in resisting centralized initiatives under conditions of well-meaning, if ineffectual *Politikverflechtung;* and (3) the strong popular predilection for local, decentralized solutions to most social and economic problems. The evident confusions and at least partial failure of *Politikverflechtung* as a "steering" mechanism does not by itself signify an enhanced capacity for the smaller communes to determine their own fate.[70]

These were the battles within and around the period of territorial reorganization in Bavaria. Much of the debate, the problems, and attempted solutions of applying to Bavaria what had been accomplished elsewhere in the intergovernmental system also stemmed from regional differences in West Germany. The North is different from the South in many ways, and Bavaria has been at one end of a range of parameters characterizing modern German society.

German Unification

In the meantime, moreover, the unification of West and East Germany, after more than forty years of communist rule, has given rise to even larger challenges of heterogeneity. As mentioned earlier, the five new East German *Länder* and the Eastern half of unified Berlin posed extraordinary challenges of integration into the existing West German federal and intergovernmental system. This was evident also from the continuing discussion of territorial realignments among the eastern *Länder,* even if nothing more came of these debates but the stillborn union of Berlin and Brandenburg. It looms largest, however, with the financial disequilibrium between East and West Germany. The East German *Länder* and municipalities have been in a state of financial dependency under suspended federal financial arrangements that still apply to the West German system.[71] The massive flow of federal and West German funds to the East continues for the fore-seeable future as long as the East remains so far behind the West.

Over the long life of West German federalism, to be sure, there have been major changes that in some cases have turned poorer *Länder* that were the recipients of funds into richer, donor *Länder*. Among other cases, the once affluent state of North Rhine Westphalia has long become some-thing akin to the rustbelt states of the American Midwest while southern states have moved from agrarian poverty to high-technology leadership. Bavaria has shared in this transformation, if in a modest way. When Ger-man unification, however, brought in a new *mezzogiorno* of poverty and depression with the Eastern *Länder*, there seemed to be no reasonable way of confirming the old system of horizontal financial equalization—funnel-ing a percentage of the above-average revenues of the richer to the poorer *Länder*—as the likely annual transfers rose sixfold from about DM 3.5 to 20 billion. Instead, an increase in the *Länder* share of the value added taxes (VAT), from 1993 on, was directed toward the new *Länder*. The en-tire system was overhauled in 1995, a process still not entirely complete in some ways. In this fashion, the intergovernmental system continued to be unsettled, if for different reasons.[72] In the meantime, the debate over the constitutional Article 104 (4) continues, especially regarding the equaliza-tion of different economic levels of capacity, the promotion of economic growth, and the abolition of "mixed [intergovernmental] financing."

Local Government in East Germany

German unification in 1990 not only reminded local officials in East and West of the striking regional differences in the organization and nature of local government in the East. It also highlighted the different develop-ments since 1945 in East and West, including the local territorial reforms of the 1960s and 1970s in most Western *Länder*. The unified election lists of the East German state Communist party (SED) had brought both the Communist party and also a substantial representation of women on post-war communal councils (16 percent) and mayors (18 percent) there. The budget laws of the 1950s furthermore incorporated all communal budgets into the national budget of the German Democratic Republic (GDR), thereby taking away the rest of their local budgetary autonomy. The GDR constitutional reform of 1952 abolished the existing five *Länder* and re-placed them with fourteen districts (*Bezirke*) in which 27 urban and 191 rural *Kreise* could be found.[73]

At the time of the Western local reforms, the GDR had some 7,500 sub-*Kreis* towns and villages of which 5,500 were smaller than one thou-sand residents (3,500 even below five hundred). By 1990 about one-fifth of the eastern population still lived in communes under one thousand in population (as compared to barely 4 percent in West Germany since the great reform, and 1 percent in Bavaria). Most of the micro-communes under five hundred were in the *Länder* where once large estates and then large collective farms played a dominant role: Mecklenburg-Vorpommern, Brandenburg, and Thuringia. It was a very different, authoritarian system than the service-oriented one emerging in the West, although the proportion of micro-communes was quite similar to that in Bavaria.

German unification promised East German local government a "veritable rebirth of communal self-government," beginning with the local elections of 7 May 1990 (that followed the fraudulent GDR elections a year earlier) and the new Communal Constitution of 17 May 1990, which in most respects introduced West German models of local government to the East. In particular, East German communes now enjoyed authority over their planning, budgets, and personnel that had been withheld under communism.[74] Yet even after unification, the East German *Kreise* resisted yielding these powers to their rightful new agents. The civic initiative groups of 1989–1990 and the round tables of the great transition had demanded real local self-government as a priority of the first order.

On the other hand, the communes still had to settle into their new roles. Some *Bürgermeister* and larger communes, for example, were reluctant to accept the regional plans, especially regarding zoning and construction (*Bauleitplanung*), when they clashed with their desire to supply large sites to giant retail centers. The communal councils still have far to go to learn to control their respective *Bürgermeisters*—a legacy of communal authoritarianism—and their communes long suffered from a general lack of financial resources, equipment, rooms, and personnel.[75]

Worst of all, there had been an extraordinary amount of turnover in communal personnel caused by the post-unification upheaval when job offers in private industry and in other locations, family pressures resulting from rising unemployment, the removal of communist political and nomenclature appointees from key offices, and general disillusionment with the blessings of democracy had their impact on the new local governments.[76] On the lower administrative levels, a lot of the old personnel remained in spite of the low salaries. Hence routine local functions were frequently vitiated by "old-boy" (or old-guard) networks, the ill-reputed *Seilschaften* (literally, those who pull the same ropes). Large communes needed to hire a lot more and well-trained staff as they followed the example of their respective West German partner cities or organizational schemes supplied by the Communal Office for Administrative Rationalization (KGSV, *Kommunale Gemeinschaftsstelle für Verwaltungsvereinfachung*).

East German local government under the GDR also underwent territorial reorganizations of sorts in 1950—when about 2,200 of 9,750 communes disappeared—and in 1973–1974 that brought another 1,200 mergers or annexations. In 1991, after unification, a new wave of reform began that, for example in Brandenburg, aimed at an average commune size of eight thousand residents and created both VGs (*Aemter*)—with at least five member communes and a total population of five thousand— and EGs.[77] In Brandenburg this resulted in 160 *Aemter* with 1,638 communes, for an average of eleven communes and 8,000 residents per *Amt*. Nearly all *Aemter* (139) take charge of their own administrative needs, though a few delegate them to one of their communes.[78]

There was an understandable reluctance to speed up local territorial reform in East Germany lest it displace and discourage large numbers of activist democratic participants at a point when East German democratic practice was still relatively new and beset by disappointments and the revival of the old communist state party (SED) in the form of the Party of Democratic Socialism (PDS) and then the Left Opposition. There was also a movement for communal constitutional reform afoot in both East and West that tried to adapt local government to its changed social environment. One of the proposed paths of reform would introduce principles of private business administration to much of the routines and thinking behind traditional German local government. Some of the eastern *Länder* also showed a pronounced preference for direct democracy on the *Land* and on the local level.[79]

Finally, the financial crisis of German local government is still around, most of all in East Germany where the German *Städtetag* had predicted early that the level of indebtedness of DM 2.2 billion in 1998 would grow and grow. The fiscal capacity of East German communes, according to *Städtetag* Director Jochen Dieckmann, was at about 42 percent of the West German level. Dieckmann described their financial condition as between "bad" and "catastrophic" and speculated that they would remain dependent on Western subsidies for a long time to come.[80] The heavy financial burden of German unification along with the structural long-term economic problems such as masses of foreign residents and of unemployed workers had spread this crisis to West Germany too. Large cities (over two hundred thousand), in particular, house half the foreign residents, half of the unemployed, and half of all the recipients of social assistance.

The *Länder* and the European Union

This survey of the larger context of German local government would not be complete if we neglected to mention the increasingly intrusive progress of European integration. Without exception, the German *Länder* have welcomed European initiatives and institutions even though they were aware that the inevitable loss of sovereign rights had a pronounced impact on their already very limited repertoire. Under Article 24 of the Basic Law, European Union (EU) regulations and international law have precedence over national and state laws. The federal government at least is represented in the European Council of Ministers and other common bodies whereas the *Länder* are not even consulted when their federal government, for example in higher education and with regard to the electronic media, transfers *Land* powers to the EU.[81]

Already before the fall of the Wall, in the 1980s, West German *Land* politicians had begun to press for protection against the erosion of their powers, both from the federal government and the European Union under the Single European Act of 1986. Their concern led to the presentation at the 1987 Conference of *Land* Minister Presidents of ten theses about their rights vis-à-vis the EU. The federal government readily conceded these points in 1987 and henceforth invited them to participate by right in preparations for other meetings and intergovernmental conferences of the EU. From these antecedents also, there came the recommendation at a July 1990 meeting of *Land* Minister Presidents, and in Art. 5 of the Unification Treaty of 1990, that federalism be strengthened in tangible ways in the federal constitution.

In 1992, the federal parliament formed a Joint Constitutional (Enquête) Commission, which proposed a number of constitutional changes, in particular additional barriers against further federal encroachment into the legislative powers of the *Landtage* (Basic Law Arts. 72, 74, 75). Of particular significance was an amendment of Art. 24 of the Basic Law to the effect that from now on the approval of the *Bundesrat* would be required for any further transfers of exclusive *Länder* powers or other vital *Länder* interests to the federal or EU level. At the same time, the *Bundesrat* also created a Europe Chamber in which all sixteen *Länder* governments, and the federal government, have a share.

In August 1990, at the time of German unification, a *Bundesrat* resolution spelled out the fears and hopes of the German *Länder* regarding the plans for a "Europe of the Regions" and the intergovernmental relations among all these levels of institutions. A consultative regional council, the *Länder* agreed, would be attached to the Economic and Social Committee that advises the EU Commission and the Council of Ministers. In the end this was not accepted by the delegation negotiating the Maastricht Treaty but the Treaty did adopt the principle of subsidiarity—decentralization in favor of the rights of smaller communities inside the larger EU community: to govern themselves as much as possible.[82]

Once the Maastricht Treaty was adopted in 1992, *Länder* ministers were given the right to appear and represent their interests when called upon by their EU member government, in this case Germany. An advisory Committee of the Regions (COR) was also created and the Joint Constitutional Commission recommended amending Article 24 of the Basic Law with respect to expanded *Bundesrat* rights in EU matters and adding a new "Europe article" (no. 23): The article guaranteed that the EU will preserve federalism and subsidiarity and that—pursuant to earlier *Länder*-federation agreements for this transition—the *Bundesrat* had to approve future transfers of sovereignty, especially when they involved *Länder* functions.[83] In fact, under a 1993 law, a two-thirds *Bundesrat* majority could even impose its position on EU matters on the federal government, another demonstration of the erosion of national sovereignty within the EU. To speed up the time-consuming process of *Bundesrat* decision-making—at least three weeks—moreover, the Europe Chamber within the *Bundesrat* could make instant decisions. The Chamber actually dates from 1988 when it was only West German and it was called the EC Chamber. It consists of only one representative per *Land* but each Land has from three to six votes, corresponding to the statutory number of seats in the plenary *Bundesrat*.

One of the first conflicts under the Maastricht Treaty involved the *Land* of Saxony and the authority of the EU Commission to approve or disapprove public industrial subsidies under certain circumstances. In 1996, the EU Commission had approved a sizable investment by the Volkswagen Co. in an area of Saxony particularly impacted by the after-effect of the pre-1990 German division, in this case with high (17 percent) unemployment. The state of Saxony, moreover, was authorized to subsidize Volkswagen's plans with DM 50 million. When the Saxonian Land government offered a subsidy nearly three times as large, the EU Commission objected and threatened to bring legal action before the European Court of Justice. At this point the federal government intervened and in 1997 effected a compromise that caused the EU Commission to withdraw its complaint. *Land* Saxony and the federal government, however, chose to further petition the European Court to clarify EU policy regarding regional subsidies in East Germany. This case suggests both the difficulties of managing market conditions in the EU and the role of federation and *Länder*.[84]

Notes

1. Quoted from Arthur Benz, *Föderalismus als dynamisches System. Zentralisierung und Dezentralisierung im föderativen Staat* (Opladen, 1985), 1.

2. Karl Ganser, "Politikverflechtung zwischen Bund und *Ländern*—Beobachtungen am Rand der Bundesverwaltung," in *Politikverflechtung im föderativen Staat*, Jens Joachim Hesse, ed. (Baden-Baden, 1978), 45–73, 45n.

3. See also the Schlussbericht der Enquête-Kommission Verfassungsreform, *Bundestags-drucksache no. 7/5924*, 166 ff. (9 December 1976); and *Gutachten der Kommission für wirtschaftlichen und sozialen Wandel in der BRD* (Göttingen, 1977).

4. See, for instance, *Regierbarkeit. Studien zu ihrer Problematisierung*, 2 vols., Wilhelm Hennis, Peter Graf Kielmannsegg, and Ulrich Matz, eds. (Stuttgart, 1977–1979).

5. See esp. Arthur Gunlicks, *Local Government in the German Federal System* (Durham, 1986), 73–81; and Hans-Georg Wehling, "Kommunale Verfassungsreform: Vergleich der Kommunalen Verfassungssysteme in Deutschland," in *Politische Bildung 31*, no. 1 (1998), 19–33. The Bavarian model is a variant of the South German council form that differs from other German regions with its first or lord mayor who is popularly elected for six years on a party ticket. The mayor is the voting chair of the council, which can add a second or more mayors. *1973 GVBl.*, as amended in *1974 GVBl.*, 502. The communal council varies from eight to eighty members depending on the size of the commune and, above a population size of three thousand, is organized into committees.

6. This accusation was common in the late sixties when German leftwing reformers saw in governmental decentralization an obstacle to their hopes. From their point of view, reactionary capitalism, the revival of old and new feudal boundaries, and American hegemony all seemed to be woven of the same cloth. But see also Carlo Schmid, "Bund und *Länder*," in *Die zweite Republik. 25 Jahre Bundesrepublik Deutschland—Eine Bilanz*, Richard Löwenthal and Hans-Peter Schwarz, eds. (Stuttgart, 1974), 244–260.

7. All of the West German *Länder*, except for Bavaria, Hamburg, and Bremen were indeed patched together by the occupying powers from smaller and earlier antecedents. See Merkl, *The Origin of the West German Republic* (New York, 1963), chapter 2. The choice of Bonn as a capital was in deliberate avoidance of the metropole of Frankfurt.

8. Ibid., 73–79 and 121–122. The Allies particularly objected to the process of equalization of financial revenues between the richer and the poorer states.

9. This feature of nearly complete separation and mutual independence between the state and federal governments is considered typical of Anglo-American federalism by such writers as the late Kenneth C. Wheare. See also United States Advisory Commission on Intergovernmental Relations, *The Condition of Contemporary Federalism: Conflicting Theories and Collapsing Constraints* (Washington, DC, 1981), 2–3.

10. United States Advisory Commission on Intergovernmental Relations, *Studies in Comparative Federalism: Australia, Canada, the U.S. and West Germany* (Washington, DC, 1981), 36; and David Conradt, *The German Polity*, 3rd ed. (White Plains, NY, 1986), 152–155.

11. German experts on the subject have also suggested that the enlarged *Bundesrat* with its increased number of less partisan *Länder* (that have coalition governments different from the alignment in Bonn) is far less under the influence of partisan divisions and, in this respect, closer to the original design of the framers of the Basic Law. See Heinz Laufer and Ursula Münch, "Die Neugestaltung der bundesstaatlichen Ordnung," in *Die Gestaltung der deutschen Einheit*, Jesse Eckhard and Armin Mitter, eds. (Bonn, Berlin, 1992), 227–228.

12. See Merkl, "Executive-Legislative Federalism in West Germany," *The American Political Science Review*, 53, no. 3 (September 1959), 732–741.

13. See also *Studies in Comparative Federalism: West Germany*, 9–10. The *Länder* need to pay also for a vast array of administrators to carry out the federal laws as well as their own.
14. Laufer and Münch, "Die Neugestaltung. ...", 231–235. The great needs of East Germany—which in comparison to areas of the original European Union is among the poorest regions, similar to Portugal and Greece—require the Federal Republic to continue precisely the kind of federal grants program (under Art. 104 [a, 4] of the Basic Law) that the framers of the constitution rejected when American occupation authorities proposed this method of financial aid.
15. Until 1990, there had been no female *Landräte* and very few female mayors in Bavaria. At that time, three female *Landräte* were elected (one each from the CSU, SPD, and a local voters' association) in run-off elections. The number of female mayors and communal councilors has been rising as well.
16. The vom Stein-Hardenberg reforms in Prussia are often erroneously reported as a glorious campaign to awaken local bourgeois pride and participation for its own sake, or for reviving medieval municipal government. But the reforms initially proposed bourgeois participation only at the provincial level in an effort to broaden the base of the Prussian state. In the long run, however, Prussian cities did gain considerably from the 1808 reforms, which enfranchised their trading and propertied bourgeoisie. See Adelheid von Saldern, "Geschichte der kommunalen Selbstverwaltung in Deutschland," in *Kommunalpolitik. Politisches Handeln in den Gemeinden*, Roland Roth and Helmut Wollmann, eds. (Opladen, 1993), 2–19; and Peter Schäfer, *Zentralisation und Dezentralisation* (Berlin, 1982), 78–89.
17. The Prussian Communal Code of 1845 already indicated the responsibility of the communes for the welfare needs of the industrial revolution. The *Reich* welfare legislation of the 1880s likewise assumed that the local level was the obvious choice for this function that was, to say the least, quite at variance with the traditional hostility shown to laboring "transients" by such large Bavarian cities as Nuremberg.
18. See also Merkl, "The Urban Challenge Under the Empire," in *Another Germany: A Reconsideration of the Imperial Era*, Jack R. Dukes and Joachim Remak, eds. (Boulder, CO, 1988), 61–72.
19. See *Kommunalpolitik im Wandel der Gesellschaft*, Oscar W. Gabriel, ed. (Mainz, 1979), 10–13, 22; and *Lokale Politik zwischen Eigenständigkeit und staatlicher Abhängigkeit*, Heinz Zielinski, ed. (Meisenheim, 1980), 16–46, esp. 28–31 where the author graphically illustrates the triumph of the service state (*Leistungsverwaltung*) over the authoritarian mission (*Ordnungsverwaltung*) in Siegen.
20. The word pseudo-federal is meant to denote the elements of authoritarian and "imperialistic" domination that are at variance with the spirit of federalism, for instance the Prussian hegemony over the rest of the federation.
21. See Merkl, *The Making of a Stormtrooper* (Princeton, NJ, 1980), 163–165. For the Saldern quote see Saldern, *Kommunalpolitik*, 6.
22. The empire had gotten along with indirect taxes, fees, and custom levies that frequently left the *Reich* government a beggar at the doors of the more affluent states. Erzberger's financial reforms put the *Reich* on a sound financial footing but neglected to assure the communes of a reasonable share of the public revenues. See also Jutta Helm, "The Politics of German Cities: A Tale of Visions, Money, and Democracy," in *The Federal Republic of Germany at Fifty: The End of a Turbulent Century*, Merkl, ed. (New York, 1999), 203–215; and Merkl, "The Financial Constitution (*Finanzverfassung*) of Western Germany," *American Journal of Comparative Law*, 6 (Spring 1957), 327–340, which describes also the 1955 campaign to give the communes a constitu-

tional claim—as the "third pillar of federalism"—on the financial resources of their *Länder*.

23. See Frido Wagener, "Milderungsmöglichkeiten nachteiliger Folgen vertikaler Politikverflechtung," in Hesse, *Politikverflechtung im föderativen Staat*, 152; and Bundesminister der Finanzen, *Finanzberichte*, various years. The federal figure for 1986 does not include the ERP funds and the EC shares in the federal budget. Also Kommission für die Finanzreform, *Gutachten über die Finanzreform in der BRD* (Stuttgart, 1966). See also the comparative tables on the local share of public expenditures, local sources of income, and debt status of West Germany, Britain, Italy, and Scandinavia in Kenneth Newton, *Balancing the Books: Financial Problems of Local Government in West Europe* (London and Beverly Hills, 1980), 9.

24. See John Shannon, *Local Finance in Great Britain, West Germany, and the United States: A Comparative Analysis*, National Urban Policy Roundtable (Columbus, OH, 1978), 2–5.

25. For excerpts from Chancellor Kiesinger's address, see *Bayerischer Gemeindetag*, January 1968, 1–2 (hereafter, *BG*); and Otto Barbarino, "Zur Reformbedürftigkeit der gegenwärtigen Finanzverfassung," in *Politikverflechtung zwischen Bund, Ländern und Gemeinden* (Berlin, 1974), 105–106 and 109–110.

26. Increased turnover or value-added taxes were expected to make up the shortfall but their likely impact on business and consumers ruled out this measure under the circumstances. In anticipation of the "harmonization" of certain taxes within the EC, the business tax seemed a logical target for a trade-off. See Peter Gröbner, "Schwierige Gemeindefinanzreform," *Bayerischer Bürgermeister*, 1968, no. 2, 33–35 (hereafter, *BB*), and the proposals themselves, 36–38.

27. See the resolution of the Bayerischer Gemeindetag, *BB*, 1968, no. 3, 50–52; and *BG*, 1968, no. 4, 93–94.

28. The president of the *Bayerischer Gemeindetag* and editor of its journal regretted the controversy between the small and the larger communes. *BG*, 1968, no. 5, 85–86. The statement is quoted in *BB*, 1968, no. 6, 152.

29. Ibid., 152–153. Strauss also warned his audience in the *Bundestag* that the communal percentage of the income taxes and the reduction of the business tax (tentatively 40 percent) had to await further study. The total business taxes raised the previous year amounted to eleven billion marks. Representatives of the only opposition party left under the grand coalition, the FDP, expressed doubts as to whether the communes would really end up with a substantial gain and there were strong objections in the CDU to the reintroduction of an "anachronistic communal income tax" before the reform was sent on to the appropriate committees of *Bundestag* and *Bundesrat*. Ibid., 155–156.

30. See *BG*, 1969, no. 2, 21–22, and no. 3, 37–40 for the reasons advanced by the Bavarian *Kreise* and *Kreis*-dependent communes against the metropolitan approach to the progressive part of the locally raised income taxes.

31. The communes had hoped for a much larger share of the income taxes. See the excerpted address of the Bavarian Finance Minister, Konrad Pöhner, in *BB*, 1968, no. 10, 249–253. Calculations suggested that communes below three thousand inhabitants might gain substantially (5–10 percent) while a town like Wasserburg would only be slightly above and one like Rosenheim slightly below their pre-reform per capita revenues. The president of the *Bayerischer Gemeindetag* used these statistics to contradict the fears that the reform would transfer big city resources in a major way to the countryside though he could not deny that communes with a larger business base stood to lose in the bargain. Ibid., 254–257.

32. Gröbner could demonstrate that while Munich and Würzburg would benefit from the whole range of income taxation, other big cities like Regensburg and Augsburg would not. *BB*, 1969, no. 1, 1–5, no. 9, 221–225, and no. 11, 277–279; and *BG*, 1969, no. 10. For the point of view of the lord mayor of Munich, Hans Jochen Vogel, see *BB*, 1969, no. 3, 57–60.

33. Wherever the *Länder* were delegated federal functions (Basic Law articles 85, 87b [2], 87c [2], 90 [2], and 120a [1]), the federation was to pay for the material costs while the *Länder* would pay for the administrative costs and personnel (Art. 104 [2]).

34. *Kursbuch Deutschland 85/86*, 123–124. In 1982, for example, the *Länder* equalization brought Bavaria 162.5 million marks, considerably less than the 299 million of 1978, in reflection of Bavaria's relative economic improvement.

35. A minimum of three *Länder* was able then to veto any constitutional amendment although a majority of the *Bundesrat* was required to stop possibly invasive implementing legislation. On all this, see Heinz Laufer, *Der Föderalismus der BRD* (Stuttgart, 1974), 77–118; and Heiderose Kilper and Roland Lhott, *Föderalismus in der Bundesrepublik Deutschland: Eine Einführung* (Opladen, 1996).

36. *BB*, 1970, no. 3, 51–62.

37. *BB*, 1971, no. 3, 57–59; and no. 4, 85–86. See also the proposals of the Enquête-Kommission Verfassungsreform des Deutschen Bundestags, *Beratungen und Empfehlungen zur Verfassungsreform*, Part II, *Bund und Länder* (Bonn, 1975).

38. See *BG*, 1975, no. 7, 129–130; and 1976, no. 2, 30. *Kreis*-dependent communes also received 10 percent less increase from the in-state equalization than the independent cities due to the formula (*Schlüsselzuweisungen*) for redistribution. See also *BG*, 1976, no. 3, 41; 1977, no. 9, 182; and no. 12, 254–259; and *Ifo-Schnelldienst 20/76*, 11. An excellent basic discussion of German communal finance can be found in Gunlicks, *Local Government*, 127–132, where the on-the-whole mixed results of the 1969 finance reform on the communes of all the *Länder* are also discussed, 132–142.

39. *Policy and Politics in West Germany: The Growth of a Semisovereign State* (Philadelphia, PA, 1987), 15–24. The author points to the rather centralized business and labor organizations, organized agriculture, and centralized policy procedures. He could easily have added the political management of the economy in general.

40. *BB*, 1979, no. 8, 9–10 and 23. In a manner of speaking, the shift from their own tax base to a share of common income taxes dated back to the Erzberger finance reforms of 1920 that had revolutionized the federal and state finances by tying them together (*Finanzverbundsystem*).

41. *BB*, 1979, no. 8, 9–10 and 23.

42. After decades of hostility to planning, the federal ministries of the grand coalition (1968–1969) became increasingly involved in it. Chancellor Brandt's planning staff in 1969 assembled nearly a thousand new plans and programs of which sixty-five were selected for action in the near future. Cabinet discussions finally picked five of these as politically opportune. The difficulties of obtaining the support of party leaders and of the federal civil servants bedeviled further efforts even before they came up against the entrenched power of the *Länder*. See Kenneth Dyson, "Improving Policymaking in Bonn: Why the Central Planners Failed," *Journal of Management Studies*, 12 May 1975, 175.

43. See, for example, the author of the earlier, much-quoted *Der unitarische Föderalismus* (1962), Konrad Hesse, "Aspekte des kooperativen Föderalismus in der BRD," in *Festgabe für Gebhard Müller* (1970), 141 ff., esp. 145; R. Kunze, *Kooperativer Föderalismus in der BRD* (Kronberg, 1968); G. Kisker, *Kooperation im Bundesstaat* (1971); and H. Ehringhaus, *Der kooperative Föderalismus in den Vereinigten Staaten von Amerika* (1971).

44. See also Klaus Stern, "Die föderalistische Ordnung im Spannungsfeld der Gegenwart," in *Politikverflechtung zwischen Bund, Ländern und Gemeinden* (Berlin, 1975), 15–38, esp. 27 and 30–33. On the system of *Politikverflechtung.* see also Jens Joachim Hesse, "The FRG from Cooperative Federalism to Joint Policy-Making," in *West European Politics*, 10, no. 4 (October 1987), 70–87.

45. In the declining years of the empire, constitutional theorists like Heinrich Triepel worried about the problem of how to compel a state to carry out a *Reich* law as it was intended by the *Reichstag* and cabinet, obviously considering the designated arbiter for such disputes, the *Reichsrat* inadequate. Triepel proposed a federal supervisory power (*Reichsaufsicht*) instead. The Basic Law, however, has once more left such complaints over noncompliance or flawed implementation to the *Bundesrat*, in effect leaving the fox to guard the chickens.

46. Quoted from a 1972 book on *Politikverflechtung* by Fritz W. Scharpf. See *Politikverflechtung: Theorie und Empirik des kooperativen Föderalismus in der Bundesrepublik*, 2 vols., Scharpf, Bernd Reissert, and Fritz Schnabel, eds. (Kronberg, 1976), I, 9 (hereafter, *Politikverflechtung*).

47. Jens Joachim Hesse in ibid., II, 10–15. The author blames the omission of the communes from the original design of the federal system for the problems that eventually brought on *Politikverflechtung*. But see also Arthur B. Gunlicks, *Local Government*, chapter 10, who sees in *Politikverflechtung* a scheme for a "unitary federal state," 182, or the critical views of Gerhard Lehmbruch who perceives policy networks in "Institutional Linkages and Policy Networks in the Federal System of West Germany," *Publius: The Journal of Federalism*, 19, no. 4 (Fall, 1989), 222 ff.

48. See Klaus von Beyme, *Das politische System der Bundesrepublik Deutschland nach der Vereinigung* (Munich, 1991), who found *Politikverflechtung* to be the logical outgrowth of the German variety of cooperative federalism. See also Franz Walter Henrich, *Kommunale Beteiligung in der Raumordnung und Landesplanung*, 2 vols. (Stuttgart, 1981), I, 7–31, 91–113, and 274–280.

49. Henrich, *Kommunale Beteiligung*, II, 10–11, 40 ff., 47–50, and 116–121.

50. *Politikverflechtung*, I, 107–108. The terminology of this study reflects the American policy studies literature with terms such as "level fixation" and "distribution" problems.

51. Ibid., I, 85–92, 97, and 111 ff.

52. Ibid., I, 123–135.

53. Ibid., I, 133–146.

54. *Städtebaubericht 1970*, quoted ibid., I, 161. It had started as early as 1962 with model programs for the renewal of towns and villages that were meant to kick off intergovernmental programs even without constitutional authority. Ibid., I, 158–163.

55. The *Länder* were also accused of playing games such as refusing to prioritize their projects, objecting formally to federal cuts, anything to assert their own role in regional planning. One *Land* even "got the federation to turn down no fewer than 55 of its projects" in order to put the blame on the federation. In 1975 a Federal Constitutional Court decision had established the rule that both levels must agree to the distribution of the funds, leaving the federation to make cuts but "with respect for *Land* priorities." There was also partisan rivalry between CDU/CSU and SPD *Länder*. Ibid., I, 166–176.

56. This had already been the practice of North Rhine Westphalia, Rhineland Palatinate, and Schleswig-Holstein before 1973. Ibid., I, 205–211, 214. In some oversupplied urban areas, it was alleged, there was an unused "mountain of beds" (*Bettenberg*) in public hospitals.

57. Ibid., I, 191–201, 218–220.
58. Ibid., I, 223–225, 230–239. See also Marianne Rodenstein, "Konflikte zwischen Bund und Kommunen," in Rolf-Richard Grauhan, *Lokale Politikforschung*, 2 vols. (Frankfurt, 1975), II, 310–325.
59. *Politikverflechtung*, II, 15.
60. A *Landtag* majority was very unlikely to stop its own parliamentary government from accepting, for example, 50 percent of the cost of university construction from the federation. See Laufer, *Der Föderalismus*, 116–118.
61. Educational policy had been a major point of partisan disagreement between the CDU/CSU and the SPD whose Young Socialists (*Jusos*) in some states had made major efforts to radicalize content and staff of the public schools. For a description of the commission and its powers see ibid., 118–124.
62. Gerhard Lehmbruch, "Verfassungspolitische Alternativen der Politikverflechtung," *Politikverflechtung*, II, 87–93.
63. See Otto Barbarino, "Zur Reformbedürftigkeit ... ," 106–118; and *Politikverflechtung*, II, 100–117. But see also Friedrich Schäfer's comments on the long-range impact of a decade of governmental and administrative reforms, *Politikverflechtung*, II, 123–128.
64. See, for example, Grauhan, *Lokale Politikforschung*, II, chaps. 3, 5, and 8.
65. See Jens Joachim Hesse, *Organisation kommunaler Entwicklungsplanung* (Stuttgart, 1976), 35, 41–49.
66. See "Forderungen der Städte und Kreise des kommunalen Bereichs nach dem Grundgesetz: Deutscher Städtetag und Deutscher Landkreistag," in *Der Städtetag*, N.F. 26 (1973), 469–470. Also Stern, *Politikverflechtung zwischen Bund, Ländern und Gemeinden*, 42, 50–52, and 57–59.
67. One objection to giving the communes seats in the *Bundesrat* was that this would change the character of the latter in the direction of a senate, and undermine the federal council type of federal system in the FRG.
68. See Henrich, *Kommunale Beteiligung*, I, 14–31, and 274.
69. Ibid., II, 47–53.
70. See esp. J. J. Hesse, *Organisation kommunaler Entwicklungsplanung*, 35–41.
71. Arthur B. Gunlicks, "The Future of Federalism in the Unified Germany," in *The Domestic Politics of German Unification*, Anderson et al., eds., 155–174, esp. 156–159 and 165. Also Laufer and Münch, "Die Neugestaltung ... ," 235–237. The reorganization proposals in West and East were extremely ambitious and it remains to be seen how much of them ever reaches realization.
72. Laufer and Münch, "Die Neugestaltung ... ," 234.
73. To the extent that the GDR territory coincided with that of pre-1947 Prussia, its local government constitutions were in part based on the 1831 and 1853 rollback of the liberal reforms of 1808 of Karl Freiherr vom und zum Stein toward state supervision and the restricted (three-class) electoral law. There had been abortive attempts in 1935 (authoritarian *Führerprinzip*) and 1947 at creating a uniform mold for the whole country, with sharp distinctions between urban and rural communes.
74. See also Helmut Wollmann, "Kommunalpolitik und -verwaltung in Ostdeutschland im Umbruch und Uebergang" in *Kommunalpolitik in Deutschland. Politisches Handeln in den Gemeinden*, Wollmann and Roland Roth, eds. (Opladen, 1993), 20–33. The East German budget reform, as a final response to the profound financial crises of all German local governments in the 1920s and early 1930s went in the opposite direction from the restoration of communal finances in the West, toward centralization.
75. To compare, West German local government emphasized the *Rechtstaat* (state of law) and juxtaposed administrative courts to police officialdom. A process of "parliamen-

tarisation" (growing initiative and control of communal council over the local executive) had weaned Western local administration from its early antecedents of paternalistic and bureaucratic authoritarianism at about the same time that democratic centralism swallowed up local initiative and autonomy. See also Siegfried Petzold, "Zur Entwicklung und Funktion der kommunalen Selbstverwaltung in den neuen Bundesländern," in Roth and Wollmann, *Kommunalpolitik*, 34–51.

76. This also applies to the East German *Kreis* administrations, which used to have large redundant staffs (two to three hundred persons) for all the supply and distribution functions of the centrally run communal economy. These old functions have now been replaced by regional planning, *Bauleitungsplanung* (zoning and construction), social assistance, and economic promotion activities. Roth and Wollmann, ibid., 24–27.

77. See Amtsordnung of 19 December 1991, for Brandenburg, *GVBl*, 682; and Petzold, "Zur Entwicklung ... ," 44–45.

78. See, for example, Hans-Georg Wehling, "Kommunale Verfassungsreform: Vergleich der kommunalen Verfassungssysteme in Deutschland," *Politische Bildung*, 31, no. 1 (1998), 19–33; and Hans H. von Arnim, "Auf dem Weg zur optimalen Gemeindeverfassung?" *Deutsches Verwaltungsblatt*, 112, no. 12 (1997), 749–761. Also Gerhard Banner, "Kommunale Verwaltungsreform und staatlicher Modernisierungsrückstand," *Politische Bildung*, 31, no. 1 (1998), 34–46.

79. See, for example, Janbernd Oebbecke, "Die neue Kommunalverfassung in Nordrheinwestfalen," *Die öffentliche Verwaltung*, 48, no. 17 (1995), 701–709; Hans H. von Arnim, "Reform der Gemeindeverfassung in Hessen," *Die öffentliche Verwaltung*, 45, no. 8 (1992), 330–338; and the contributions of Gert Hillmann and Axel Saipa in the same journal. Also Uwe Anderson, "Kommunalpolitik als Experimentierfeld für Reformen—eine Einführung," in Wehling, "Kommunale Verfassungsreform ... ," 5–18.

80. See *Süddeutsche Zeitung*, 6 June 1998; and Göttrich Wever, "Die Krise der Kommunalfinanzen," in Wehling, "Kommunale Verfassungsreform ... ," 47–61. See also the bibliographical footnote 1 in Helm, "Citizen Initiatives ... ," and the description of financial transfers from West to East in von Beyme, *Das politische System*, 349–360.

81. See Arthur Gunlicks, "50 Years of German Federalism: An Overview and Some Current Developments," in *The Federal Republic of Germany at 50*, Merkl, ed. (London and New York, 1999), 186–202.

82. See *Maastricht and Beyond: Building the European Union*, Andrew Duff, John Pinder, and Roy Price, eds. (London and New York, 1994), 27–29, 162, 167–169, 280–282; and D. M. Harrison, *The Organisation of Europe: Building a Continental Market Order* (London and New York, 1995), 50. Also, see *Federalism, Unification, and European Integration*, Charlie Jeffrey and Roland Sturm, eds. (London, 1993).

83. The original Art. 23 served to unify East Germany, state by state, with West Germany and, having accomplished this purpose, became obsolete. Regarding Article 24, see also Donald Kommers, "The Basic Law and Reunification," in *The Federal Republic of Germany at 45*, Merkl, ed. (London, 1989), 193–197.

84. The EU Commission's subsidy policy had become contested when it chose to authorize a French state subsidy of FF 20 billion for Air France. It was a very controversial decision. See also Gunlicks, "50 Years ... ," and von Beyme, *Das politische System*, 346–364.

Chapter 6

Conclusion

"There is now an active concern for the viability of the small town and small towners. In part, that concern may be in reaction to the big city and large scale bureaucracies—private and public—that have come to dominate American life. The revitalization of small communities is part of the general search for smallness, simple (appropriate) technology, alternative lifestyles, and environmental conservation."[1]

For some decades now, Americans have worried about the decline and death of the small town and rural center[2] although our definitions of such units tend to vary.[3] American communities with a population under twenty-five hundred make up 69 percent of all American communities, but less than 8 percent of the population. Those under ten thousand are 89 percent of the communities, but only 22 percent of the population. This can be compared to the 6.2 percent of the West German population that lived in communities under two thousand in 1980 (after local territorial reorganization in most states)—in 1871 it was still 64 percent and in 1910 still 40 percent.[4] Already in the heyday of American small towns, in the second half of the nineteenth century, there were the first laments of their dying—especially in New England and later in the upper Midwest as young people moved on toward big cities and to places farther out west.[5] Today the "dying" is connected with the lingering crisis of American family agriculture that affects the country towns as well. Following the overexpansion of Midwestern farm investment in the 1970s,

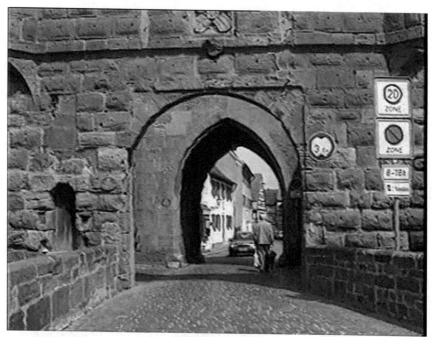

Illustration 6.1. Man at Wolframs-Eschenbach gate.
Photo by Peter Merkl.

the 1980s brought a tidal wave of farm foreclosures and, inevitably, failures of many banks and crucial businesses in rural towns, for example farm equipment and retail stores, restaurants, and taverns.

The reasons why we worry so much about their "dying" are not hard to guess: small towns have tended to be viewed as microcosms of human life, wellsprings of American values and national character, and through nostalgic eyes as everyone's innocent childhood, before the temptations and corruptions of adulthood or big-city life destroyed the primal wholeness of the old habits of the heart.[6] Small country and village towns, including small urban places, in other words, are really a state of mind and an object of dreams and myths as much as they are places of real flesh, populated with real people, and heirs to real problems.[7]

Germans have looked upon their small towns in very similar ways, including the towns that date back much farther than those of the New World. The nineteenth century, *Biedermeier* idol of the German small town and village had already been superimposed on the much older, medieval and later hometowns that Mack Walker has described so well—cities with walls, gates, and turrets, though not always with the large populations we expect of them today. German literature and art of the last two hundred years are replete with the images of the passing of the village and small-town way of life. To the present generations of Germans, as to Americans—most of whom were also born in non-metropolitan settings—small towns appear through a profoundly ambivalent lens, partly as a source of authentic values, not unlike *la France profonde* to the French,[8] and partly as scenes of oppressive, narrow-minded prejudice and provinciality: Outsiders, minorities, and the lower classes led marginal lives, preyed upon by established elites and patricians.[9] No matter how contradictory, both visions boast a certain amount of truth. It is against this ambivalent backdrop that we should view the subject matter of this book: On the one hand there is the character and soul of each community, its integral, moral character-building mission, and also its primal right to live its life with democracy and citizen participation and without major outside interference even though no one will deny that each small place or medium-sized town is inevitably tied to the larger system around it.

On the other hand, there has occurred the singular intervention of communal territorial reorganization in all the larger *Länder*, which we have described above in considerable detail from long before to long after. This reorganization has been ostensibly for the communities' own good and yet it raises more basic questions than it ever set out to resolve. What did this do to the soul and character-building mission of the communities? Did it make them less of a source of an individual's hometown identity, or of a spiritual locus of the national soul? Were the mini-towns and micro-communes not long overripe, "hollowed out" in their original, self-contained substance by social change before they were incorporated into the larger units of the territorial reform, the VGs, or neighboring centers? Was there really something left of the small communal way of life that was not already nearly dead before the great reform allegedly killed it?

Mini-Towns and Micro-Communes

The thrust of this question about the integrity of the original sense of community and local identity, of course, applies particularly to the small communities we examined in West Middle Franconia, some of them mini-towns dating back to the medieval splendors of city walls and a half-millennium of civic pride, others part of old agrarian cultures, inward-looking and set in their ways. To be sure, such ancient antecedents are merely a small part of the present sense of local identity of some of their citizens, overshadowed by the more recent exigencies of survival in a world of war and depression, agricultural and economic changes, population losses, and the spread of the national media culture with its own world of values—or the lack of it, depending on one's own views.[10] As small-town daily life becomes indistinguishable from life in big cities and even abroad, the original form and function of that hometown or village in the small-towners' mind may also fade from view. Well-intentioned educational reforms, the erosion of local business and trade, and the atrophying of local festival activity in most of these micro-communes further alienate the remaining citizenry and especially the young from the memories of the old way of life. Today the typical village and small-town life that so many nineteenth- and twentieth-century writers still described in great detail, if not always very kindly, is a matter of the past.

Is there no alternative except for inexorable decline or state-planned reassembly into larger, synthetic communities—administrative unions (VGs) or unitary small centers (EGs)—for the likes of Mitteleschenbach or Ornbau? There are some alternative models in areas attractive to tourism but they are hardly a viable choice for most of these micro-communes. The Bavarian local territorial reform pointedly allowed well-established tourist attractions of small population size to survive the cull, an option less realistic for the flat country we have examined. Alpine ski tourism, in particular, has found its own formulas that are not likely to be followed elsewhere. In Austrian Tyrol in the Upper Inn Valley, for a striking example, Serfaus, a former mountain village of one thousand residents, has embarked upon a new conception of Tyrolean mountain tourism that attempts to follow a hazardous path between the environmental abyss of mass tourism and the economic vagaries of part-time bed-and-breakfast,[11] namely seasonal ski tourism, while still living off a declining mountain agriculture. This new "Tyrolean Way" aims at limiting new hotel construction and prohibiting the establishment of new ski lifts and downhill runs in the hope of improving the quality of existing capacities.

Like many other skiing resorts, Serfaus went through the typical development from one thousand years of subsistence mountain agriculture via the first skiers and new hotels in the 1920s and 1930s, until tourism overtook agriculture as the foremost source of income by 1970. Today, with more than forty-two hundred beds available, Serfaus no longer has any truly independent farms. It imports all its milk, cheese, meat, and sausage for the hotels and restaurants from the outside. Even the remaining local cattle is slaughtered and the milk processed in nearby agricultural Fiss before it can be consumed in Serfaus. Mountain farms (Almen) with a high Alm cabin and rich grazing slopes that once nourished the cattle now receive subsidies from the hotels and ski lifts to maintain the atmosphere and the Alm facilities with ski slopes where the cattle used to roam each summer. Nearby the entire village now consists of hotels. Except for a few old barns there are no real farmhouses left. The hotels follow the old Tyrolean, large farmhouse look, however, with concrete and wooden beams, and chalet balconies that are ringed with geraniums in the summer. The hotels include four- and five-star establishments and appropriately expensive restaurants. There are a few night spots for the tourists but not a single old-style tavern for the locals whose BMW and Mercedes automobiles ostentatiously try to keep up with the affluent visitors, belying the high indebtedness of many of the new hoteliers. To keep the traffic of daytime tourists from clogging up the access to the funicular and from fouling the air, finally, Serfaus spent $20 million to have a subway built from the edge to the center of town. Only overnight guests are permitted to park in town or near their hotels. The daytime visitors have to leave their vehicles outside town and take the subway. The investments needed to "preserve nature" for this luxury tourism do not end here, but have required additional refinements with the lift capacity and provision for ample artificial snow production in case nature should fail its $100–200 a day worshippers.

This appears to be one way out for the survival of micro-communes but there are many critics and scoffers who doubt that the new Tyrolean way can be trodden by more than a very few micro-communes among many. In Upper Bavaria too, it will be remembered, a few small resort communities of far fewer year-round inhabitants than had been required by the local territorial reform were rescued by Minister President Strauss's "reform of the reform." But how many skiing and hiking resorts can survive in a finite market, or how many resorts of any kind can share in the limited number of customers? In parts of West Middle Franconia too, it will be recalled, there are recreational attractions and "vacation on a farm" programs, though nothing quite on the scale of the fabulous skiing slopes and mountain scenery of Tyrol or the Bavarian ski resorts.

In some places, there has also occurred an influx of senior retirees or elderly but active persons from urban habitats. Frequently, they originally came from small-town or rural environments, or at least would like to retire somewhere, where life is slower and more gentle than in the city. This is a phenomenon well known in other developed countries like Great Britain or the US where it has led to the expansion of mountain and lake communities with seasonal recreation facilities. Some of these retro-migrants only want to live out their years in peace. Others may make their presence in a small attractive place into a business to supplement their income or make their retired years more interesting. There may also be some culture and arts tourism, or historical attractions of note.

There are also other solutions such as agribusiness, or the next "stages of community development" that we described above (chapter 1). And there are compromises between the touristic route and the original village or small-town character, as, for example, Serfaus's neighbors in Fiss achieved. Caught a decade behind the tourist boom in Serfaus, the eight hundred or so Fissers were "backward" enough not to abandon their farming and farmhouses even though by now nearly everyone there is also involved in tourism as a sideline or as their main income. Today Fiss is booming in the ski season and it still lives in its characteristic, heavy old farmhouses of quarry stone, its old taverns, and its typical hearty Tyrolean food and wine. But the road to today's modest riches was long and included many a long dry stretch of dire agrarian poverty when most farm children were routinely sent off to spend summers working and being fed on (German) Suebian farms. The overcrowded old houses were so full of bodies, hungry old and young bodies, that people would mark off their respective territories with chalk on the floor. In Fiss, bountiful nature still means simply a lot of snow (without too many avalanches) and the natural panorama of mountains, ski slopes, and propitious weather to enjoy them. There is a common ski pass for Fiss and Serfaus but there is no subway and no four- and five-star hotels, and the Fissers like it this way. It seems not to bother them much that haughty Serfaus looks down upon their lot.

There are many ways of looking at the ambitious local territorial reform in Bavaria—which thought to split the Gordian knot of micro-commune survival with one blow—depending on the vantage point of the observer, and we have quoted some of them above. The foremost determinant of the view of what has transpired among the mini-towns and micro-communes we discussed seems to hinge upon whether a community (or its spokespersons) thought it was capable of a bright economic future on its own—such visions probably varied considerably even within the same community, not to mention between the locals, their *Landrat,* and the *Land* government's regional planners. Just as among enterprises in a market economy, strong and naturally favored small communes (like Serfaus) were more likely to rely on their own initiative while the weaker and weakest communes hoped for aid and comfort from the state and its planners. The "losers" among mayors, local councillors, and small communes, for the most part, had no dreams of fame and fortune in their knapsacks either. They were protesting because they felt robbed even of the opportunity to opt for the status quo of isolation and poverty. And many of them were disappointed because they felt purposely sidelined and retired before the onrush of an ambiguous "progress."

The vast majority of those who accepted the dramatic mergers and were willing to find a modest role for themselves within the reorganized local settings, conversely, appeared to accept the verdict that their old communes had been "hollowed out" by inexorable trends of multiple social change in non-metropolitan Bavaria over a quarter century or more. They agreed that their familiar old mini-town or micro-commune had lost the capacity to live on its own, with its local sense of identity, and its original mission in the world. They knew that the motorization of the countryside, agricultural transformation, and the atrophying of autonomous parish churches and businesses would remove much of the incentives for their young generation to stay with their communities. Once the hope of a revival or restoration of the old foci of life had faded, it was possible to think of building a new, more inclusive life and identity, retaining at least for a while the partial identity of an *Ortsteil* commune that might still be founded on traditions, however ephemeral. New forms and institutional arrangements could be developed, given adequate subsidies for the transition, and perhaps new identities and modern cultural adaptations would flourish in time in the enlarged EGs and VGs. But cultural flowering too requires an economically and ecologically viable community base.

The Search for Roots

In the preceding chapter on the broader intergovernmental framework that surrounds these local changes and reorganizations we reminded the reader of the striking reversal of German postwar urban migration and orientation patterns in the seventies. Just as the federal law on spatial order (*Raumordnung*) and the reorganizations of local boundaries got underway in the late sixties and early seventies, the trends of rural flight toward the metropoles (along with general population increases) and toward governmental centralization began to stall and, in part, to reverse themselves. The big cities suddenly seemed to have lost their enormous attraction—in considerable measure perhaps for the very reasons of excessive traffic density, noise, air and water pollution, and shortages of good housing and recreational facilities that had caused the *Raumordnung* planners to call for decentralization—and smaller towns and rural communes (especially some at the edge of cities) seemed more livable again.

The relevant polls among West German adults between 1950 and 1980 reveal the surprising change in sentiment even while the economic disparities between city and countryside remained nearly unchanged, and this in spite of the infusion of tens of billions of federal marks into the infrastructure of rural and depressed areas, especially before 1989 along the Iron Curtain.

The Allensbach polls ascertained a massive change of popular preferences regarding what kind of a community one preferred to live in during the 1970s. While the respondents were not asked to specify where they might draw the line between "in the country," "small town," and

Table 6.1. West German preferences of residence, 1950–1980 (in percent)

	1950	1970	1980
In the country	25	27	35
In small town	20	18	22
In medium-sized city	24	26	25
In large city	27	27	14

Question: If you could choose freely, where would you prefer to live?

Source: *The Germans: Public Opinion Polls, 1967–1980*, ed. by Elisabeth Noelle-Neumann. Copyright © 1981 by Elisabeth Noelle-Neumann. All rights reserved. Reproduced with permission of ABC-CLIO, LLC, Santa Barbara, CA.

"medium-sized city," we can assume that the first two categories might correspond to our fifteen communities in West Middle Franconia, possibly separating the more agrarian from the mini-towns typical of the area. Rothenburg o. T., Dinkelsbühl, and Ansbach were probably perceived as medium-sized cities by the respondents. As the table shows, the pronounced preference of the fifties and sixties for living in medium-sized or large cities—51–53 percent vs. 45 percent in small places—reversed itself in the seventies to a majority of 57 percent for rural or small-town living vs. 39 percent for big or medium city residence.

The change began already in 1972 when the rural or small-town preferences rose to around 54 percent (55 percent in 1976 and 63 percent in 1977). The local territorial reforms had begun in 1967–1970 in Rhineland Palatinate and North Rhine Westphalia and, except for the city states Hamburg, Bremen, and West Berlin, nearly everybody completed their reforms before Bavaria did. The 1980 poll in the Federal Republic also revealed a sharp generational split in that respondents under forty-five years of age—that is roughly equivalent to the "68-er generation" and younger cohorts—opted more for medium and large-city living while those over forty-five preferred small-town and rural life at a ratio of more than two to one.[12] Farmers also shared this preference while professional people and blue collar workers opted for the medium and large cities.

The perceived advantages of the more urbanized settings were mostly in the availability of educational, job, and cultural opportunities. The great attraction of small-town and country living, on the other hand, was the lower cost of living, the clean environment, and good housing. When asked in 1976 whether their residence was a single-family house, in fact, 69 percent of rural and 51 percent of small-town respondents responded in the affirmative as compared to only 42 percent of medium-city and 14 percent of metropolitan respondents. Forty-one percent of all adult respondents said they lived in such a house, but 76 percent referred to it as their "ideal home."[13] With the rise of consumer expectations over the decades in West Germany, it seems likely that the desire for a house of their own, as well as for better ecological and cultural advantages—especially with the advent of better roads and other infrastructural improvements—tilted the balance toward a preference for small-town and rural living. Or, to remain in tune with the rise of a new "post-materialist" consciousness, lifestyle issues won out over the higher incomes available in a larger urban setting.[14]

Revisiting Wolframs-Eschenbach

The final upshot of the extraordinary reform of small Bavarian communities in 1978 came to light for me on Pentecost Sunday (31 May 1998) when I revisited Wolframs-Eschenbach, which twenty years earlier seemed lost in the bureaucratic coils of the VG Triesdorf I, along with the five other towns—some with the remainders of medieval walls around them, some with the title "market towns"—named in chapter 1 of this book. Upon my visit twenty years earlier, Wolframs-Eschenbach was a dispirited sight, its historic buildings unkempt and wet in the rain, its walls, gates, and moat almost overgrown by a landscape that did not give the ancient city the prominence it deserved. Comparisons with its famous and successful neighbor on the Romantic Road, Rothenburg ob der Tauber, seemed far-fetched indeed at that time.[15] In the light of the territorial reform of 1978, Wolframs-Eschenbach seemed just another road casualty along the juggernaut route of the bureaucratic reformers. But now, in the glorious sunlight of this Sunday and amid crowds of tourists, the town sparkled as a double-walled, gated, moated, and towered jewel on a hill, located on the *Burgenstrasse* (castle road) in the Franconian countryside, its ancient St. Mary's Ascension church (dating from 1230) surrounded by two dozen authentic old buildings, with half-timbered exteriors. The town claims to date back to the middle of the eigth century. In its days of glory, around 1500, it had about one thousand residents and was half the size of Ansbach, twelve miles away. The Thirty Years War (1618–1648) initiated its long decline.

We cannot be entirely sure this was the birthplace of the poet, Wolfram von Eschenbach (1170–1220), the author of the medieval epic Parzifal, whose statue graces the Wolfram von Eschenbach Platz and who is said to be buried in Mary's Chapel in the ancient church. The town still boasts the one-time headquarters of the crusading Teutonic Knights (*Deutschritterorden*) that controlled the town for centuries. They last fought at the eastern borders of Prussia and then turned to more religious and medical missions. Napoleon dissolved the already secularized order whose quarters by then had moved to Bad Mergentheim in Württemberg. Its Grand Master (*Hoch- und Deutschmeister*), the Hapsburg Archduke Anton-Victor (1804–1835), held forth in Vienna. The order then had scattered possessions in Germany and Hapsburg Austria, that is in today's Czech, Yugoslav, and South Tyrolean (Italian) lands. It still exists, despite repeated dissolutions, but is exclusively religious today, not military.

I interviewed the *Bürgermeister*, Anton Seitz, who had been in office since 1984, about the striking improvements in his town. He blamed the ineptness and advanced age of his predecessor and inattention of the

Illustration 6.2. Palace of Teutonic Knights and Wolfram-von-Eschenbach Square.
Photo courtesy of the city of Wolframs-Eschenbach.

Ansbach *Landrat* at the time for Wolframs-Eschenbach's temporary relegation to being a mere member commune of the VG Triesdorf I. In fact, the mayor hinted that his letter to the new Bavarian minister president of 1979, Franz Josef Strauss, had triggered Strauss's spectacular "reform of the reform" of that year that, among about a few hundred revisions, also freed Wolframs-Eschenbach by dissolving the VG Triesdorf I and replacing it with VG Triesdorf II and a new VG Wolframs-Eschenbach that has only one other member, Mitteleschenbach. Wolframs-Eschenbach (its present name was conferred in 1917 by the last monarch) was permitted to annex seven dwarf communes and, with 2,672 (1996) residents, became the seat of a VG of 4,200 residents. In 2010 the town had 2,879 residents all told. Its *Bürgermeister* was now the presiding officer of the VG.[16]

The mayor also took credit for having wiped out the large debt of the town and accumulated a substantial surplus. With the town's pride salvaged, the new mayor evidently succeeded in mobilizing several major state Urban Renewal grants to restore the city, its historic edifices, and the land surrounding wall and moat. The wall is a mile long, up to thirteen feet high and completely encloses the old town. Several new businesses including hotels and restaurants were added to the tax base of the

Illustration 6.3. Franz Josef Strauss plaque at Wolframs-Eschenbach Rathaus.
Photo by Peter Merkl.

Illustration 6.4. Glass Annex to old Rathaus of Wolframs-Eschenbach.
Photo courtesy of the city of Wolframs-Eschenbach.

town. Small wonder that a plaque commemorating the 1980 "reform of the reform" and with Strauss's image graced the entrance to the historic old *Rathaus* of Wolframs-Eschenbach, then still next to the Palace of the Teutonic Order. Governor Strauss, by the way—who had been the conservative (CDU/CSU) candidate for federal chancellor against Helmut Schmidt that year—was a member of the Teutonic Knights, as was Chancellor Konrad Adenauer in his time. It is not yet clear if the economic fortunes of the town will continue to improve.

In 2010 I revisited the town and chatted with the new mayor, Michael Dörr, a young-looking native of Wolframs-Eschenbach who for years had travelled all over the globe as a representative of the Edeka grocery chain. His quarters were now in a gleaming new glass-and-steel city hall near the old church. As he proudly explained, the town now had nearly three thousand residents and was doing well. My wife and I had parked at the foot of the hill on which all the streets were being resurfaced with asphalt. Mayor Dörr also showed us a large new children's park that appeared to be a great draw to families with small children. Outside of weekends and special holidays like Pentecost, Wolframs-Eschenbach still does not get enough tourists who instead are drawn by other old towns like Rothenburg or two attractive lakes, the Altmühlsee and the Brombachsee, in the neighborhood. Twelve years ago already, the town had more than doubled the number of tourist beds available, but the tourists have not shown up in the expected fashion. Or, in the view of the locals, Rothenburg is too far away and the lake resorts are not willing to share their tourists. "German tourists don't really care about medieval sights," Mayor Seitz had sighed. The economic and especially the unemployment problems of the nearest metropolitan area, Nuremberg/Fürth also weighed upon the whole region of Middle Franconia and the industrious people of Wolframs-Eschenbach, in the mayor's opinion.

It should be emphasized that, among the small Franconian communities where our inquiry started, even the good fortune of Wolframs-Eschenbach was rather rare. There were some other cases of successful population growth (including through annexation) between 1961 and 2010, especially in the 1980s, such as Weihenzell, Langfurth, Burk, and Stadt Ornbau—which had been a part of the VG Triesdorf I in 1979. A second group held steady or rose modestly since the 1980s, such as Bruckberg, Röckingen, and Steinsfeld. But there was also a third group that has kept on losing population throughout the years in question, for example Adelshofen, picturesque Ohrenbach, wine-growing Ippesheim, and neighboring Weigenheim—both in the VG Uffenheim of Kreis Neustadt an der Aisch/Bad Windsheim—or Markt Berolzheim and neighboring Meinheim in the VG Altmühltal of Kreis Weissenburg/Gunzenhausen. The "success stories" often show the impact or incentives of the territorial reform of 1978 itself, including the shock of demotion from previous independence to junior membership in a VG. Wolframs-Eschenbach and Mitteleschenbach provide good examples of such an impact, if tempered by their rescue through the 1980 "reform of the reform."

Finally it is no coincidence that the success stories among our small Franconian communities tended to be among those that were most advanced in their type of community development (see chapter 1) in 1970. Wolframs-Eschenbach,[17] Langfurth, and Burk were already considered manufacturing communities (#4) then, and Weihenzell, Ornbau St., and Mitteleschenbach "agrarian-residential (#3). The "loser group," on the other hand, was mostly "agrarian" (type #1 and #2) in 1970, for example Weigenheim, Adelshofen, and Ohrenbach (all #1). The vicinity of expanding larger towns, or the annexation of largely agricultural villages, as in the case of Steinsfeld (#4 in 1970) confuses the pattern somewhat. In any case, the number of farms in the whole state of Bavaria has still dropped another two fifths since 1978 so that less than 5 percent of the gainfully employed now work in agriculture while the tertiary sector claims a majority.[18] All of our small communities lost a lot of farms but the "losers" lost fewer than did the "winners."[19] On the other hand, the structural changes in the Bavarian economy favored particularly the growth of tourism: The number of available tourist beds tripled since 1960 and the number of restaurants and inns rose 7 percent in the last dozen years before 2000 alone while the number of persons employed in this sector increased one-third and the turnover ballooned by almost two-thirds. Depressed Middle Franconia more or less kept up with this development.[20]

The Response of the State

If the reform in 1978 had been in the manner of benevolent absolutism, from the top down and deliberately closing off most avenues of protest from below, democratic politics reasserted itself first with the "reform of the reform" of 1980 when, in response to complaints, the new Minister President Franz Josef Strauss moved to undo over a hundred of the most resented local mergers and confinements to a VG. This did not grease all the squeaky wheels among the reorganized communes but it raised the general expectation that, given time, the reform would settle down and the discontents become mollified. By the time I first revisited the state, indeed, sixteen of nineteen *Bürgermeisters* of the small communities—I added four to the original fifteen because they were impacted by the formation and dissolution of the VGs involved—had been elected only after 1978, five of them as recently as 1996. Only three *Bürgermeisters* had been in office at the time of the reform. The *Landräte* and Bavarian Ministry of the Interior officials involved, and even the experts at the communal association, the *Bayerische Gemeindetag*, similarly had come into office only after the reform so that their memories mostly reflected what they had heard rather than the event itself.

Still, there continued to be complaints and controversies and in the eighties and early nineties, the public debate resumed over the merits of the 1978 reform. In 1987, one high official of the Ministry of the Interior, Emil Wiebel, reviewed the *Kreis* and local reforms and pointed out that the drastic *Kreisreform* of 1972 had generated far less protest: only in three of the 71 new *Landkreise* was there any doubt expressed about the reform which in fact sixty-four of the *Kreise* "found good." Many of the communes, however, are far older than the *Kreise*, which were already fairly well adapted to a modernized environment before 1972. The parameters of the VGs had to be revised already in 1979—one year after the reform—when Strauss's intervention resulted in the dissolution of forty-eight of them. Two hundred and two member communes thus became independent again, often leaving others even more frustrated. Three were freed by court decisions. A second law about communes belonging to a VG in 1985 released seven communes and dissolved five more VGs while one was newly formed. The Bavarian Administrative Court, on the other hand, settled 149 lawsuits by 1987, and the State Constitutional Court sixty-three, and these mostly by ruling against the plaintiffs.[21] Wiebel's new 1987 totals came to 2,051 communes (including the twenty-five *Kreisstädte*), of which 958 were EGs and 1,068 belonged to 341 VGs.

Finally, the chief reformer, *ancien* minister of the interior Bruno Merk,[22] felt compelled to justify his reform all over again. "The organization of state and communes," he wrote in the official *Bayerische Verwaltungsblätter* in 1993, "is not a purpose in itself, but a means to the end of the efficient performance of differentiated tasks at economic cost." His point that the federal (Basic Law Art. 28) and Bavarian constitutions never meant to guarantee the existence of individual communes but only the right to local self-government in general is supported by court decisions and expert opinion. The Bavarian Constitutional Court ruled that the state is obliged to create strong local administrations, similar to traditional images of community, and the legislature "must balance" the elements of government capacity, identity, and closeness to the citizenry (*Bürgernähe*).[23] The organization of local government needs to be adjusted periodically to the drastic social changes. In other words, and quite contrary to Anglo-American ideas of local self-government, existing local units were merely one means to carry out the legitimate (and constitutionally sanctioned) functions of local self-government and could be replaced by better-functioning instruments. Merk reconstructed the history of the planning of the reform under several ministers of the interior and its beginnings under Minister President Alfons Goppel who had been in office since 1966. The third Goppel administration in 1971 announced the beginning of the *Kreisreform* and introduced the concept of the *Verwaltungsgemeinschaft* (VG) to the public.[24] Ex-minister Merk claimed there had been a consensus on the need for reform since the fifties and once again enumerated the goals of his reform as follows: strengthening communal administration and securing its effectiveness, economy, and *Bürgernähe*, decentralizing self-government functions onto strengthened local institutions, restoring the unity of living conditions and investment space, and reducing the differential between urban and rural administrative capacity.[25]

By the early nineties, however, a major shift of opinion had occurred in the Bavarian *Landtag* and among political leaders such as the next minister president, Edmund Stoiber, who had already readjusted some boundaries and helped to redistribute state land among the communes in 1989.[26] In 1992, the *Landtag* passed an amendment to the Communal Statute (*Gemeindeordnung*), Art. 11(3), creating new rules for releasing a member commune from a VG, provided the district (*Regierungsbezirk*) government supported the action. This was the first time since the "reform of the reform" that new general criteria and procedures had been officially developed for this purpose. The old Art 11(2) had, in effect, barred all territorial changes, especially for the restoration of communes, except for mergers or annexations. The amendment permitted restoration if: (1) it would redound to the public benefit—an "elastic clause" of dubious legal significance; (2) the commune in question had reached a population of two thousand, the minimum for an EG; and (3) if communal council majorities of two-thirds in all the member communes supported it.

In practice, this meant that returning a commune's independence was all right if, (1) it put long-standing strife to rest; (2) it was within 10 percent of the population minimum—substantial tourism measured in 36,500 available tourist beds/nights a year was counted in lieu of one hundred additional residents; and (3) if there was "not too much resentment" of its departure among the remaining member communes to block the action. There was also some reference to the old criteria of the reform of 1978 and the three corrective laws since, as well as to a Federal Constitutional Court decision of 12 May 1992 regarding "retro-reorganizations" (*Rückneugliederungen*) in which the court had cautioned that such actions must: (1) not override the presence of strong economic and social linkages within the VG; (2) that its advantages must exceed the counterindications; and (3) that it must strengthen local self-government. "If the capacity of the existing local arrangement was truly burdened by the nonacceptance of it by significant parts of the citizenry," and it was not just a temporary mood of dissatisfaction, the court reasoned, the state should give in and make an adjustment.[27]

There were several more such adjustments made, beginning with the Fourth Law on Changes in Communes and VGs (1993) and a Fifth Law in 1997. It was understood that, under the new rules, every new *Landtag* would seriously consider communal complaints and free communes that met the new or old rules. If a commune contemplated leaving a VG, but fell short of the minimum population for independence, it would have to have a new VG in mind that welcomed it and its departure must not leave its old VG "weakened." In fact, the Fourth Law dissolved fifteen VGs and modified another fourteen, mostly by loss of member communes. Five "unified communities" (EGs) lost parts of their annexed territory. Four new EGs and three new VGs were formed.[28] In some cases, annexations too were reversed. For example, the long-contested annexation of Ermershausen to Markt Maroldsweisach was undone and Ermershausen instead was made a member of the VG Hofheim (County Hassberge, Lower Franconia).[29]

Four years later, in 1997, a Fifth Law on Changes in Communes and VGs dissolved yet another six VGs and modified another six, releasing seven communes. It also raised two towns along the Romantic Road, Dinkelsbühl and Donauwörth, to the rank of *Grosse Kreisstadt*.[30] As of this date, then, the final tally was 319 VGs with 1,015 member communes and 1,019 EGs, a far cry from the figures of the original reform of 1978.

To sum up, the great communal reform in Bavaria is still intact and widely accepted in its broad outlines even though the minimal size limits have been greatly modified, for example from a minimum of five thousand residents for EGs to one of more or less two thousand. It certainly brought down the total number of all communes from over 7,000 to 2,034 by eliminating all independent micro-communes. What looked like a pressure cooker bound to explode sooner or later—namely the authoritarian imposition of this dramatic reorganization with practically no recourse for communal complaints—had been remedied in that the amended Communal Statute now offered a viable path to communities like Ermershausen whose complaints have not gone away as have most of the others. In the sense of the Federal Constitutional Court decision, Ermershausen's unrelenting twenty-year refusal to accept the dictate of yesterday—and the similarly unyielding attitude of Maroldsweisach[31]—signified the lack of capacity of this local self-government to function. Eventually, the *Landtag* allowed Ermershausen to escape the grip of Maroldsweisach even though the amended Communal Statute specifically limits retro-reorganization to cases of "peaceful secession" and the Bavarian Constitutional Court never required the consent of all the communes affected by annexation or subordination to a VG for such action.[32]

Unlike the US where we might have expected the remedy to come from the courts, the Bavarian Constitutional Court in any case not only rejected most communal complaints against the reform of 1978, including the most recent one of Markt Pleinting near Passau; it had been debating how much longer it should even consider such grassroots suits (*Popularklagen*) arising from the 1978 reform.[33] In other words, the process of democracy, or government by consent, won out over the *étatist* bureaucracy in the end, if only in cases where local resistance did not succumb to the passage of time and generations.

Re-Interviewing the *Bürgermeisters*

Problems of local reorganization are often extremely complicated and hard to summarize. For a first impressionistic test of our assessment of the situation of small communes twenty years after the reform, we re-interviewed the *Bürgermeisters* of the original fifteen small Middle Franconian communes that had lost their independence in 1978, bearing in mind that all but one current *Bürgermeister* had attained office only after the reform. Our first question had to do with the frequently observed problems of integrating annexed or merging micro-communes into the surviving, larger commune. After twenty years, the mayors responded, few problem cases remained alive. One was that of small Wöltendorf that had become part of Stadt Wolframs-Eschenbach. As the mayor of the larger town remarked, the lag in complete integration was connected to the continued attendance of Wöltendorf elementary school children at a school outside Wolframs-Eschenbach. "Experience has taught us that integration succeeds best when the schools, churches, and associations of all the parts are organized [exclusively] within the main commune," he added with a twinkle in his eye.

The *Bürgermeister* of Weihenzell expressed satisfaction with the integration of four small entities but pointed to difficulties where an *Ortsteil* (partial commune) was as big as the host commune and still had its own parish, voluntary fire brigade, and an active singing club. For the sport clubs, at least, Weihenzell was in a position to make playing fields, gun club, and other indoor facilities available to all. The continuing rivalry between merged communes of similar size is an old story that could be observed in many cases. The *Bürgermeister* of Langfurth, now an EG, also reported good cooperation but expressed his reservations about the representatives from the communal councils of two *Ortsteile* of the 1970s of his town because they appeared to take an interest only in the problems of their original micro-communes even though they were elected by all the residents of unified Langfurth. The mayor of wine-producing Ippesheim also reported good cooperation among the three part communes that now formed the town. He attributed this harmony to the shared associations, and furthermore to growing up together in the communal kindergarten. The other *Bürgermeisters* reported either that their present communes had not been merged or that they had not experienced integration problems. The mayor of the city of Ornbau attributed the successful integration of his town to its centrality: It had always been the central place where people from smaller, now annexed micro-communes had to come to shop, attend church, or bring their children to kindergarten.

The *Bürgermeisters* had supportive comments also to three other questions presented to them. Asked whether they found their VGs a useful focus of cooperation, they all said so. In one case they stressed the need for a VG branch office in a less central, member commune, in two others dissatisfaction with a branch office manned by only a half-time secretary. This generally positive if cautious reaction to the VG was confirmed in my 1998 interviews by representatives of the Bavarian rural community association (*Gemeindetag*) even though they were well aware of the possible rivalries among VG members. With computers—which were one of the improvements in local government that were already talked up twenty years ago—some small-town mayors believed they were in a much better position than before to keep their records and to stay in touch with their VG staff. The progress of computer literacy and the example of the computerized VG operations evidently have created new capacities that go far beyond those of the old micro-commune mayors of the 1970s. In the last twenty years, computer literacy in Germany has gradually grown beyond the younger cohorts and the better-educated and more urban groups so that, by now, only some of the oldest (over seventy-five) may not possess any.

The mayors were also questioned whether any of the dire predictions of the 1978 reform—that it would destroy the close contacts between the citizenry and local government (*Bürgernähe*), or ruin the distinctive character, or even take away the name of a historical place—had come true. All of them answered No. (Unlike in 1978, by the way, there were now considerable numbers of Bavarian women mayors, including one newly elected in Bruckberg, one of our fifteen communes: 50 of 2,034 Bavarian mayors and 2 of 71 *Landräte* were female.) Finally, the *Bürgermeisters* were surprisingly positive and content with the functions and finances allocated to their small communes. Only one mayor out of fifteen complained that state and federal mandates for the communes were forever outrunning their resources. The early doubts about the lagging "functional reform" and the local financial crisis thus seem to have been attenuated.

The Changing Role of the *Bürgermeister*

Few changes would seem to typify the great reform better than the final departure of the traditional kind of *Bürgermeister* of rural micro-communes, the *père de famille* of his village, a respected and well-to-do farmer who not only represented his constituents, but handed out personal, especially economic and even psychological advice on family relations as well. He often remained in his honorary office for a lifetime and was reelected without fail by the vast majority of his constituents, perhaps even by near-unanimity like many leaders in the Third World. His numbers (there were no women mayors then) greatly diminished with the near-disappearance of communes under one thousand residents in Bavaria. In 1996 there were still over a thousand honorary mayors in the state, slightly more than half of the total. Three-fourths of them served in communes of less than two thousand population and, surprisingly, they had the largest number of women mayors among them. On the other hand, there were nearly as many *Bürgermeisters* who had, by training and certification, attained the qualifications for a civil service career. Four-fifths of these civil servant (*berufsmässige*) *Bürgermeisters* served in communes of three thousand and more. Two-thirds of them tended to have been nominated for mayor by the major political parties, sometimes (15.6 percent) together with local voters "associations." Four-fifths of the honorary mayors, by contrast, were nominated exclusively by such local non-partisan voters groups.[34]

In Middle Franconia as a whole, there were disproportionately more *berufsmässige* mayors and more partisan nominations. Among our fifteen communes and neighboring towns, however, voters associations seemed to predominate[35] and so did the longer terms: There were six mayors serving since 1990 or earlier (three since 1978) who were reelected by over 90 percent of the vote, two even by near-unanimous votes, 99.8 percent (Ohrenbach) and 98.2 percent (Röckingen), most of them in rural villages and some of these long-lived mayors indeed were farmers. Newly (since 1996) elected Bavarian mayors, on the other hand, typically drew only a bare majority of 51 to 55 percent of the vote in their communes. But only a handful of these West Middle Franconian *Bürgermeisters* appear to have the civil service qualifications. The statistical trend borne out in the state statistics still appears to be weak among them. Asked about this, they replied as follows: The then *Bürgermeister* of Wolframs-Eschenbach felt that a full commitment of the presiding mayor to the task at hand strongly suggested *berufsmässig* qualifications. Others echoed this thought, but really more in the form of a wish: The old mayor of Weihenzell who had been in office since 1966, for example, thought of himself as probably the last old-time honorary *Bürgermeister*, even in his rural area. However, there were still several other honorary mayors and they tended to say that their VG had taken over the hardcore administrative functions anyway, especially those newly assigned by state law, and thus spared their commune the expense of a *berufsmässig* mayor. A self-confident, upbeat note often speaks from their statements, such as that of the mayor of Burk who wrote: "I have been mayor of the commune of Burk since 1996, an honorary mayor, and I am a baker master by trade. It is my opinion that I know and understand my fellow-citizens better than does the administrative personnel." On the other hand, we can also point to the relative loss of power of communal *Ortsteil* councils in VGs since almost one half of the new common VG council membership consists of the mayors of the member communes. A rather different atmosphere indeed can be observed in these gatherings than obtains in typical communal councils.[36]

As for their partisanship, we would expect the Bavarian mayors, honorary or civil service, to reflect the absolute majority of the Christian Democrats (CSU) in state elections. Fifty of the seventy-one *Landräte* were indeed nominated by the CSU, and another six by the SPD. However, this dominance does not quite hold for the mayors: Of 2,031 Bavarian mayors in 1996, only 560 were nominated by the dominant party, although another 338 owe their nomination to a joint action of the CSU together with another organization, usually a local voters association.[37] In any case, the CSU is obviously ahead of the SPD, which only nominated 227 mayors (plus 82 on joint tickets), although the ratio between CSU mayors and the opposition SPD favors the CSU quite a bit more (3:1) than the 2:1 ratio of the vote prevailing in the *Landtag*, a sign of the more rural roots of the CSU as compared to the labor-based SPD. Among the honorary, small-commune mayors, indeed, the SPD is 1:5 behind its CSU rivals. There are other parties, the FDP, the Greens, and the Republicans, but they only accounted for two of the 2,031 nominations.

One most striking aspect of local partisanship, however, lies in the fact that the vast majority of the mayors—1,244 of the 2,031 overall, and as many as 800 of the 1,065 honorary mayors—were *not* simply nominated by either one of the major parties alone but by action of non-partisan local voters associations, with or without partisan concurrence. This is very significant, both because it shows the limits of the German party state at the local level[38] and because it evokes Stein Rokkan's theories of the "mobilization of the periphery" in European national development.[39] The strong presence of independent local voters associations and even their co-sponsorship with political parties represents the resistance of the periphery to the actions of the center (or centers), including the high-handed local territorial reforms of 1978. Evidently, much of the Bavarian rural periphery has not yet been successfully penetrated by the CSU party state. And in some cases, as we have seen in Wasserburg am Inn, CSU city councillors provoked by the *Kreisreform* even dropped out of the party in protest and formed the long-lived Wasserburger Block. It goes without saying that the penetration from the center in the form of the prevalence of the Bavarian (and federal German) party system is farther advanced among the civil servant mayors of the larger towns where mayors nominated strictly by either the CSU or the SPD alone (522) outnumber those who owe their nomination only to non-partisan voters associations. Among the honorary mayors the ratio is quite different, 265 party-nominated to 509 non-partisan voters associations, and even the share of joint nominations is more than 50 percent larger.

Our last question regarding partisanship and its opposite juxtaposes the Old Bavarian districts of Upper and Lower Bavaria with regard to the mobilization of the periphery to the four "booty Bavarian" districts, including Upper, Middle, and Lower Franconia. The differences are not overwhelming but the partisan nature of mayoral nominations is indeed greater in Old Bavaria than in the other Bavarian districts. Among honorary mayors, on the other hand, non-partisan nominations have the edge in the newer districts. Especially in Middle Franconia, local non-partisanship outweighed the share of party nominations 8:1, as compared to a ratio of about 4:3 in Old Bavaria. As in the last two hundred years, Middle Franconians such as the people of our fifteen small communes tended to feel the resentment of the rural periphery toward the center in Munich even more than does the rural periphery in general in Old Bavaria. What about our small West Middle Franconian communes and their neighbors? Of nineteen communes, eleven of the mayors were nominated by a local voters association, seven jointly by a party and a local association, and only one directly by the CSU. A map in back of the official mayors' directory (*Bürgermeisterverzeichnis*) shows the geographic concentration of non-partisan local endorsement: The whole northwest of Bavaria, including our area, has mostly local voters associations as the source of formal nominations.

Small Town and Village in Bavaria

The Bavarian monarchy is long gone even though there is still considerable public affection for the House of Wittelsbach and its few surviving offspring. Some Bavarians particularly revere the long dead Ludwig II (1864–1886), "mad king Ludwig," as their "*Kini*," who built all those dream castles and rode a golden sled pulled by white horses through wintry woods. They also pay tribute to his forebears, Ludwig I (1825–1848) and Maximilian II (1848–1864) and their Munich city architecture, monuments, and treasures. That original Bavarian state that some Bavarian historians date from when Pfalzgraf Otto von Wittelsbach in 1180 was given the Duchy of Bavaria by Emperor Frederick Barbarossa has changed its shape and extent a dozen times over the centuries.[40] Average people in the street feel neither particularly beholden to that state—which in its well-established old absolutistic way imposed the recent local territorial reform on them—nor do they hate it, although their opinion of state "bureaucrats" is not the highest. The Bavarians feel rather more affection for its vast historical architectural and art treasures even though a deeper appreciation of their finer aspects is probably limited to the better-educated among them.[41] Average Bavarians more likely see them as of one piece with the varied beauties of the landscape of their *Land*. This may in fact be their chief link to distant history and traditions extending back beyond their parents and grandparents.

The feelings of average Bavarians are far more intensely bound up with their hometowns, villages, and regions, and perhaps even with a kind of simplified idea of the identity of their big cities, their mythical image or images.[42] These social habitats, after all, are their lives, their intimate friends and enemies, their customers and rivals, their neighbors. In the days before the breakdown of the village and small-town community that we have charted here, the vast majority of villagers and small towners under the spell of church and school perhaps felt more deeply connected to their place of birth and residence. As compared to Americans, Bavarians move around very little—especially the rural and small-town folks—although they have probably moved more often in the postwar era than ever before in their history. Learning a lot more about the great wide world out there through travel may also have made them more beholden to their homeland.

They do know their villages and small towns well and, as we have seen, they also know their mayors and communal councilors as few big city dwellers ever get to know their elected officials. In a small community where everyone indeed knows everyone else, their family and individual history, voting for an office holder is a very different thing than voting among the distant and abstracted figures of state and national politics. Just how different was brought home to me when a North German colleague, also a political scientist, told me of his own growing up in a rural Lower German area near the North Sea and of occasional visits to his native village where people only speak *plattdeutsch* (Lower German) dialect. This German colleague had no problem reviving his own *plattdeutsch* skills when needed, but he found it most difficult to chat with Lower German rural villagers about such abstractions as political ideologies and parties, not to mention the complexities of the politics and institutions of the Federal Republic, then in distant Bonn. There seemed to be no words for any of this in *plattdeutsch village* talk, he said, but the villagers were happy to discuss the personalities of their local politicians, their faults and virtues, and what villagers might remember of their past actions.[43] It is surely no accident that the vast majority of old-time Bavarian mayors of small communities tended to receive near-unanimous support at the polls and that they often held office for decades, even life. At the small community level, politics is still very personal and the often patriarchal relationship between citizens and their mayor fits into their daily lives much as the patriarchal relations within the family did.

The transformation or modernization of local government in this setting, therefore, is only in small part a matter of administrative efficiency or even of supplying needed services better to rural and small-town citizens. Rather, such a reform runs the risk of destroying family-like communities and trust in the *père de famille* mayor who is at once avuncular counselor, psychiatrist, agricultural expert, and father image to his flock and, only secondarily, a (rather inadequate) administrator. For these small communities, the reform may have warped identities, social trust, and communal feelings without offering much to replace them although it is easy to exaggerate the suddenness of the transition, from autonomous micro-commune to *Ortsteil* (partial commune), which often retained its name and some of its representatives. Larger towns and medium-sized cities such as Ansbach or Rosenheim obviously suffered no such loss of identity or community. At worst they gained some unhappy and hence rebellious little communes at their periphery that may have sued or fought against their takeover. To the extent, then, that the reform was a game of winners and losers, it was mostly the smallest, more or less rural communes that suffered a painful loss—their citizenry, aside from losing the closeness (*Bürgernähe*) to their chosen councilors and *Bürgermeister*, received considerable compensation in the form of the benefits of improved administration and infrastructure.

In my long academic career, I frequently have tried to explain America to the Germans just as I have tried to explain aspects of German politics past and present to Americans. In this vein I once related in a German textbook on American government how Americans sometimes achieve social change not by confronting it head-on, but by frequently moving from place to better place: "*Wanderung statt Wandlung*" (migration instead of change)[44] made for a good German slogan and it applies also to the modernization of rural and small-town Bavaria. In the half century from 1950 to 2000, American demographic studies reveal that half the American population moved to the suburbs of big cities (which themselves hardly changed their one-third share of the increasing population of the nation): The suburban share rose from 23 percent in 1950 to 50 percent in 2000, as people evidently pulled up their rural and small-town roots (perhaps without giving them up entirely) and moved closer to an urban way of life. At the same time, the remaining non-metropolitan share of the US population dropped from 43.9 percent in 1950 to a mere 19.7 percent in 2000.[45] By now, thinned by age and the population emigration especially in the Midwest, countless rural and small-town communities have lost farms, shops, and taverns to sinking commodity prices and job-destroying farm technology, and the village and small-town folk have died or moved away. In Bavaria, where small-town and village people are slower to move, urban life instead came to them, both in the form of social change and via the great local territorial reform.[46]

Notes

1. From *Small Towns and Small Towners: A Framework for Survival and Growth*, Bert E. Swanson, Richard A. Cohen, and Edith P. Swanson, eds. (Beverly Hills, CA, 1979), 17.

2. See, for example, William Simon and John Gagnon, "The Decline and Fall of the Small Town," *Transaction 4*, April 1967, 51 f.; and Glenn Fuguit, *The Growth and Decline of Nonmetropolitan Cities and Villages* (Madison, WI, May 1976). Fuguit nevertheless found that there had been more than five times as many new American nonmetropolitan incorporations between 1900 and 1970 than failures of such units.

3. The Census Bureau has worked with a size of twenty-five hundred to ten thousand inhabitants, but separate from urbanized areas (usually "Standard Metropolitan Statistical Areas") with centers of fifty thousand or more. Smaller communities under twenty-five hundred are called "rural non-farm," which still leaves unincorporated population concentrations unaccounted for. The author of this book has lived nearly forty years in such an area of over seventy thousand inhabitants in the Goleta valley outside Santa Barbara, California, until it partially incorporated in 2001 as the city of Goleta.

4. German towns below a size of ten thousand housed 87.5 percent in 1871 and 65.3 percent in 1910. Today, only 6.5 percent of the Bavarian population still lives in 133 communes under one thousand, including member communes of VGs. Another 592 Bavarian communes are between one and two thousand (28.8 percent). There are 375 communes between two and three thousand (18.2 percent) and another 407 between three and five thousand (19.8 percent of the state's population). *Jahrbuch BRD 2008*. See also Wolfgang Köllmann, "The Process of Urbanization in Germany

at the Height of the Industrialization Period," in *The Urbanization of European Society in the 19th Century*, A. and L. Lees, eds. (Lexington, KY, 1976), 28–44.

5. Richard Lingeman tells of these population movements and of articles in the 1890s with names like, "The Doom of the Small Town." *Small Town America* (New York, 1980), 326–327.

6. See also the catalogs of small-town studies in Robert Redfield, *The Little Community* (Chicago, 1955); and Colin Bell and Howard Newby, *Community Studies* (New York, 1973). Also Dennis Poplin, *Communities* (New York, 1972).

7. Swanson et al., *Small Towns and Small Towners*, chap. 2, devote a whole chapter to the values, real and attributed, of small towns in America and how they differ from those of big cities.

8. For an example of a mid-nineteenth century paean to small-town moral life as contrasted to the evils of the big city, see Wilhelm Heinrich Riehl, *Die Naturgeschichte des Volkes als Grundlage einer deutschen Social-Politik*, vol. I: *Land und Leute* (Stuttgart, Tübingen, 1954). A lengthy quotation from this work appears in English in Lees et al., *Urbanization*, 58–64.

9. The unfavorable image of small-town and rural village life emerges clearly from a wide range of Bavarian literature, including *Die Chronik von Flechting* by Oskar Maria Graf and Ludwig Thoma earlier in the twentieth century. Among contemporary German writers, there is Anna Winschneider, Otmar Franz Lang, and Herbert Rosenberger. Few have skewered small-town provincialism more effectively than Hermann Glaser, for example in *Spiesserideologie*, rev. ed. (Cologne, 1974). For examples of the literature and art, see also *König Max I Joseph*, I, 448 ff. and Tafel 84 f., and II, 328 ff., 367–431, and 451–456.

10. A large part of German television programs consists of American television schlock and other European fare with almost no local or even Bavarian referents, and a vast array of cable and satellite programs of similar provenance. There is a Bavarian TV channel that shows quite a few folk comedies. Also, Bavarian radio still plays a lot of folk music.

11. We are not referring to the luxury type of historical bed-and-breakfast inns comparable to American and British practice but to the renting out of rooms with breakfast in farms and private residences for supplementary income.

12. The 68-er generation of student rebels and their non-academic coevals was mostly born between 1940 and 1948. See also chapter 3 above, where 1980 Bavarian polls are reported from five rural counties in which 28 percent of the rural and small-town population would rather move to a larger town or to the edge of a big city. Respondents under fifty, women, and the well-educated particularly voiced this preference. Big city dwellers over fifty and the less-educated, on the other hand, would rather move to a village or small town.

13. *The Germans*, 14. Sixty-eight percent of the metropolitan and 48 percent of the medium-sized city dwellers said they lived in an apartment house while only a minority of 36 percent of small-town and 18 percent of village residents said they did.

14. For definitions of postmaterialism, see esp. Ronald Inglehart, *Culture Shift* (Princeton, NJ, 1990), chapters 2 and 4.

15. Rothenburg originated with an ancient castle that Hohenstaufen emperor Konrad III acquired early in the twelfth century. It took shape in the middle of the same century and grew into its present Renaissance pattern in the thirteenth and fourteenth centuries, with walls and gates surrounding its Gothic St. Jakob's church, the old *Rathaus*, and the merchants' houses. Wolframs-Eschenbach's antecedents were documented with excavations of eighth-century graves and the settlement was first

mentioned in records in 1058 when the bishop of Eichstätt, Gundekar, consecrated a church there. The bishop owned the small settlement until the twelfth century when it was given in fief to the counts of Wertheim and Rieneck. Seitz, *Wolframs-Eschenbach*, 13–19.

16. Mitteleschenbach has a VG administrative branch office (*Aussenstelle*) and three (its mayor and two councilors) of the seven seats of the VG assembly.

17. Wolframs-Eschenbach's population already consisted of 58.2 percent employed in manufacturing in 1970 and the town substantially gained in the number of handicraft, manufacturing, and service firms in the eighties.

18. The agricultural share of employment was still 30.6 percent in 1950 and 10.1 percent in 1978. *Jahrbuch Bayern 1997*. The number of farms declined by two-thirds in spite of the town's agricultural annexations since 1949.

19. Wolframs-Eschenbach, for example, went from 111 farms in 1979 to 90 in 1987.

20. In the non-agricultural, non-tourist sector, however, the number of retail outlets was halved in that period while food and beverage stores increased. For details, see *Arbeitsstätten des Gastgewerbes in Bayern. Ergebnisse der Handels- und Gaststättenzählung 1993*, Beiträge zur Statistik Bayerns, Heft 497, 14, 53. See also Heft 495, 19, and Heft 496, 14.

21. A third law dissolved another four VGs and freed four communes. For the text of these two laws, see *BVBl.*, no. 14 (1985), 270, and no. 18 (1989), 369. See Wiebel, "Die kommunale Gebietsreform im Rückblick," *BVBl.* (1987), Heft 22, 677–679.

22. Merk credited his predecessors Ankermüller and Junker with the specifics of the plan and then-Minister President Alfons Goppel with the earliest proposals (1961) for merging micro-communes of three hundred residents or less. The 1961 plans for administrative reform and rationalization were abandoned in the face of protest. But with Goppel's and Merk's advent to office in 1966, they were taken up again in the name of reducing authoritarian administration and administrative costs, and of strengthening the maintenance and promotional activities. See *Landtagsdrucksache 4/106* (1961), and Bruno Merk, "Sinn und Ziel der Gebietsreform," *BVBl.* (1993), 385–386.

23. See Otto Madejczyk, *Das Selbstverwaltungsrecht der bayerischen Kreisangehörigen zwischen staatlicher Reglementierung und europäischer Integration* (Munich, 1995), 63–64.

24. There was an early plea of dissent that called the 1978 reform a "setback for democracy." See Christine Stang, *Die Gemeindegebietsreform—ein Rückschlag für die Demokratie* (Munich, 1978), and esp. the preface by Peter C. Mayer-Tasch, 8. Also the 1978 memorandum of the Bayerischer Städteverband, ibid., 26–28.

25. Merk, 385–387. See also the oft-cited reports of his immediate successor, Minister of the Interior Süss, "Funktionalreform in Bayern," *BGVbl.* (1975), 1 ff., (1976), 449 f., and (1978), 417 f.

26. Regarding the distribution of *gemeindefrei* state lands, there had been 594 such state plots in 1972, but only 313 in 1987. See also *BGVbl.*, no. 29 (1989), 697–700.

27. See also Michael Deubert, "Die Aenderung des Art. 11 Bay GO—(k)ein missverständliches Signal zur Bewältigung von 'Problemfällen,'" *BVbl.*, 124 (1993), Heft 3, 65–68. Also *BGVbl.*, no. 27/1993 for the Fourth Law on Changes in Communes and VGs (November 1993) and the *Landtag* draft, *Drucksache 12/11340* of 18 May 1993.

28. *Landtagdrucksache 12/11340*, 1–4, and *BVbl.* 124, no. 3 (1993), 831–832. None of these reorganizations affected any of our fifteen small communes in Middle Franconia.

29. After getting off to a bad start when a police action was employed to confiscate their records, the citizens of Ermershausen for sixteen long years had contested their annexation and there had been a series of lawsuits, penalties against them, and boycotts

against the administrators. In 1986, a referendum in the former commune drew a 90 percent turnout and 89.4 percent of those voting endorsed the demand for restoration of their commune. Maroldsweisach did not make compromise any easier by its resentment and obstruction. An added complication was Ermershausen's location at the border with the GDR that contributed to the economic marginality of the area until German unification occurred.

30. BGVbl., no 16 (1997), 309–310. This was to take effect, with the exception of some clauses on 1 January 1998. The explanation in the draft bill concluded with resignation that additional costs would be incurred with the promotion of some member communes to EGs and that their departure would weaken their old VGs. It also listed a number of cases waiting to be decided. See Landtag, Drucksache 13/7893 of 18 April 1997. My 1998 interviews with the Bavarian Gemeindetag also confirmed the sense that the reform, despite, or perhaps because of, the concessions made on minimal population size, seemed to be holding firm. The smallest recently restored EG has only 1,430 residents.

31. The Maroldsweisach Communal Council voted twelve to three against letting Ermershausen secede again, and it also blocked an effort to give the unhappy community a vice mayorship of the EG.

32. The amended Art. 11 of the Communal Statute still waffles on this point: In clause 11(2.2) it asserts that in cases of "urgent reasons of the general welfare (öffentliches Wohl) reforms can be imposed against the will of a commune" but clause 11(4) insists that, in contested cases, the residents from now on must have an opportunity to vote on the matter.

33. See column "Rechtsprechung" (court watch), BVbl (1997), no. 24, 751 ff. The Bavarian Constitutional Court decided in 1987 that the right to initiate complaints against a one-time organizational action ran out after a few years. In particular, it would not be fair to the parties relying on the validity of a reorganization if the court continued to accept new complaints "initiated six or seven or, in one case, seventeen years after the reform." Regardless of these doubts, however, the court found the substance of the complaint of Markt Pleinting against Stadt Vilshofen (Lower Bavaria) unfounded.

34. My interviews with representatives of the Bavarian Gemeindetag confirmed that, while there are still many old-style mayors, the trend has been toward the newer model.

35. See Bürgermeisterverzeichnis 1996, 12–13. The mayor of Wolframs-Eschenbach, Seitz, was no exception. In office since 1984, he was reelected by 93.2 percent in 1996.

36. This was already predicted in 1978 by Christine Stang who also pointed out that the big reform would greatly diminish the numbers of honorary communal office-holders that had stood at 55,284 back in 1969. Die Gemeindegebietsreform, 23, 33, 50. See also Konrad Hesse, Grundzüge des Verfassungsrechts der Bundesrepublik Deutschland (Karlsruhe, Heidelberg, 1977). The mayor of Burk, by the way, thought the school district reform (which assigned school children from his commune and VG to four different school locations) should have been the precedent for the local territorial reform. He would have preferred coinciding boundaries for the school, church, and government districts.

37. There are some differences between honorary and civil servant mayors. The latter, who represent more often larger communes, also have been more often nominated by the CSU alone (337) rather than by joint tickets (118). Of the twenty-five largest cities, the Kreisstädte of Bavaria, eleven lord mayors were nominated by the CSU, ten by the SPD. Verzeichnis der Bürgermeister und Landräte. Kommunalwahlen in Bayern am 10. März 1996, of Beiträge zur Statistik Bayerns, Heft 502.

38. The CSU in particular has a reputation of strong and effective party organization in all parts of Bavarian society. See also Merkl, "Factionalism: The Limits of the West German Party State," in *Faction Politics: Political Parties and Factionalism in Comparative Perspective*, Frank P. Belloni and Dennis C. Beller, eds. (Santa Barbara, CA, 1978), 245–264, esp. 254–259, where the speculations about voters associations in the 1960s were discussed.

39. See Stein Rokkan, with Angus Campbell, Per Lorsvik, and Henry Valen, *Citizens, Elections, Parties* (Oslo and New York, 1970), 14–16; and Rokkan, "Electoral Mobilization, and National Integration," in *Political Parties and Political Development*, Joseph La Palombara and Myron Weiner, eds. (Princeton, NJ, 1966), 241–265.

40. Most recently, Bavaria lost the Palatinate left of the Rhine (1946) and before that, it was augmented with Franconia and eastern Suebia (1806). There have also been varying ties with Austria, especially in the eighteenth century, which at times placed Bavaria directly under the control of Hapsburg.

41. See the chapters on art and culture in *Freistaat Bayern*, ed. by Siegfried Lengl (Munich, N.d.), 109–168.

42. This linkage may be more debatable because big cities are far too complex to be easily identified with or even *überschaubar* (transparent) for the average resident. Some may be more involved with their city, and know a lot more about it, than most other residents.

43. They also felt more confident in judging particular federal politicians—such as Helmut Kohl or Gerhard Schröder, if only they could get reliable information about them—than they knew what to make of the national parties, the CDU/CSU and SPD.

44. Merkl and Dieter Raabe, *Politische Soziologie der USA. Die konservative Demokratie* (Wiesbaden, 1977), 9 ff.

45. *Demographics of the U. S.: Trends and Prospects* (Ithaca, NY, 2003), 336–337.

46. *Jahrbuch BRD 2008*, 40.

Appendix

TABLES

A1. Population change 1961–2008 (in present boundaries)

Commune	1961	1970	1979	1987	Dec. 2008
		Resident Population			
Bruckberg	1,235	1,267	1,249	1,233	1,337
Weihenzell	1,636	1,649	1,754	2,110	2,819
Langfurth	1,690	1,878	1,886	1,963	2,148
Röckingen	713	705	670	705	750
Burk	893	959	1,020	1,011	1,168
Ornbau Stadt	1,294	1,360	1,387	1,476	1,627
Markt Berolzheim	1,323	1,297	1,175	1,246	1,367
Meinheim	908	876	785	788	877
Mitteleschenbach	1,134	1,300	1,322	1,378	1,579
Wolfr.-Eschenbach	1,997	2,018	2,019	2,096	2,870
Adelshofen	1,225	1,180	1,025	988	925
Ohrenbach	863	840	766	713	627
Steinsfeld	1,313	1,238	1,179	1,180	1,245
Ippesheim	1,483	1,362	1,183	1,159	1,095
Weigenheim	1,105	999	931	968	1,021

SOURCE: Calculated from Bayerisches Statistisches Landesamt *Die Gemeinden Bayerns*, Heft 377 der Beiträge zur Statistik Bayerns, Munich 1980, *Gemeindedaten 1980*, *Gemeindedaten 1988*, and *Gemeindedaten 2009*.

A2. Stages and types of community development in West Middle Franconia, 1950–1980

Commune	1950	1961	1970	Pre-territorial reform May 1970	Post-reform 1980	Within the borders of 2007
Bruckberg	6	6	6	6	*	6
Weihenzell	1	1	1	3	3	5
Langfurth	2	2	4	4	2	4
Röckingen	1	1	1	2	*	2
Burk	4	4	4	4	4	4
Ornbau Stadt	2	3	3	3	3	4
Markt Berolzheim	2	2	5	5	*	5
Meinheim	1	1	1	3	2	2
Mitteleschenbach	1	1	3	3	3	3
Wolframs-Eschenbach	2	4	4	4	4	4
Adelshofen	1	1	1	1	1	2
Ohrenbach	1	1	1	1	1	2
Steinsfeld	1	2	2	4	2	3
Ippesheim	1	1	1	2	2	2
Weigenheim	1	1	1	1	1	1

* No territorial change

A3. Gainfully employed persons in Bavaria by sector (1882–2008) and position (1939–2008)

(a) By Sector		
	Agriculture	Manufacture	Other
---	---	---	---
1882	59.3	24.3	16.4
1925	45.1	32.2	22.7
1950	30.6	41.4	28.0
1978	10.1	45.1	44.8
1987	5.1	44.0	50.9
2008	3.1	32.4	64.5
Germany:			
2007	2.1	25.4	72.5

(b) By Position					
	1939	1950	1961	1977	1985	2008
---	---	---	---	---	---	---
Independents	17.4	17.1	15.1	10.7	10.2	12.1
Family Help	24.7	19.8	15.1	7.5	5.2	1.5
Civil Servants	5.3	3.7	5.9	8.5	8.3	5.3
Employees	10.3	12.9	19.6	30.4	35.4	54.5
Workers	41.8	46.5	44.3	42.9	40.9	26.7
TOTALS	100.0	100.0	100.0	100.0	100.0	100.0

SOURCES: *Jahrbuch Bayern 1981, 1987, 2009*, and *Kreisdaten 1987. Jahrbuch 2009 for Germany.*

A4. Residents and commuters in fifteen communes in 2008

	Residents I	Residents II	Out-Commuters	Percentage of Out-Commuters	Balance of In-and Out-Commuters
Bruckberg	380	56	271	71.3%	+367
Weihenzell	1,128	326	973	86.3%	−795
Langfurth	848	172	753	88.8%	−670
Röckingen	284	34	271	95.4%	−244
Burk	451	451	386	85.6%	−168
Ornbau Stadt	602	116	538	89.4%	−480
Berolzheim M.	477	150	428	89.7%	−327
Meinheim	308	79	277	89.9%	−222
Mitteleschenbach	655	103	601	91.8%	−552
Wolfr.-Eschenbach	975	450	799	81.9%	−519
Adelshofen	324	87	296	92.0%	−229
Ohrenbach	205	127	182	88.8%	−70
Steinsfeld	444	315	394	88.7%	−129
Ippesheim	387	153	349	90.7%	−226
Weigenheim	367	67	337	91.8%	−300
Middle Franconia	617,269	663,607	368,827	58.8%	+46,686
Bavaria	4,450,187	3,044,632	2,842,164	63.9%	+68,614

NOTE: Residents I pay social insurance at residence, residents II at place of work. *Gemeindedaten 2009*.

A5. Changing employment patterns before the reform in fifteen communes (1939–1970), in percent

	Agriculture		Manufacturing		Services	
	1939	1970	1939	1970	1939	1970
Bruckberg	45.1	10.2	20.6	21.1	34.3	59.7
Weihenzell	93.6	46.5	3.9	32.5	2.5	21.1
Langfurth	61.9	26.0	30.6	58.2	7.5	15.8
Röckingen	86.3	51.5	9.6	33.1	4.2	15.4
Burk	65.6	21.4	32.2	64.5	2.2	14.1
Ornbau Stadt	62.2	18.8	26.8	51.8	11.1	29.4
Markt Berolzheim	61.0	22.8	23.9	46.3	15.1	30.9
Meinheim	81.4	51.8	11.9	28.7	6.8	19.5
Mitteleschenbach	76.0	28.1	19.4	61.4	4.6	10.5
Wolfr.-Eschenbach	61.7	20.4	24.0	58.2	14.4	21.3
Adelshofen	91.1	68.5	5.5	21.2	3.4	10.4
Ohrenbach	92.2	69.7	6.2	21.6	1.6	8.7
Steinsfeld	80.2	49.7	15.0	32.1	4.8	18.1
Ippesheim	81.0	60.0	13.5	24.6	5.5	15.4
Weigenheim	83.8	60.5	11.3	28.1	5.0	11.4
Middle Franconia	29.5	11.5	44.2	50.6	26.3	37.9
Bavaria	38.6	13.2	36.7	47.2	24.8	39.6

SOURCE: *Gemeindedaten 1970*.

A6. Number and size of Bavarian farms (in percent), 1949–2007

	1–5 Acres	5–12.5 Acres	12.5–25 Acres	25–50 Acres	50–125 Acres	125+ Acres	Absolute Numbers
1949	18.0	28.0	28.0	18.8	6.7	.5	477,067
1960	17.3	23.4	28.5	22.9	7.4	.5	426,795
1970	16.6	19.6	24.6	27.8	10.7	.7	347,230
1978	17.3	17.3	21.6	26.6	15.9	1.1	308,078
1985	10.0	16.3	22.4	28.2	21.3	1.8	244,791
1999	15.5		19.9	25.7	30.2	8.7	149,057
2007	15.1		16.6	25.0	28.5	14.1	117,867

SOURCE: *Agrarbericht 1980*, Tabellenband, 13, and *Jahrbuch Bayern 1987* and *2009*.

A7. Changing farm numbers and sizes in the fifteen communes (in percent and absolute numbers)

Commune	% Change 1939– 1970	% Change 1971– 1979	% Change 1979– 1987	In absolute numbers (2009)		
				Smallest (<25 acres)	Largest (>75 acres)	All Farms
Bruckberg	−6.7	−15.4	−29.4	3	5	9
Weihenzell	−6.9	−7.5	−7.5	27	34	88
Langfurth	−24.8	−22.4	−8.2	18	5	34
Röckingen	−17.4	−9.5	−20.8	7	9	23
Burk	−13.7	−12.8	−32.8	6	2	13
Ornbau Stadt	−44.2	−2.7	−23.5	14	9	44
Mark Berolzheim	−10.6	−13.6	−23.0	9	8	26
Meinheim	−28.9	−17.3	−7.6	17	8	46
Mitteleschenbach	−6.0	−5.4	−14.7	13	8	38
Wolfr.-Eschenbach	−17.6	−5.9	−20.5	15	25	64
Adelshofen	−18.3	−4.0	−10.0	17	21	69
Ohrenbach	+0.2	−6.5	−10.8	8	21	53
Steinsfeld	−17.0	−7.2	−9.5	9	24	52
Ippesheim	−18.2	−11.8	−9.4	46	13	94
Weigenheim	−10.7	−12.5	−2.2	30	15	75

NOTE: In Middle Franconia, including metropolitan Nuremberg and Fürth, the number of farms declined by 16 percent in the period 1939–1970, by 10 percent in 1970–1979, and by 14 percent in 1979–1987. In Bavaria, the decline was 28 percent, 11 percent, and 13 percent, respectively.

Source: *Agrarbericht 1980*, Tabellenband, 13, and *Jahrbuch Bayern 1987* and *2009*.

A8. Taverns, restaurants, and inns by size of population (1960) in small communes

Size of population	No. of Communities	Taverns & Restaurants	Pensions, Inns & Hotels	Turnover in 1,000 DM	Beds for Guests	Employees
up to 499	3,779	5,539	1,044	138,560	9,782	14,879
500–999	1,753	4,375	1,268	180,374	16,277	14,120
1,000–1,999	928	3,414	1,691	239,569	26,011	16,174
2,000–4,999	448	2,722	2,143	310,784	39,182	19,543
5,000–10,000	126	1,460	1,325	219,317	25,615	13,222

SOURCE: Bayerisches Statistisches Landesamt (special survey).

A9. Handicraft enterprises and their employees (1956, 1968, and 1977) in fifteen communes

	Enterprises			Gainfully Employed (incl. owner)		
	1956	1968	1977	1956	1968	1977
Bruckberg	26	14	15	98	60	56
Weihenzell	31	24	29	76	60	81
Langfurth	59	41	26	149	186	132
Röckingen	19	16	14	51	64	51
Burk	36	26	22	168	168	192
Ornbau Stadt	25	19	12	65	65	68
Markt Berolzheim	35	27	22	84	106	86
Meinheim	29	17	10	60	31	43
Mitteleschenbach	20	12	12	50	51	59
Wolfr.-Eschenbach	42	34	29	135	150	175
Adelshofen	37	25	14	73	51	54
Ohrenbach	20	13	7	45	23	11
Steinsfeld	36	25	16	132	133	121
Ippesheim	42	25	20	104	91	57
Weigenheim	26	21	11	58	48	38
Lkr. Ansbach	3,570	2,612	1,968	12,019	13,228	13,032
Lkr. Neustadt/ Aisch-Bad Windsheim	2,157	1,527	1,117	7,166	6,802	6,814
Lkr. Weißenburg- Gunzenhausen	1,738	1,312	950	6,229	6,373	6,184

SOURCE: *Gemeindedaten 1980*, Bayerisches Statistiches Landesamt, and *Jahrbuch Bayern 1981*.

A10. One-way distance in miles to nearest railroad station in fifteen communes (1950 and 1981)

	1950	1981
Bruckberg	4.8	same
Weihenzell	4.8	same
Langfurth	7.2	same
Röckingen	2.7	same
Burk	4.2	7.2
Ornbau	1.8	same
Markt Berolzheim	Station	6.0
Meinheim	1.4	7.2
Mitteleschenbach	3.0	same
Wolframs-Eschenbach	3.0	5.4
Adelshofen	4.2	5.4
Ohrenbach	4.0	4.2
Steinsfeld	1.2	4.2
Ippesheim	1.8	4.2
Weigenheim	3.9	same

SOURCE: Bayerisches Statistisches Landesamt, Bayerische Gemeinde- und Kreisstatistik 1949–1950, Heft 177 of *Beiträge zur Statistik Bayerns*, Munich, 1952; *Gemeindedaten 1987*.

A11. Ownership of passenger cars and motorcycles (1950–1989) in Bavaria

	Motor-cycles	Ownership of Motorcycles (% Inhabitants)	Cars & Vans	Ownership of Cars & Vans (% Inhabitants)	Total Vehicles per (% Inhabitants)
1947	64,626	.73	39,482	.44	1.17
1950	282,877	3.08	112,400	1.22	4.30
1954	520,960	6.23	262,362	2.86	9.09
1957	551,985	6.09	452,836	4.94	11.03
1960	413,808	4.40	775,731	8.23	12.63
1964	196,459	2.00	1,435,352	14.50	16.50
1968	70,058	.70	1,046,115	19.80	20.50
1971	42,284	.40	2,647,495	24.90	25.30
1974	50,754	.50	3,055,065	28.20	28.70
1979	142,000	1.30	3,945,000	36.40	37.70
1986	310,270	2.81	4,909,672	44.50	47.30
1989	312,826	2.97	5,489,445	49.70	52.50

SOURCE: *Jahrbuch Bayern 1990* and *Kreisdaten 1989*.

A12. Territorial reorganization in seven areas of West Middle Franconia (1966–1980), including annexations

	1966	1972	Name & Seat of VG after Reform	1978	Reform of the Reform 1979
County Neustadt a. d. Aisch/Bad Windsheim					
1.	Ippesheim & 4 others; (still in Cty. Kitzingen, Dis. Lower Franconia) Weigenheim & 1 other; 23 other communes	Ippesheim & 1 other; Weigenheim; 7 others	*VG Uffenheim* (1974) Uffenheim St.	Ippesheim; Weigenheim & 8 other member communes	Same
County Ansbach					
2.	Adelshofen & 4 others; Steinsfeld & 3 others; Ohrenbach & 2 others; 13 other communes	Adelshofen & 1 other; Steinsfeld & 3 others; Ohrenbach & 1 other; 6 others	*VG Rothenburg*: (Steinsfeld mayor presiding in Rothenburg)	Adelshofen; Steinsfeld; Ohrenbach & 5 other communes	Same
3.	Langfurth & 2 others; Röckingen; 10 other communes	Langfurth & 1 other; Röckingen	*VG Hesselberg*: (Langfurth mayor presiding in Ehingen)	Langfurth; Röckingen & 4 other member communes	Langfurth a separate (1,863) EG; otherwise the same
4.	Burk; 12 other communes	Burk; 2 others	*VG Dentlein am Forst*: Dentlein am Forst	Burk & 2 other member communes	Same

(continued)

A12. Continued

	1966	1972	Name & Seat of VG after Reform	1978	Reform of the Reform 1979
5.	Ornbau St. & 1 other; Mitteleschenbach; Wolframs-Eschenbach & 2 others; 12 other communes	Ornbau St.; Mitteleschenbach; Wolframs-Eschenbach & 4 others; 6 other communes	VG Triesdorf I: (Ornbau mayor presiding in Weidenbach)	Ornbau St.; Mitteleschenbach; Wolframs-Eschenbach & 3 other member communes	Two VGs, two EGs: VG Triesdorf II (Ornbau & seat Weiden bach); VG Wolframs-Eschenbach (with Mitteleschenbach); Arberg M. (1,938) now EG; Merkendorf St. (2,232) EG
6.	Weihenzell & 6 others Bruckberg; 2 other communes	Weihenzell & 2 others; Bruckberg; 2 other communes	VG Weihenzell: (Weihenzell mayor presiding)	Weihenzell; Bruckberg & 1 other	Same
County Weißenburg/Gunzenhausen					
7.	Meinheim & 2 others; Markt Berolzheim & 8 others	Meinheim & 1 other; Markt Berolzheim; 6 other communes	VG Almühltal: (Meinheim mayor presiding)	Meinheim; Markt Berolzheim	Same

SOURCE: *Die Gemeinden Bayerns und Zielplanung der Regierung Mittelfranken* (1975), and Reigl et al., *Kommunale Gliederung*.

A13. No. of Bavarian communes, EGs, VGs, and member communes (1855–2008) by population size

	0–499	500–999	1,000–1,999	2,000–2,999	3,000–4,999	5,000–9,999	10,000–19,999	20,000–49,999	50,000–99,999	100,000+	Total
1855	5,435	1,924	536	81	34	23	12	5	1	1	8,052
1910	4,834	2,089	727	153	90	54	15	14	5	3	7,984
1939	4,737	1,923	781	311		76	24	20	5	5	7,882
1950	3,206	2,121	1,166	280	168	112	35	18	6	4	7,116
1970	3,546	1,700	1,002	294	203	157	68	20	9	5	7,004
2008											2,056
1978 EGs*	—	1	20	129	236	213	119	30	11	6	765
1978 Member Communes	2	253	658	216	75	43	40	—	—	—	1,287
1978 VGs	—	—	—	7	+150	212	24	—	—	—	393
1980 EGs	—	1	80	213	269	225	121	31	11	6	965
1980 Member Communes	2	252	587	129	82	31	—	—	—	—	1,083
1980 VGs	—	—	—	23	++158	150	14	—	—	—	345
1987 EGs	—	1	70	213	291	236	124	34	11	5	985
1987 Member Communes	3	211	598	130	90	36	—	—	—	—	1,068
1987 VGs	—	—	—	25	+++138	160	17	—	—	—	340

*Including Independent Cities

\+   Of these, 53 were between 3,000 and 4,000

++   Of these, 72 were between 3,000 and 4,000

+++ Of these, 54 were between 3,000 and 4,000

SOURCE: Bayerisches.Statistisches Landesamt, Reigl et al, *Kommunale Gliederung*, 45–46 and appendix; and *Gemeindedaten 1988, 2009*.

A14. Comparing the *Länder* reforms (1965–1980)

	Bavaria	Baden-Würtem.	Hesse	Lower Saxony	N.Rh. Westph.	Rhinel. Palatin.	Saar-land	Schleswig Holstein
Rural Counties								
Before	143	63	39	60	57	39	7	17
After	71	35	20	37	31	24	5	11
1980								
Independent Cities	25	5	6	9	23	12	*1	4
Other Communes	2,023	1,111	422	1,028	396	2,322	50	1,150
Of these, EGs	940	179	416	276	373	36	50	45
Of these, VG Members	1,083	923	—	743	—	2,274	—	1,101
VG-type Associations	345	272	—	142	—	164	—	122
Pre-Reform Communes	7,073	3,379	2,684	3,976	2,334	2,905	345	1,378

*Metropolitan Association Saarbrücken

SOURCE: Reigl et al., *Kommunale Gliederung*, 44–45.

A15. Survey of "winners" and "losers" among communes: social indicators

	104 New EGs	87 New VG seats	Losers I: 51 Members of VGs	Losers II: 11 Annexed by EGs
Population Increase (%) since 1961	28.5	9.8	8.8	16.4
Population Increase (%) since 1970	9.6	3.2	2.2	—
Density (persons per km²)	216	125	94	178
No. of agricultural enterprises in 1976	270	204	183	122
Industrial enterprises with 10 or more employees	6.1	3.5	1.3	1.8
Industrially employed persons 1976	689	251	36	301
Tourist overnight stays 1976	46,730	23,527	11,144	2,315
Local tax capacity (per capita)				
DM real property tax	276	256	220	226
DM turnover tax (business transactions)	65	60	52	—
DM communal share of income tax	177	165	136	115
DM total communal taxes raised 1976	389	360	306	273

SOURCE: *Die Gemeinden Bayerns, Gemeindedaten zur Gebietsreform*, Bayerisches Statistisches Landesamt, 1978, and *Gemeindedaten*, 1973.

SELECT BIBLIOGRAPHY AND GOVERNMENT DOCUMENTS

Select Bibliography

Albertin, Lothar. "Local Territorial Reform in the Context of West German Social Development," in *New Local Centers in Centralized States*, Peter H. Merkl, ed. (Lanham, MD, 1985), 128–131.

Albrecht, Dieter. "Von der Reichsgründung bis zum Ende des ersten Weltkrieges (1871–1918)," in *Bayerische Geschichte im 19. und 20. Jahrhundert, 1800 bis 1970*, 2 vols., Max Spindler, ed. (Munich, 1978), I, 283–386 (hereafter, Spindler, *Bavarian History*).

Ammann, Hektor. "Wie groß war die mittelalterliche Stadt?" in *Die Stadt des Mittelalters*, 3 vols., Carl Haase, ed. (Darmstadt, 1969), I, 408–412.

Anderson, Christopher. "Necessary Illusions: The Transformation of Governance Structures in the New Germany," in *The Domestic Politics of German Unification*, Christopher Anderson, et al., eds. (Boulder, CO, 1993), 124–126.

Anderson, Uwe. "Kommunalpolitik als Experimentierfeld für Reformen—eine Einführung," *Politische Bildung*, vol. 31, no. 1 (1998).

Banner, Gerhard. "Kommunale Verwaltungsreform und staatlicher Modernisierungsrückstand," *Politische Bildung*, vol. 31, no. 1 (1998), 34–46.

Barbarino, Otto. "Zur Reformbedürftigkeit der gegenwärtigen Finanzverfassung," in *Politikverflechtung zwischen Bund, Ländern und Gemeinden*, Schriftenreihe der Hochschule Speyer no. 55 (Berlin, 1974), 105–110.

Bayerischer Bauernverband. *Zehn Jahre Bayerischer Bauernverband* (Munich, 1955).

Beer, Rüdiger. *Die Gemeinde: Grundriß der Kommunalpolitik* (Munich, 1970).

Bell, Colin, and Howard Newby. *Community Studies* (New York, 1973).

Belloni, Frank, and Dennis Beller, eds.. *Faction Politics* (Santa Barbara, CA, 1978).

Bendixen, Ernst, and Helmut Harbeck. "Zur sozialen Sicherung in der Landwirtschaft," in *Produktion und Lebensverhältnisse auf dem Land*, Onno Poppinga, ed., special issue of *Leviathan*, no. 2 (1979).

Benz, Arthur. *Föderalismus als dynamisches System. Zentralisierung und Dezentralisierung im föderativen Staat* (Opladen, 1985).

Berkenbrink, Gerd. *Wandlungsprozesse einer dörflichen Kultur* (Göttingen, 1974).

Borgerding, Albert, et al.. *Kommunale Politik: Rahmenbedingungen, Strukturen, Entscheidungsprozesse* (Bonn, 1978).

Bosl, Karl. "Die historisch-politische Entwicklung des bayerischen Staates," in *Bayern, Handbuch der historischen Stätten*, 2nd ed., Karl Bosl, ed. (Stuttgart, 1974).

———. "Was sind Stämme und welche Rolle spielen sie im modernen bayerischen Staat?" in *Freistaat Bayern*, 3rd ed., Rainer Roth, ed. (Bayreuth, 1983), 129–131.

Brockmann, Anna D., ed. *Landleben* (Reinbek/Hamburg, 1977).

Clout, Hugh D., ed. *Regional Development in Western Europe* (London, 1975).

DDR Handbuch (Cologne, 1975).

Deubert, Michael. "Die Aenderung des Art. 11 Bay GO—kein missverständliches Signal zur Bewältigung von 'Problemfällen,'" *Bayeriche Verwaltungsblätter* 124 (1993), 65–68.

Deuerlein, Ernst, and Wolf D. Bruner. "Die politische Entwicklung Bayerns 1945 bis 1972," in *Bayerische Geschichte im 19. und 20. Jahrhundert, 1800 bis 1970*, 2 vols., Max Spindler, ed. (Munich, 1978).

Duff, Andrew, John Pinder, and Roy Price, eds. *Maastricht and Beyond: Building the European Union* (London and New York, 1994).

Dyson, Kenneth. "Improving Policy-making in Bonn: Why the Central Planners Failed," *Journal of Management Studies*, 12 (May 1975), 175.

Eckhard, Jesse, and Armin Mitter, eds. *Die Gestaltung der deutschen Einheit* (Bonn and Berlin, 1992).

Ehringhaus, H. *Der kooperative Föderalismus in den Vereinigten Staaten von Amerika* (Stuttgart, 1971).

Ellwein, Thomas, and Gisela Simpel. *Wertheim: Fragen an eine Stadt* (Munich, 1969).

Emenlauer, R., et al. *Die Kommune in der Staatsorganisation* (Frankfurt, 1974).

Festschrift 90 Jahre Freiwillige Feuerwehr Mitteleschenbach, broch. (1964).

Friedrichs, Christopher R. *Urban Society in an Age of War: Nördlingen, 1580–1720* (Princeton, NJ, 1979).

Fuguit, Glenn. *The Growth and Decline of Non-metropolitan Cities and Villages* (Madison, WI, 1976).

Gabriel, Oscar W., ed. *Kommunalpolitik im Wandel der Gesellschaft* (Mainz, 1979).

Ganser, Karl. "Politikverflechtung zwischen Bund und Ländern—Beobachtungen am Rand der Bundesverwaltung," in *Politikverflechtung in föderativen Staat*, J. J. Hesse, ed. (Baden-Baden, 1978), 45–73.

Gibson, Patricia R. "Local Territorial Reform in Bavaria," in *New Local Centers in Centralized States*, Peter H. Merkl, ed. (1985).

Glaessner, Gert-Joachim. *The Unification Process in Germany: From Dictatorship to Democracy* (New York, 1992).

Glaser, Hermann. *Spiesserideologie* (Cologne, 1974).

Golde, Günter. *Catholics and Protestants: Agricultural Modernization in Two German Villages* (New York, 1975).

Grauhan, Rolf-Richard, ed. *Großstadt-Politik: Texte zur Analyse und Kritik lokaler Demokratie* (Gütersloh, 1972).

———. *Lokale Politikforschung II* (Frankfurt, 1975).

Gröbner, Peter. "Schwierige Gemeindefinanzreform," *Bayerischer Bürgermeister*, no. 2 (1968), 33–38.

Grünemann, Willem. "Konzentration und Zentralisation in der Agrarindustrie und in den Genossenschaften," in *Produktion und Lebensverhältnisse auf dem Land*, Onno Poppinga, ed., special issue of *Leviathan*, no. 2 (Opladen, 1979).

Grunwald, Karl. "Das 'Wassertrüdinger Modell,'" *Unser Auftrag*, no. 1 (1976).

———. "Unsere Landgemeinden sind seelsorgerliches Notstandsgebiet," in *Korrespondenzblatt*, 96, no. 2 (1981).

Gunlicks, Arthur B. "Die parteipolitischen Präferenzen beim niedersächsischen Entscheidungsprozess für eine Gebietsreform im Spannungsfeld von Effizienz, Gleichheit und Freiheit," *Zeitschrift für Parlamentsfragen*, no. 7 (1976), 472–480.

———. "The Future of Federalism in the Unified Germany," in C. Anderson, *The Domestic Politics of German Unification* (1993).

———. *Local Government in the German Federal System* (Durham, NC, 1986).

———. "The Reorganization of Local Governments in the Federal Republic of Germany," in *Local Government Reform and Reorganization: An International Perspective* (Port Washington, NY, and London, 1981).

———. "Restructuring Service Delivery Systems in West Germany," in *Comparing Urban Service Delivery Systems*, Vincent Ostrom and Frances P. Bish, eds. (Beverly Hills, CA, 1977).

———. "50 Years of German Federalism: An Overview and Some Current Developments," in *The Federal Republic of Germany at 50*, Merkl, ed. (London and New York, 1999), 186–202.

Haase, Carl, ed. *Die Stadt des Mittelalters*, 3 vols. (Darmstadt, 1969).

Hall, Peter. *Urban and Regional Planning*, 4th ed. (London and New York, 2002).

Hansen, Niles M., ed. *Public Policy and Regional Economic Development: The Experience of Nine Western Countries* (Cambridge, MA, 1974).

Helm, Jutta. "Citizen Initiatives in West Germany," in *Western European Party Systems: Trends and Prospects*, Merkl, ed. (New York, 1980), 576–596.

———. "The Politics of German Cities: A Tale of Visions, Money, and Democracy," in *The Federal Republic of Germany at Fifty: At the End of a Turbulent Century*, Merkl, ed. (New York, 1999), 203–215.

Hennis, Wilhelm, Peter Graf Kielmannsegg, and Ulrich Matz, eds. *Regierbarkeit. Studien zu ihrer Problematisierung*, 2 vols. (Stuttgart, 1977–1979).

Henrich, Franz Walter. *Kommunale Beteiligung in der Raumordnung und Landesplanung*, 2 vols. (Stuttgart, 1981).

Hesse, Jens Joachim, ed. *Politikverflechtung im föderativen Staat* (Baden-Baden, 1978).

———. *Politikverflechtung II* (Kronberg im Taunus, 1977).

———. "The FRG from Cooperative Federalism to Joint Policy-Making," in *West European Politics*, 10, no. 4 (October 1987), 70–87.

Hesse, Konrad. *Der unitarische Föderalimus* (Darmstadt, 1962).

———. "Aspekte des kooperativen Föderalismus in der BRD," in *Festgabe für Gebhard Müller* (Stuttgart, 1970).

———. *Grundzüge des Verfassungsrechts der Bundesrepublik Deutschland* (Karlsruhe, 1997).

Hirschmann, Gerhard. "Die evangelische Kirche seit 1800," in Spindler, *Bavarian History* (Munich, 1978), II, 883–913.

Hochschule Speyer, eds. *Politikverflechtung zwischen Bund, Ländern und Gemeinden* (Berlin, 1975).

Hoffman, Helmut. *Bayern, Handbuch zur staatspolitischen Landeskunde der Gegenwart*, 2nd rev. ed. (Munich, 1974).

Hofmann, Christa, and Dagmar Schmerbeck. "Die Gemeinde-Gebietsreform in Bayern: Dargestellt am Beispiel der Eingemeindungen von Seebach und Natternberg nach Deggendorf," in *Sozialwissenschaftliche Beiträge zur Raumforschung*, Universität Augsburg, Institut für Soziooekonomie, 5 (1979).

Horak, Karl, "Volkslied und Volksmusik in Altbayern," in *Bayerische Symphonie*, 2 vols., Herbert Schindler ed., (Munich, 1968), II, 279–287.

Hubensteiner, Benno. *Bayerische Geschichte: Staat und Volk, Kunst und Kultur* (Munich, 1977).

Institut zur Förderung Öffentlicher Angelegenheiten, ed. *Die Bundesländer* (Frankfurt, 1950).

Isbary, Gerhard. *Zentrale Orte und Versorgungsnahbereiche* (Bad Godesberg, 1965).

Jarausch, Konrad H. *The Rush to German Unity* (New York, 1994).

Jeffrey, Charlie, and Roland Sturm, eds. *Federalism, Unification and European Integration* (London, 1993).

Kazepov, Yuri, ed. *Cities of Europe: Changing Concepts, Local Arrangements and the Challenge of Urban Cohesion* (Oxford, 2005).

Kern, Rudolf. "Die Gemeindestrassen in Bayern," in *Bayern in Zahlen*, 17 (May 1963).

———. "Bayerns Gastgewerbe," in *Bayern in Zahlen* (May 1971).

———. "Das Gaststätten- und Beherbergungsgewerbe in Bayern," in *Bayern in Zahlen* 31, no. 9 (September 1977).

———. "Struktur und Entwicklung der Unternehmen des Handels und Gastgewerbes in Bayern," in *Bayern in Zahlen* 35, no. 1 (January 1981).

Keyser, Erich, and Heinz Stoob. *Bayerisches Städtebuch*, 2 vols. (Stuttgart, 1974).

Kilper, Heiderose, and Roland Lhotta. *Föderalismus in der Bundesrepublik Deutschland: Eine Einführung* (Opladen, 1996).

King, Leslie J. *Central Place Theory* (Beverly Hills, CA, 1984).

Klein, Ernst. *Geschichte der deutschen Landwirtschaft im Industriezeitalter* (Wiesbaden, 1973).

Köllmann, Wolfgang. "The Process of Urbanization in Germany at the Height of the Industrialization Period," in *The Urbanization of European Society in the 19th Century*, A. and L. Lees, eds. (Lexington, KY, 1976), 28–44

Kohler-Hezinger, Christel. "Lokale Honoratioren," in *Dorfpolitik*, Hans-Georg Wehling, ed. (Opladen, 1978).

Kornrumpf, Martin. *In Bayern Angekommen* (Munich, 1979).

Laufer, Heinz. *Der Föderalismus der BRD* (Stuttgart, 1974).

Laufer, Heinz, and Ursula Münch. "Die Neugestaltung der bundesstaatlichen Ordnung," in *Die Gestaltung der deutschen Einheit*, Jesse Eckhard and Armin Mitter, eds. (Berlin, 1992), 227–228.

Lehmbruch, Gerhard. "Verfassungspolitische Alternativen der Politikverflechtung," in *Politikverflechtung II*.

———. "Institutional Linkages and Policy Networks in the Federal System of West Germany," in *Publius: The Journal of Federalism*, 19, no. 4 (Fall 1989).

Lingeman, Richard. *Small Town America* (New York, 1980).

Lütke, Friedrich. *Geschichte der deutschen Agrarverfassung* (Stuttgart, 1966).

Madejczyk, Otto. *Das Selbstverwaltungsrecht der bayerischen Kreisangehörigen Orte zwischen staatlicher Reglementierung und europäischer Integration* (Munich, 1995).

Mayer-Tasch, P. C., ed. *Kulturlandschaft in Gefahr* (Munich, 1976).

Merk, Bruno. "Sinn und Ziel der Gebietsreform," in *Bayerische Verwaltungsblätter* (1993), 385–386.

Merkl, Peter H. "Executive-Legislative Federalism in West Germany," *The American Political Science Review* 53, no. 3 (September 1959), 732–741.

———. "Factionalism: The Limits of the West German Party State," in *Faction Politics*, Frank Belloni and Dennis Beller, eds. (Santa Barbara, CA, 1978).

———. *The Federal Republic at Fifty* (London and New York, 1999).

———. *The Federal Republic at Forty-Five* (London, 1995).

———. "The Financial Constitution (*Finanzverfassung*) of Western Germany," in *American Journal of Comparative Law*, 6 (Spring 1957), 327–340.

————. *German Unification in the European Context* (University Park, PA, 1993).

————. *Germany: Yesterday and Tomorrow* (New York, 1965).

————. "How Communities Decline," in *New Local Centers in Centralized States*, Merkl, ed. (Lanham, MD, 1985), 29–94.

————. *The Making of a Stormtrooper* (Princeton, NJ, 1980).

————, ed. *New Local Centers in Centralized States* (Lanham, MD, 1985).

————. *The Origin of the West German Republic* (New York, 1963).

————. "Territorial Reform and Bavarian Local Politics: Patterns of Resistance," in *New Local Centers in Centralized States*, Merkl, ed. (Lanham, 1985), 95–122.

————. "The Urban Challenge Under the Empire," in *Another Germany: A Reconsideration of the Imperial Era*, Jack R. Dukes and Joachim Remak, eds. (Boulder, CO, 1988), 67–72.

Moeller, Robert G., ed. *West Germany Under Construction: Politics, Society and Culture in the Adenauer Era* (Ann Arbor, MI, 1997).

Nassmacher, Karl-Heinz. *Kommunalpolitik und Sozialdemokratie* (Bonn-Bad Godesberg, 1977).

Newton, Kenneth. *Balancing the Books: Financial Problems of Local Government in West Europe* (London and Beverly Hills, CA, 1985),

Nicholas, David. *The Later Medieval City, 1300–1500: A History of Urban Society in Europe* (Westport, CT, 1997).

Noelle-Neumann, E., ed. *The Germans: Public Opinion Polls, 1967–1980*, Institut für Demoskopie Allensbach (Westport, CT, 1980).

Oebbecke, Janberud. "Die neue Kommunalverfassung in Nordrheinwestfalen," in *Die Oeffentliche Verwaltung*, 48, no. 17 (1995).

Petersen, Edward N. *The Limits of Hitler's Power* (Princeton, NJ, 1969).

Petzold, Siegfried. "Zur Entwicklung und Funktion der kommunalen Selbstverwaltung in den neuen Bundesländern," in *Kommunalpolitik in Deutschland: Politisches Handeln in den Gemeinden*, Helmut Wollman and Roland Roth, eds. (Opladen, 1993), 34–41.

Planck, Ulrich. *Die Landgemeinde*, Österreichisches Institut für Agrarsoziologie und Agrarrecht (Linz, 1978).

Poplin, Dennis. *Communities* (New York, 1972).

Poppinga, Onno. "Bauern in der Bundesrepublik Deutschland," in *Landleben*, Anna D. Brockmann, ed. (Reinbek and Hamburg, 1977).

————. "Gebrauchsanleitung zum Agrarbericht," in *Produktion und Lebensverhältnisse auf dem Land*, Onno Poppinga, ed., special issue of *Leviathan*, no. 2 (1979).

Pross, Helge. *Über die Bildungschancen der Mädchen in der Bundesrepublik* (Frankfurt, 1969).

Rausch, Heinz, and Theo Stamm, eds. *Aspekte und Probleme der Kommunalpolitik* (Munich, 1972).

Reble, Albert. "Das Schulwesen," in Spindler, *Bavarian History* (1978), I, 978–988.

Redfield, Robert. *The Little Community* (Chicago, 1955).

Reigl, Otto, Josef Schober, and Gerhard Skoruppa, eds. *Kommunale Gliederung in Bayern nach der Gebietsreform* (Munich, 1978).

Riehl, Wilhelm Heinrich. *Die Naturgeschichte des Volkes als Grundlage einer deutschen Socialpolitik*, vol. 1: *Land und Leute* (Stuttgart, 1954).

Ritter, G. A., and J. Kocka, eds. *Deutsche Sozialgeschichte 1870–1914* (Munich, 1982).

Rodenstein, Marianne. "Konflikte zwischen Bund und Kommunen," in *Lokale Politikforschung 2*, Rolf-Richard Grauhan, ed. (Frankfurt, 1975).

Röder, Christoph, ed. *Bürgernahe Kommunalpolitik* (Munich, 1977).

Rörig, Fritz. *The Medieval Town* (Berkeley and Los Angeles, 1967).

Rokkan, Stein. "Electoral Mobilization and National Integration," in *Political Parties and Political Development*, Joseph La Palombara and Myron Weiner, eds. (Princeton, NJ, 1966), 241–265.

———. Angus Campbell, Per Lorsvik, and Henry Valen. *Citizens, Elections, Parties* (Oslo and New York, 1970).

Rowat, Donald C., ed. *International Handbook on Local Government Reorganization: Contemporary Developments* (Westport, CT, 1980).

Schäfer, Peter. *Zentralisation und Dezentralisation* (Berlin, 1982).

Scharpf, Fritz W., Bernd Reissert, and Fritz Schnabel. *Politikverflechtung: Theorie und Empirik des kooperativen Föderalismus in der Bundesrepublik* (Kronberg im Taunus, 1976).

Schmid, Carlo. "Bund und Länder," in *Die zweite Republik. 25 Jahre Bundesrepublik Deutschland—Eine Bilanz*, Richard Löwenthal and Hans-Peter Schwarz, eds. (Stuttgart, 1974), 244–260.

Schmid, Hans. "Musik," in Spindler, *Bayerische Geschichte* (1978).

Schofield, John, and Alan Vince. *Medieval Town*, 2nd ed. (London and New York, 2003).

Schreyer, Klaus. *Bayern—ein Industriestaat* (Munich, 1969).

Shannon, John. *Local Finance in Great Britain, West Germany, and the United States: A Comparative Analysis* (Columbus, OH, 1978).

Sharpe, Laurence James, ed. *The Local Fiscal Crisis in Western Europe: Myths and Realities* (London and Beverly Hills, CA, 1981).

Simon, William, and John Gagnon. "The Decline and Fall of the Small Town," *Transactions* 4 (April 1967), 51 ff.

Sonthofen, Wolfgang. *Der Deutsche Orden: 800 Jahre Geschichte* (Freiburg, 1990).

Spindler, George, et al. *Burgbach: Urbanization and Identity in a German Village* (New York, 1974).

Spindler, Max, ed. *Bayerische Geschichte im 19. und 20. Jahrhundert, 1800 bis 1970* (or Spindler, *Bavarian History*), 2 vols. (Munich, 1978).

Stang, Christine. *Die Gemeindegebietsreform—ein Rückschlag für die Demokratie* (Munich, 1978).

Stern, Klaus. "Die föderalistische Ordnung im Spannungsfeld der Gegenwart," in *Politikverflechtung zwischen Bund, Ländern und Gemeinden* (Berlin, 1974).

Stollreither, Konrad, ed. *Verfassung des Freisstaates Bayern und Grundgesetz für die Bundesrepublik Deutschland* (Munich, 1977).

Swanson, Bert, Richard A. Cohen, and Edith P. Swanson. *Small Towns and Small Towners: A Framework for Survival and Growth* (Beverly Hills, CA, 1979).

Treiberg, Werner. *Grundfragen der Kommunalpolitik* (Mainz, 1970).

Treml, Manfred, ed. *Politische Geschichte Bayerns* (Munich, 1989).

United States Advisory Commission on Intergovernmental Relations. *The Condition of Contemporary Federalism: Conflicting Theories and Collapsing Constraints* (Washington, DC, 1981).

———. *Studies in Comparative Federalism: Australia, Canada, the U.S. and West Germany* (Washington, DC, 1981).

Volk, Ludwig. "Bayern im NS-Staat, 1933 bis 1945," in Spindler, *Bavarian History* (1978), I, 518–537.

von Arnim, Hans H. "Auf dem Weg zur optimalen Gemeindeverfassung," in *Deutsches Verwaltungsblatt* 112, no. 12 (1997).

———. "Reform der Gemeindeverfassung in Hessen," *Die öffentliche Verwaltung* 45, no. 8 (1992), 330–338.

von Beyme, Klaus. *Das politische System der Bundesrepublik Deutschland nach der Vereinigung* (Munich, 1991).

von Saldern, Adelheid. "Geschichte der kommunalen Selbstverwaltung in Deutschland," in *Kommunalpolitik: Politisches Handeln in den Gemeinden*, Roland Roth and Helmut Wollmann, eds. (Opladen, 1993).

von Unruh, Georg-Christoph. *Gebiets- und Verwaltungsreform in Niedersachsen, 1965–1978* (Hannover, 1978).

Vries, Jan de. *European Urbanization 1500–1800* (Cambridge, MA, 1984).

Wagener, Frido. "Reform kleiner Gemeinden in Europa," *Verwaltungsarchiv* 62, no. 2 (1971), 97–113.

———. "Milderungsmöglichkeiten nachteiliger Folgen vertikaler Politikverflechtung," in J. J, Hesse, *Politikverflechtung* II, 152 ff.

———. "West Germany: A Survey," in Rowat, *International Handbook on Local Government Reorganization: Contemporary Developments* (1980).

Walker, Mack, *German Home Towns: Community, State, and General Estate* (Ithaca, NY, 1971).

Weber, Max. "Die Stadt," in *Archiv für Sozialwissenschaft und Sozialpolitik* 47 (1921), 597–605.

Wehling, Hans-Georg, ed. *Dorfpolitik* (Opladen, 1978).

———. "Kommunale Verfassungsreform: Vergleich der kommunalen Vefassungssysteme in Deutschland," in *Politische Bildung* 31, no. 1 (1998), 19–33.

Weis, Eberhard. "Die Begründung des bayerischen Staats unter König Max I: (1799–1825)," in Spindler, *Bayerische Geschichte* (1978).

Wells, Roger H. *German Cities: A Study of Contemporary Municipal Policy and Administration* (Princeton, NJ, 1932).

Wever, Göttrich. "Die Krise der Kommunalfinanzen," in Wehling, *Dorfpolitik*, 47–61.

Wiebel, Hans. "Die kommunale Gebietsreform in Rückblick," *Bayerische Verwaltungsblättert* (1987), Heft 22, 677–679.

Witetchek, Helmut. "Die Katholische Kirche seit 1800," in Spindler, *Bavarian History*, II, 914–945.

Wollmann, Helmut, and Roland Roth, eds. *Kommunalpolitik in Deutschland: Politisches Handeln in den Gemeinden* (Opladen, 1993).

Wollmann, Helmut. "Kommunalpolitik und -verwaltung in Ostdeutschland im Umbruch und Uebergang," in Wollmann and Roth, *Kommunalpolitik in Deutschland: Politisches Handeln in den Gemeinden* (1993), 20–33.

Zielinski, Heinz, ed. *Lokale Politik zwischen Eigenständigkeit und staatlicher Abhängigkeit* (Meisenheim, 1980).

Zoll, Ralf. *Wertheim III: Kommunalpolitik und Machtstruktur* (Munich, 1974).

———, ed. *Gemeinde als Alibi: Materialien zur politischen Soziologie der Gemeinde* (Munich, 1972).

Zorn, Wolfgang. "Die Sozialentwicklung der nichtagrarischen Welt (1806–1970)," in Spindler, *Bavarian History* (1978), II, 846–882.

Government Documents

Baden-Württemberg, Innenministerium, *Denkmodell der Landesregierung zur Kreisreform in Baden-Württemberg* (Stuttgart, 1969).

———, "Gutachten zur Kreisreform," in *Staatsanzeiger für Baden-Württemberg* (July, 1970), supplement, 10–15.

———, Kommission für die kommunale Verwaltungsreform, *Teilgutachten A, B, C.* (N.d.).

———, Landtag, 5, Wahlperiode *Drucksache* V/3300 (15 October 1970).

Bayern, Landesamt für Statistik und Datenverarbeitung, *Amtliches Gemeindeverzeichnis für Bayern: Gebietsstand* (31 December 1987).

———, "*Arbeitsstätten des Gastgewerbes in Bayern. Ergebnisse der Handels- und Gaststättenzählung* (1993).

———, *Bayerische Gemeindestatistik* (1970–2007).

———, *Bayerische Gemeinde- und Kreisstatistik 1949/50* (1952).

———, *Die bayerische Landwirtschaft, ihre Struktur und Entwicklung* (1975).

———, *Bayerischer Agrarbericht* (1980, 2004, 2006, and 2007).

———, *Bayerns Wirtschaft, Gestern und Heute* (1980).

———, *Betriebsstruktur der Landwirtschaft in Bayern* (1979).

———, *Bürgermeisterverzeichnis* (1967, 1973, 1978, 1984, 1990, 1996, and 2004).

———, *Gemeindedaten* (1973, 1975, 1978, 1980, 1988, 1990, 1994, and 2009).

———, *Kommunalwahlen in Bayern am 18. März 1990, Endgültige Ergebnisse* (1990).

———. *Statistisches Jahrbuch für Bayern* (1971, 1972, 1978, 1981, 1987, 1990, 1995, and 2009; or *Bayern Jahrbuch*, with the year).

Bayern, Staatskanzlei, *Verwaltungsreform III* (Munich, 1973).

———, Staatsministerium des Inneren, *Gebietsreform Bayern. Gemeinden in der Reform* (1975).

———, Staatsministerium für Landesentwicklung und Umweltfragen, *Landesentwicklung Bayern. Zentrale Orte und Nahbereiche in Bayern* (1972)

———, Staatsministerium für Landesentwicklung und Umweltfragen, *Die Gemeinden Bayerns, Änderung im Bestand und Gebiet von 1840 bis 1975* (1975).

———, Staatsministerium für Landesentwicklung und Umweltfragen, *Die Gemeinden Bayerns, Gemeindedaten zur Gebietsreform* (1978).

———, Staatsministerium für Landesentwicklung und Umweltfragen, *Die Gemeinden Bayerns* (1980).

———, Staatsministerium für Landesentwicklung und Umweltfragen, *Gutachten zum Stadt-Umland-Problem in Bayern* (December 1974).

Bayern, Staatsregierung, *Landesentwicklungsprogramm Bayern*, Teil C, Entwurf (1974), A, B, and C.

———, *Raumordnungsbericht* (1971, 1976, and 1978).

———, *Region Westmittelfranken*, Kartenbeilagen, Marktheidenreid (1975).

———, *Verwaltungsgemeinschaft in Bayern* (December 1973).

Deutsches Reich, *Statistisches Jahrbuch für das Deutsche Reich* (annual).

Federal Republic, (West), Bundesamt für Statistik, *Datenreport* (Bonn, 1992).

———, *Deutschland im Wiederaufbau*, later *Deutsche Politik* (Bonn, 1952–1963; ministerial activity reports with the year).

———, *Jahresbericht der Bundesregierung* (Bonn, 1968–1978; annual government reports, with the year).

———, *Tatsachen über Deutschland* (1979).

———, Bundesminister der Finanzen, *Finanzberichte* (annual).

———, Bundesminister des Innern, *Die Neugliederung des Bundesgebietes* (Bonn, 1955).

———, Bundesminister für Städtebau und Raumordnung, *Städtebaubericht* (1970).

———, Bundesregierung, *Raumordnungsbericht der Bundesregierung* (1966, 1971, 1972 and 1974).

———, Bundestag, Enquête-Kommission Verfassungsreform des Deutschen Bundestags, *Beratungen und Empfehlungen zur Verfassungsreform*, parts I and II, *Bund und Länder* (Bonn, 1975 and 1977).

———, *Schlussbericht der Enquête Kommission Verfassungsreform*, Bundestagsdrucksache no. 7/5924 (9 December 1976).

————, Kommission für die Finanzreform, *Gutachten über die Finanzreform in der BRD* (Stuttgart, 1966).

————, Kommission für wirtschaftlichen und sozialen Wandel in der BRD, *Gutachten der Kommission für wirtschaftlichen und sozialen Wandel in der BRD* (Göttingen, 1977).

————, Statistisches Bundesamt, *Datenreport 1992* (Bonn, 1992).

————, Statistisches Bundesamt, *Statistisches Jahrbuch für die BRD* (annual).

German Democratic Republic, *Statistical Pocket Book of the GDR* (1973).

Hessen, Deutsches Institut für Urbanistik, *Organisation kommunaler Entwicklungsplanung* (Stuttgart, 1976).

————, Innenministerium, *Hessen, Gemeinden und Landkreise nach der Gebietsreform, eine Dokumentation* (1977).

INDEX